1st ed   2f

400

BSA

Hidden Hierarchies

Hidden Hierarchies

THE PROFESSIONS AND GOVERNMENT

by Corinne Lathrop Gilb

 HARPER & ROW, PUBLISHERS

NEW YORK AND LONDON

Grateful acknowledgment is made to the following authors and publishers for permission to quote material:

Encyclopedia of Associations. Vol. I: *National Organizations of the U.S.* Used by permission of Gale Research Company.

Oliver Garceau, *The Political Life of the American Medical Association.* Used by permission of Harvard University Press.

E. E. Schattschneider, *The Semi-Sovereign People,* copyright © 1960 by E. E. Schattschneider. Used by permission of Holt, Rinehart and Winston, Inc., publishers.

Table of health-service occupations, by Herman M. and Anne R. Somers. Copyright 1958 California Law Review, Inc. Reprinted by permission.

Reginald Heber Smith of the American Bar Association for Edson R. Sunderland, *History of the American Bar Association and Its Work.*

Edgar B. Wesley, *NEA: the First Hundred Years.* Used by permission of Harper & Row, Publishers, Incorporated.

FIRST EDITION

LIBRARY OF CONGRESS CATALOG CARD NUMBER: 66–13940

C-Q

Acknowledgments

The research and writing of this book spread over so many years that my debts of gratitude to those who have been of assistance are large and numerous: to Thomas I. Cook, of Johns Hopkins University, who first interested me in political theory; to the faculty in American Civilization at Harvard, and most particularly Louis Hartz, Robert McCloskey, and the late Perry Miller; to the late Dixon Wecter; to Lawrence A. Harper and Berton J. Ballard, who first fostered my interest in the legal profession; to the late Vernon Smith and to Dean Frank Newman, of the University of California Law School; to all of the many people in the professions, on the staffs of professional associations, in politics, and in government who have granted me interviews and given me information (several hundred all together); to the Social Science Research Council and (in the final stages) to the University of California's Center for the Study of Law and Society (with aid from the Russell Sage Foundation) for financial assistance, with special thanks to Philip Selznick and Leonard Cottrell of the latter two institutions; to Sheldon Messinger, of the Center, for his editorial comments on portions of the manuscript; to Mary Moore Skinner and my good friend Elaine FitzGibbon for their research assistance; to Saxon Stern and Katharine Wilson for editorial assistance and to Marion Madsen and Helen Rulison for typing the manuscript. I am indebted to Joan Meinhardt of Harper & Row for her thorough and meticulous copy-editing. I also owe a very special debt of gratitude to W. Stull Holt, of the University of Washington, for his faith and encouragement over many years, and to Tyrell Gilb for his patience, wisdom, belief in me, and unwillingness to let me quit. Needless to say, responsibility for what I have written is entirely my own.

CORINNE LATHROP GILB

Contents

vii

PART IV
Epilogue: The Dialectic Continued and Revised

Tables

Tables

PART I

Introduction

Historical Trends
and Political Theories

The American vista today offers a series of paradoxes: separation and unity, freedom and conformity, individualism and collectivism, free enterprise and public regulation, a status society and a mass society, conservatism and rapid change. Ordinarily these traits are pictured as contradictory, as mutually threatening. In political debate the dichotomies are stressed. This book contends instead that these elements of the American system need each other and are the essential parts of a workable and working whole. Although the immediate emphasis is on the professions, professional associations, and their relationship to government, the aim nonetheless is (using the professions as points of departure) to illuminate this development of the American system as a whole and the relationships between its various parts.*

Why use the relationships between the professions and government as a point of departure? Because both the professions and govern-

---

* Since the subject matter is so large and complex, supporting evidentiary detail has often been omitted so that the main themes and interpretations would be more clear. The reader is asked, therefore, both to trust that the more narrow generalizations rest on a painstaking scrutiny of factual detail and to take the larger, more daring generalizations as hypotheses for further discussion, debate, and research.

3

ment are so much more conspicuous today than they were 150 years ago and because their conspicuousness is symptomatic of other major trends. The number of professional and technical workers in the American work force increased from approximately 3 percent in 1870 to 8.5 percent by 1950.[1] More recently this trend has been accelerating as the maturing of the industrial revolution has brought with it more and more research and automation, and a rising per-capita income permits the spending of a higher percentage of consumer dollars on services.[2] Over the past century, nursing, social work, librarianship, accounting, and many other vocations have become professions. The older professions have made dramatic gains in glamour, power, and prestige. Many vocations never before considered professional are becoming "professionalized" (even farm and business management). An "age of professionalism" seems to have arrived. The increased importance of government is manifest. The growth of professional licensing boards, the wholesale entry of public government into scientific research and development, and public debate over the financing of education and health services illustrate the more intensified relationships between the professions and government.

What does all this mean? To answer the question we must widen the scope of our inquiry to take in the broad vistas of historical development and, at each stage of that development, the theories that have arisen to explain what is or should be the relationships between the work system and the political system, society and government, private associations and the state. Theories about the distribution of consumption have not been so well articulated (at least in political-science terms), though each era has had its characteristic attitudes toward the consumer that have paralleled those toward government and work.

THE DIALECTIC OF ANGLO-AMERICAN HISTORY

Although no event, no era, is ever exactly like one that went before, a child may bear a startling resemblance to his great-great-grandfather. So, many present American institutions and values "look like" some of the institutions and values of medieval Europe and of medieval England particularly. Despite numerous exceptions and qualifications, over the past nine hundred years Anglo-American civilization has moved not only from professionalization of work, to nonprofessionalism, back to professionalism again, but also—

—from an economic system with an interdependent division of nonagricultural labor that tended to keep a man doing the same kind of work throughout his life, to a society in which a man—working independently or in combination with only a few others—might turn his hands both simultaneously and sequentially to a wide variety of tasks, back to an economic system requiring a high degree of specialization and interdependence;

—from a hierarchical organization of authority, to an atomized society of relatively equal individuals, back to hierarchies of authority;

—from many, to few, to many organizations;

—from combined guild and public regulation of nonagricultural work, to little or no regulation of work, back to guild-public regulation;

—from status, to contract, to status as the basis of many private rights;

—from a fusion of governmental authority with socioeconomic authority, to at least a theoretical separation of government and society, back to a fusion of authority, with related changes in the nature of law;

—from collective concern for consumer welfare, to no concern, back to collective concern; and

—from community, to contract, back to community as the basis of law.

The Medieval Situation[3]

Most nonagricultural work in the Middle Ages, too, was specialized and professionalized, and defined and regulated by self-governing guilds. This was true of skilled craft work as well as of the labors of lawyers and scholars.[4] The master-journeyman-apprentice organization of labor in the crafts had its parallel in the fields of scholarship and the law (the words "journeyman," "bachelor," and "barrister" being roughly equivalent).[5] As R. M. MacIver put it, all cultivated "the long apprenticeship, the distinctive training, the small-scale unit of employment and the intrinsic—as distinct from the economic —interest alike in the process and the product of the work."[6] The Inns of Court and the great English universities resembled the craft guilds in function and structure.

This professionalism of nonagricultural work fitted well into the whole medieval socioeconomic system. The feudal agricultural and military systems and the medieval Catholic Church were roughly pyramidal in structure. The Church hierarchy of authority and function, from laymen to parish priests, moved up the ladder to bishops, archbishops, cardinals, and the pope himself;[7] a chain of vassals, bearing lesser titles, up from the serfs, the peasants, and the gentry, supported each feudal lord; and the lords in turn presumably served as vassals of the king.[8] A pluralistic, not a monolithic, system of power groupings, nevertheless theoretically all were united in a comprehensive pyramid whose apex was God himself—a hypothetical unity despite the actual pluralism of the parts. The individual was linked with the social organism through ties of loyalty and obligation to specific persons immediately above and below him on the social scale, and with the past and to the future by the ties of kinship that led father and son and grandson through the same channels of status and function. Each man was supposed to keep his place, not strive to rise out of it, to do his work, not to further his own self-interest, to articulate and sustain his particular status contributing his allotted share to the organically interdependent whole. He could not freely buy or sell his castles or plots of land—he did not hold ultimate title or absorptive ownership in property. Men did not "own," they had "rights." Along with economic rights went social, civil, and "governmental" rights and obligations. Both rights and obligations, generally speaking, were the prerogatives of a particular status; they did not adhere to the individual as individual apart from his status.[9] The guilds, the medieval counterpart of contemporary professional associations, defined the position of the guildsmen in the hierarchy of authority; defined and if necessary defended their rights, which in turn were correlated with their economic function; and defined and if necessary enforced their obligations, civic as well as economic.

The governing principle of the Middle Ages was that life on earth was brief and the main concern of man was the afterlife; man should minimize worldly striving, the better to concentrate on the ultimate. Medieval men thought in terms of mutual obligations, of service to one another as part of the larger duty of service to God.[10] Social regulation and social pressures were designed to maintain the status quo, to sustain a populace static geographically (except for war), socially, and economically. Guild monopolies were designed to keep out itinerant merchants. Towns passed vagrancy laws to discourage men from moving out of their traditional locations. The teachings of the Church and the ethic of the guilds proscribed competition and the pursuit of self-interest and emphasized cooperation and mutual aid. Property rights were not an end in themselves; property was an instrument for the fulfillment of one's role and obligations. Production was not for profit but for consumption, to maintain the order of things. The Church forbade usury, not only to protect borrowers but also to keep moneylenders from becoming too powerful. The guilds regulated prices or fees, apprenticeship, the size of the product, and the quality of workmanship to assure a "just" price and high craft standards for consumers and perhaps to curtail "unfair" competition,[11] and the guildsman learned to serve the community rather than himself. Guilds were required to contribute work and financial support to the government.[12] Each community was to be responsible for its poor; the brotherhood of the guild looked after the widows and orphans of its members and gave service to the sick and destitute.[13] The principle of noblesse oblige presumably governed the feudal nobility. All regulation conspired to keep the parts of the social organism in their place. Sumptuary laws were concerned not only that the actuality but also that the outward signs of social stratification be maintained. Some—but not all—of these traits have begun to reappear; some are, in fact, the very essence of "professionalism."

In medieval England there was no clear-cut distinction between what was public and what was private. Organizations (the Church, guilds, etc.), each within its own sphere, had responsibility for "finding" and applying the law. Just as the guild had its rules and enforcement procedures, so the Church had its canons and courts, and the lord of the manor administered the feudal laws. Although the guilds were generally self-governing, sometimes the local lords or municipal authorities might nominate guild officials and examine or even modify guild ordinances.[14]

Government and society interpenetrated to the extent that they were not separate entities; therefore no question arose about the structure or mechanism of their interrelationship. Since the norms that governed the social system were already given in the customary and common law, the canons and dogma of the Church, and in a widely accepted body of economic ideas, a full-scale lawmaking or consensus-reaching apparatus was unnecessary. Jurisdictional problems occurred, to be sure—questions of the division and overlapping of authority between the priesthood and the kings and of the division and overlapping of authority between the towns and the guilds within the towns. Yet there was no atomistic pluralism, there were no completely autonomous private governments, because of the institutional and legal web of the feudal system and the universality of Christian value assumptions. All presumed themselves to be functional parts of a single organism.[15] The law of custom kept each institution in its circumscribed sphere. None was sovereign. Nor did the individual relate directly as an individual to any abstract all-embracing state or nation. The feudal aristocracy intermarried and lords acquired "rights" across what later came to be national boundaries. As late as the French Revolution, "citizen" was a heady word, as evocative as "comrade" later came to be.

Despite the medieval design to maintain the status quo, change inevitably came. The causes and manifestations were many: the stirrings of trade and commerce; improved communication and transportation; the rise of capitalism and the factory system of production outside the walls of the towns and beyond the effective reach of the guilds; application to the whole country as a commonweal, through the mercantilism of the sixteenth to the eighteenth century, the principles that once applied to towns as self-contained units; nationalization of the Church; and the emerging power of kings as national sovereigns.

Seventeenth-Century Transitions

By the seventeenth century private organizations, although still enjoying considerable governmental autonomy, were legally subordinate to the state. In England Parliament had passed laws to restrict entry into apprenticeship and to regulate wages and prices and terms of apprenticeship when the guilds could no longer do so effectively, but much parliamentary intervention bolstered the declining guild system. The king had now replaced the pope as head of an established church, but the Church still possessed many of the attributes of a private government. England relied upon "private" joint-stock trading companies, operating under a charter from the crown, to colonize huge land areas abroad and to govern the colonies. These "private governments" represented a transition between the medieval order and the later liberal conception of the state, for though they exercised almost full sovereignty within their sphere, the sovereignty had been delegated by the crown. In the modern manner, they were contractual voluntary associations, partly like guilds, partly like partnerships; and presumably, within the limits of the charter, all full members of the company shared in decision-making.[16]

The Puritan movement, which so affected American institutions, was also partly medieval, partly "modern" in its thinking. Early-seventeenth-century English Puritans, battling the idea of the divine right of kings, clung to the traditional medieval concepts of a decentralized organization of authority with customary rights and

obligations for groups as well as for individuals, rights defined and
protected by the fundamental law, in turn interpreted by an independent judiciary and bar. Their ideas of limited government and
individual rights were traditional, not modern, in origin, their view
of group-state relationships conservative.[17] The Puritans who migrated
to New England did so under the aegis of private companies with
charters from the crown, one of the few instances in which a
private government has had almost complete jurisdiction over a
geographical area. And so the structure of government in early
Massachusetts had some of the characteristics of a government of a
joint-stock trading company. Over the years this early-day equivalent
of the company town evolved into a self-governing state, yet without
representation in Parliament and subject to the laws of England
and the ultimate jurisdiction of the crown—a pattern consistent
with its private-company origins. The New England churches, too,
with their congregational organization based on covenants, resembled
in structure a joint-stock trading company, but a more autonomous
one. They were truly private governments, with considerable public
impact. And yet, at the same time, the Puritans who migrated to
America attempted to establish, in the New World, medieval concepts of social stratification in a fixed, interdependent economic order,
so that the regulatory authority wielded by the churches, self-
regulating guilds, and self-contained towns approximated medieval
pluralism within unity. (The Bible, of course, served as the guide
for civil as well as for church government.[18]) There was public
concern for the consumer and the poor.

The seventeenth century was an age of transition in England, for
out of internecine religious battles, civil war, and the demands of
Parliament against the crown were hammered modern conceptions of
the state, abstract citizenship, representative government, lawmaking,
and separation of state and society.

The New World's immigrants came from many places, severing
their former social bonds. Few aristocrats came, and opportunity
existed for social and geographic mobility. It became impossible to
maintain medieval concepts of fixed social stratification and social

regulation; the new ideas of government developing in England and in France had found a congenial social setting.

Social Atomism and Liberal Democracy

In America, by the end of the eighteenth century most of the strands of the complex medieval web had broken. Society was atomized. Most business enterprises were run by individuals or by partners.[19] The majority of Americans lived as yeomen farmers, more or less economically independent and more or less equal. Property law had gradually returned to the Roman conception of property, emphasizing tangible things in which ownership was regarded as indivisible and unique, absorbing the object owned, and including the right not only to use the property and receive its fruits but also to dispose of it freely.[20] In the United States, by the end of the eighteenth century primogeniture and entail had been abolished and land was held in fee simple. Men were no longer linked to the land and one another by a complex system of rights.

The American yeoman farmer of necessity was a jack-of-all-trades; he built his own shelter, made his own household goods, wove his own cloth, and even cobbled his own shoes.[21] The frontier storekeeper functioned also more than likely as the community doctor and lawyer, perhaps doing a little farming and schoolteaching on the side. This versatility reached its apogee in such men as Benjamin Franklin (printer, publisher, philosopher, scientist, author, diplomat, statesman) and Thomas Jefferson, and led quite naturally to the notion of the Jacksonian era that anybody could do anything and ought to be allowed to try! No dedication to craftsmanship characterized the America of the 1830's and 1840's. As late as 1869, Harvard Medical School had no entrance requirements and awarded medical degrees upon oral examination after a brief period of residence.[22] Apprenticeship in most fields diminished almost to the vanishing point, as did standards for admission to practice medicine and the law.[23] Nonexperts filled government posts, according to the canons of the spoils system. On the frontier the first waves of farmers camped on the soil and took the most readily accessible of nature's gifts.[24] The tradition of craftsmanship declined further in the early stages of the industrial revolution, as mass production, using machines and unskilled workers, replaced custom production.

The Renaissance and discovery of the New World, the rise of nationalism, and the industrial revolution all played their share in bringing about the eventual atrophy of the guilds in England. Torn by struggles between the masters' and journeymen's associations, the craft guilds in America virtually disappeared in the period after the War of 1812.[25] The resentment of debtors against the role of attorneys in assisting creditors, and the general mood of egalitarianism of the Jacksonian period, created a climate that made it impossible for bar associations any longer to enforce guild standards for admission.[26] Medical societies, too, were inadequate as enforcement agencies. To be effective, guild regulation required that the guild have a monopoly over a controllable area and that the population be reasonably stable and nontransient, in a geographical and in a socioeconomic sense. The American population of the 1820's and 1830's was too mobile and dispersed for this.

In the 1790's and early 1800's, such organizations as existed, and they were few, had dwindled in strength or significance.[27] Cut free from the bonds of intermediary corporate bodies and the social organism, without the interdependence that goes with a division of labor, Americans found themselves on a flat social terrain, separated not only from their contemporaries but also from their ancestors and descendants. As Alexis de Tocqueville put it, the woof of time was at every instant broken, the track of generations effaced, and the American thrown back upon the solitude of his own heart.[28]

Rights and obligations were no longer a prerogative of status. Eighteenth-century Americans thought in terms of the Lockean principle of inalienable natural rights adhering to the individual as individual. They began to accept Adam Smith's and Jeremy Bentham's arguments for an inevitable harmony between private interests and the public good. Competition could be treated as an effective substitute for honesty; in serving his own interest the individual could

be expected automatically to fulfill a social function.[29] Regulation
was unnecessary, according to the new theory, whether by government or by guilds.[30] In both the ethical and the organizational spheres
guildism succumbed to individualism and laissez faire. The prevailing
ethic was caveat emptor: let each man look after his own interest;
let the buyer beware. No man was his brother's keeper. Individual
acquisition of material things became the goad and guide of life.[31]
Relations between individuals were governed by the cash nexus and
the principle of contract (voluntary agreement between two or more
freely assenting and hypothetically equal people, a contract that
could be unmade as facilely as it could be made). Even the professions
of law and medicine, although they never completely gave up their
older ethic, responded to this change.

Men were now citizens of a state, in a relationship that functioned
presumably without benefit of group intermediaries, according to
laws "made" by a representative government. Liberal democracy
(with its emphasis on limited government, protection of minority
rights, decision-making by those with a stake in society, and rule by an
aristocracy of talent)[32] was evolving into a more thoroughgoing
egalitarian, majority-oriented democracy, which in turn saw the evolution of mass-based political parties out of the earlier legislative
caucuses; the newer democracy was welded by the heat of national
patriotism.[33] By the end of the eighteenth century what was public
began to be clearly distinguished from what was private; more and
more activities were thought to be private. A brief period (so brief
as to be almost apocryphal) followed, when the older mercantile
system was dying, with its implications that corporations were arms
of the state, exercising delegated authority, subject to regulation
for the commonweal; when states began to enact general incorporation laws on the theory that corporations were private associations[34]
(the courts eventually went as far as to treat them as private persons);[35] and when the new uses of the state by industrial capitalists
had not yet fully matured. More than in any other time in our history,
the classical definitions of free enterprise and democracy were most
nearly realized in practice.

Prevailing theories about group-state relationships dating from that time can be paraphrased as follows: Government is distinct and separate from society, and government is and should be the instrument of an abstract sovereign state administering an impartial rule of law in the public interest. Organizations should be treated as part of society, having no governmental functions or any special ties to government.[36] (Corporations, said the Jacksonians, should be treated as voluntary associations of private individuals, not monopolistic arms of the state.) How is the public interest defined? Some eighteenth-century theorists said, by the use of *reason,* exercised by those with a special talent to use reason (a natural aristocracy, not an aristocracy by birthright) to interpret the natural law for the public good. Some nineteenth-century Americans said, by the use of *intuition* or *individual judgment,* exercised by all men, since all had access to the universal Oversoul or to a common fund of common sense. The more practical nineteenth-century American politician said, by the expression, through the ballot box, of *individual will,* voting on choices articulated and organized through political parties, with the majority wish as the ultimate standard.

The Problem of Group-State Relationships in the New Order

No sooner had the pendulum of history moved away from medieval institutions than it began moving back again, with the industrial and organizational revolutions. Industrial growth came, among other reasons, because Americans had moved into the heartland of their continent, where few rivers flowed from East to West. They needed roads, canals, bridges, steamboats, railroads. It was unfeasible to transport raw products in bulk, and inland farmers, therefore, needed mills, packing houses, refineries, and distilleries. The soldiers and pioneers needed guns.[37] The scale of new business enterprise required capital in quantity. The corporation, capable of garnering capital from sundry and far places, assuring the investors that their liability would be limited, lending itself to rational organization of labor and centralized control, erected everywhere new pyramids on the American social terrain.

Village communities, in which all inhabitants could relate to one another without formal organization, gave way to cities, heterogeneous in population, where those of like mind and circumstance felt compelled to seek one another out and provide institutionalized channels for communication, fellowship, and the attainment of common purposes. This, too, led to a multiplication of organizations; and in the country scattered farmers—on the defensive—formed their own organizational bonds.[38]

Unification, centralization, nationalization, stabilization, bureaucratization: these were the patterns toward which the new organizations moved. Through mergers, interlocking directorates, financial manipulation, holding companies, and the trust, industries began to integrate vertically and horizontally and to operate over an ever-widening market area.[39] The Protestant churches, fragmented in the early nineteenth century over the division of power between laymen and clergy, missionary policy, and the slavery issue, by the end of the century were beginning to reunite; and those that had been more or less locally autonomous began to form state, regional, and national conferences and committees—new layers of authority.[40] From the federal Pendleton Act in 1881 to the city and state civil-service reforms of the Progressive movement, the American government tended toward the elimination of the spoils system, with its egalitarian implications, and the substitution of a rationalized, bureaucratized division of labor and hierarchy of authority.[41] Business organizations, too, moved in this direction—and beyond.

By the end of the nineteenth century Thorstein Veblen was calling industrial magnates "robber barons,"[42] and W. J. Ghent was writing about the "new feudalism."[43] Veblen emphasized the exploitive aspects of early industrial capitalism. More recently Bertrand de Jouvenel has said that the pattern of contemporary corporations represents a return to the medieval flight of individuals to the protection of the feudal lords.[44] Twentieth-century business enterprise is reminiscent of the more benevolent aspects of the feudal system. Giant American corporations, sometimes controlling assets greater than the national assets of such countries as Spain or Norway, offer their employees security, a sense of identity, and a way of life that gives the individual a feeling of total integration with the corporate life of the institution.[45] Sickness and accident benefits, pension plans, company psychiatrists and family counseling services, company dances and picnics, football and bowling teams, company magazines and newspapers, company stores, sometimes company towns and even a company uniform lure a new breed of "organization men" more interested in security and status than in salary and rapid advancement, completely loyal to the corporation, well suited to their slots in the hierarchy, relating primarily to their peers and those immediately above and below them in the chain of command, thinking in terms of a lifelong commitment.[46] The "robber barons" and their corporal and corporate offspring have subsidized churches, museums, libraries, hospitals, homes for the poor and the sick, philanthropic organizations, publishing enterprises, colleges and universities, the work of artists, musicians, researchers, scholars—phalanxes and flying buttresses serving to extend and perpetuate the power of the corporation, since subsidy is seldom, if ever, gratuitous.[47] The dialectic has moved nearly full circle from American individualistic egalitarianism back again to a socioeconomic order bearing some resemblance to medieval corporate society.

Leaving aside for the moment the factor of "small-scale unit of employment," characteristic of work in medieval towns, the trend in the United States in the past century has clearly been back to a definition of work and an attitude toward work implying "the long apprenticeship, the distinctive training . . . and the intrinsic—as distinguished from the economic—interest alike in the process and the product." The tendency of modern times, as Max Weber has said, has been toward rationalization of all aspects of life, toward selection of workers according to standards of "fitness determined by technical competition tested by rational procedures and generally requiring long formalized training."[48]

In the older professions, as knowledge accumulates and is compounded by technical research, the professional man has had to know more and more and to have had longer training in order to claim even a minimal mastery of his field. With urbanization and industrialization in the nineteenth century, mastery of the law became more difficult not only because of the accumulation of written opinions and statutes but also because society and human relations themselves had become more complex. Urbanization and industrialization not only made a more complex division of labor possible but also led city dwellers and employers to expect more of the professional men who served them, in turn making mandatory longer and more rigorous professional training.

Increased selection of professional and skilled workers by "technical competition tested by rational procedures" has been due to the need to attain higher levels of expertise, and to make more predictable and interchangeable (at any given level) the human parts of the vastly more complex, interdependent economic system and to provide warranties of competence where geographical mobility and urbanization have made men strangers to one another.

The emphasis on service rather than on profit is not so easily explained, but it illustrates one more contemporary trend away from the cash nexus, a fundamental part of the nineteenth-century economic theory.

To articulate and sustain the new and needed levels of professionalism, and to hold their own in a society whose various other members were increasingly organized, the professions, too, formed organizations. The American Medical Association was organized in 1848, the American Society of Civil Engineers in 1852, the American Institute of Mining Engineers in 1871, the New York and Chicago bar associations in the early 1870's, the American Economic Association in 1875, the American Chemical Society in 1876, the American Bar Association in 1878, the American nursing association in 1896—as well as hundreds of other associations. The details and the results of this organizational revolution among the professions will be explored throughout this book.

Certainly one result, not only of professional organization but also of the whole organizational revolution, in which professional organization came relatively late, has been an alteration in the relationship between the individual and government, between groups and government, between government and society. Although most people would agree that a change has taken place, they disagree about empirical details and applicable theories. Over the past century, Anglo-American theories about the nature of government and its relationship to groups have run the gamut from those that ignore the existence of groups (or of organizations as private governments), to those that in effect would deny the existence of a separate public government, to those that commingle groups and government in varying degrees.

Looking primarily at the lawmaking process, one view retains the American concepts of the state, government, and the public interest dating from the eighteenth and early nineteenth centuries and considers organized pressure groups as simply one more set of institutions through which the public communicates its interest and expresses its will. The natural-law theorist can treat group pressures and claims as a useful body of data, informative but not necessarily compelling. Those who believe public officials should be the agents of public will face all the dilemmas of measuring and weighing the various expressions of interest and of will. It is not easy to reconcile with democratic theory the facts about groups as they actually operate. This theory also tends to ignore the relationship of groups to government in the tasks of social control and the administration and enforcement of law, either public law or the rules of private organizations.[49]

Another view, originating somewhat later in the nineteenth century, does look primarily at the impact of government on groups rather than vice versa and sees government relating to warring groups as a playground supervisor does to the activities of the boys under his jurisdiction: government (in the public interest, expressing the public will) should set the basic rules, restore the balance of power when one group gets out of hand or another is too weak, and take care of interests universally conceded to be general in character, not otherwise taken care of. Private associations carry out the remaining tasks of social control.[50] This is the way government does appear to function when it sets the rules for private collective bargaining between labor and management; when it enacts special social legislation for women and children, minimum-wage laws for the economically helpless, laws permitting subsidization for small business and agriculture, and antitrust laws and tax laws directed against the too-powerful; and when it otherwise confines itself to coining money, building highways, operating postal services, preparing for national defense, and similar functions necessarily or at least more conveniently handled by a centralized government. This theory leaves much power and activity in the hands of organized groups, yet it makes government the ultimate coercive force: it still has the power to step in in the case of a dispute, if necessary, in an impartial way. Some pluralists contend that freedom resides only in the interstices between organizations, that freedom for the individual consists of the right and opportunity to change organizational allegiances or to be only partially committed to organizations, that this freedom can exist only when there is a variety of organizations to choose from, and therefore the proper role of government is to enforce a pluralism among private organizations.[51]

Political Darwinists argue that government cannot adhere to principles of abstract justice or right when it attempts to affect power distribution in the social system because government is merely the arena in which organized groups struggle for survival or supremacy. Each group reconciles the conflicts within its own ranks, then, with its forces marshaled, goes out to contest other groups on the battlefields offered by political parties and the legislature. Cited as evidence are the facts that most of the testimony within political parties at the time platforms are being written is the testimony of organized groups and organized groups first drafted or suggested most bills introduced in the legislature. Legislative public hearings and investigating committees are described as instruments of interest-group propaganda. Earl Latham has said: "The legislature referees the group struggle, ratifies the victories of the successful coalitions, and records the terms of the surrenders, compromises, and conquests in the form of statutes."[52] Legislators and other governmental officials, according to this theory, do not stand apart from the group struggle; they are a part of it—in a metaphorical and sometimes even in a real sense, its mercenaries. Final decisions depend not on detached reason but on the power to win.

Contending groups do make their claims in the name of public interest. The National Association of Manufacturers argues that what is good for business is good for the country. The AFL-CIO believes that what is good for labor is good for the country. When many citizens' organizations whose members include doctors, lawyers, college professors, or suburban housewives talk about the general welfare or the public interest, they appear to take for granted that what seems reasonable and good to the middle class is reasonable and good for the country. Made cynical by these conflicting claims, "realists" have concluded that there is no absolute public interest just as there is no absolute truth. The concept of public interest is merely a conceptual mask for the realities of power;[53] and the primary locus of power is in private organizations, in some more than in others.

Some pluralists have proposed that sovereignty be divided, that government should be only one organized group performing one set of functions just as other groups perform other sets of functions.[54] Some forms of guild socialism imply this kind of arrangement or even that there should be no government at all, only self-governing groups.[55] Although these pluralists sometimes point to the medieval system as a prototype, they forget the web of interconnections that bound medieval organizations together. Their view is instead a kind of philosophical anarchism, with groups rather than individuals as the units. They presume a minimum of conflict, a natural harmony, and a natural equilibrium. To most observers of the world as it is, these presumptions seem unrealistic.

The basis for Harold Laski's suggestions along these lines has been a fear: "To make the state omnicompetent is to leave it at the mercy of any group that is powerful enough to exploit it."[56] This fear, in turn, rests on a line of reasoning to be found in Karl Marx's contention that government is the instrument of those who own the means of production and in the polemics of those who talk about a power elite.

A different point of view is that of E. E. Schattschneider: "The function of democracy has been to provide the public with a second power system, an alternative power system, which can be used to counterbalance the economic power. . . . The most significant difference between the private domain and the public domain is that in private conflict the strong prevail whereas in the public domain the weak combine for self-defense. . . . In some ways the public interest resides in the no man's land between government and business." The public chooses between the options made available to it by the contending forces; the public would be powerless if there were not competing groups to make such choices possible.[57]

Another theory contends that the distinctions between public and private activities, between government and society, have become blurred, that the old distinctions between government and organized groups are no longer valid. One of the chief characteristics of American statutory and case law today is a gradual moving of the line between public and private to include more and more organizations (such as trade unions) in the halfway zone called quasi-public.[58] Government is an arm of the organized groups, but so are organized groups arms of the government; both are forms of collective action to serve the needs of large numbers of people. "The administration in the modern state," Lane Lancaster has said, "tends more and more to stand face to face with the governed, not in the relationship of ruler and ruled, but rather as collaborators in the task of social control. . . ."[59]

Those who emphasize group-government collaboration generally believe that the state retains ultimate sovereignty, just as the crown retained it in the sixteenth and seventeenth centuries when it chartered joint-stock trading companies to govern overseas colonies. However, evidence indicates that government officials do not always retain ultimate power. It sometimes appears that the balance of power

lies with the private organizations rather than with the government
agencies with which they collaborate. So powerful are some private
groups that it has been seriously questioned whether contemporary
American democracy works at all in the ways described by classical
democratic theory.[60] (Just as it has also been questioned whether
antitrust efforts, pursuing the old image of an atomized economic
order, can stem the tide of history moving in an opposite direction.[61])

No major American school of thought has adopted an interpretation comparable to Bosanquet's observation, first published in 1899,
that man belongs to a gradation of communities, that the state is
merely an idea force holding together a complex hierarchy of
groups, and that there may be a return to medieval conditions where
there is no true sovereign state, although Mary Follett has suggested that this would be a desirable direction in which to move.[62]

The various theories of group-government relationships break
down into three categories: those that visualize groups as private
and government as a detached instrument of the sovereignty resid-
ing in the people or exercised in their name; those that see groups
as atomized units and government either as one of the units or one of
the arenas in which the units battle; and those that see an integral
relationship between what we think of as government and social
and economic structures of power.

The answer to this confusion is, of course, that all of the theories
are partially right. Different theories have been applicable to different stages of modern development. Today each of the theories
describes a part of the whole, but the whole is bigger than all of
these parts.

The contention here is that—by and large—the structure and
process of group-government relationships for consumer issues are
different from those for producer issues. The structure and process
for resolving consumer issues are closer to those perceived by
classical American democratic theory. On these issues the drum and
thunder of public debate resound. The whole political apparatus is
brought into play, and this embroiling of the public paradoxically
helps to provide cohesion for the whole American system, a cohesion

that transcends the divisions inherent in the smaller system of work.

For resolution of producer (work) issues, on the other hand, the participants in the debate are much fewer, and the process is not like that presumed by classical democratic theory. The Lockean, later Jeffersonian, concept of the separation of state and society, at first an ideology, a weapon against the Establishment, became in early-nineteenth-century America a reasonably accurate description of the facts. Since then many new large organizations and associations have taken on such quasi-governmental characteristics that the actual process of governing often occurs at levels other than the public government. These private governments are not *imperia in imperio*. The structure of these private governments and the process of law-making and law enforcing within and between them are so closely integrated with the structure and process of public government that there is no clear-cut separation between public and private. Both are part of an integral whole. The concept of separation of state and society need not be abandoned altogether, but it must be greatly modified.

Another major premise of the Lockean-Jeffersonian conception of government was the idea of law as command, in the United States the command of the sovereign people. Many group theorists have struggled in vain to reconcile the facts about group pressures with the theories of popular sovereignty and law as command; others have abandoned the latter theories altogether. Although there are some circumstances in which law may still be conceived as command, it also may accurately and usefully be conceived in other ways. The premise here is that for the regulation of the work system there are degrees of law, ranging from inarticulate custom through informal rules, written private codes, and formal intergroup treaties to the public law—a degree of law for each stage or degree of government.

In the cohesion provided by new attitudes toward the consumer, by a renewed concept of the commonweal, as well as in the stratified but integrated work-governmental system, the United States today is closer to the medieval order than to Jacksonian America.

This resemblance is not, of course, complete. Redistribution of consumption takes place through political processes similar to those of Jackson's day. The processes of lawmaking for both consumer and producer issues result in a dynamism of the American system unlike the static medieval order and also unlike the theory, but not necessarily the practice, of late-eighteenth-century democracy. While the traditional democratic conception of government included provisions for orderly change, it was essentially a-historical. It assumed that the forms of government would remain fairly constant. It visualized the lawmaking process as a series of independent decisions occurring on a contemporaneous time plane. The contention here is that the interaction between public government and private quasi-governments has differed in form and degree at different stages of the organizational revolution, that changes in private organizations have produced changes in the structure of public government and the process of public lawmaking, which in turn have played a functional role in the growth patterns of private organizations. Law-as-enacted should be regarded as only one stage in a long law-germination process; the dynamics of development of individual laws, from the time it is first a gleam in society's eye until the time when it has virtually withered away on the statute books, is integral with the dynamics of development of different aspects of the socio-economic-political system. Law germination helps to sustain an organization's cohesiveness and purposiveness from one generation to the next and to bind different segments of the social system together in continuing dialogue. It is this importance of linear time thrust that distinguishes the contemporary merger of public and private from the medieval model, with its more static social order. On this point, and on others, the medieval analogy is only partially valid.

PART **II**

↝

The Growth of the Professions

CHAPTER I

Bread-and-Butter Professionalism

The patterns of growth of professional associations, their ethic and activities, and their changing relationships with public government have been reactions to, and play a functional role in, the evolution of an interdependent, increasingly complex, industrialized (hence urbanized) economic system.

What is a profession? Members of different professions have defined the term differently, and their definitions vary from era to era, but all stress the application of special knowledge requiring long training, the exercise of discretion, and a commitment to some kind of standard to which the pursuit of self-interest is subordinated.

The nineteenth century saw three stages of growth of professional associations, paralleling three more or less distinct plateaus in the evolution of the industrial system.

In the first half of the nineteenth century, when business and most transportation systems were still local in orientation, there were also local and regional professional associations, and only a few state associations. During this period the corporate form of business organization and the factory system became well entrenched, primarily to serve local or regional needs.

By the 1870's intersectional economic conflict had reached a white heat and the issue of national unity had been resolved by civil war; the westering process and transcontinental railroads were laying the groundwork for national economic integration. The last half of the nineteenth century saw a major wave of organization of national and state professional associations, the peak being the 1870's. Because the population was still mobile, and because work roles in new industrial, urban conditions had not yet become clearly defined, the new professional associations were founded by men in high position, often in government, and were elitist in orientation and loosely integrated.

For the industrial system a third plateau came between the 1890's and the First World War, when national economic integration in basic industries was well established, when urbanization had reached a peak, and when skilled labor had settled on a mode of organizing. For the professions these same years saw a wave of reoganization —away from what might be called company unionism and toward "bread-and-butter" professionalism. They now sought more inclusive membership and closer integration of the associations at different geographical levels. Their vocational aims were more practical; they were no longer the stepchildren of men in government, but pressure groups lobbying government from the outside.

As the economic system in the twentieth century has become more differentiated and articulated, so have professional associations. Local associations and special organizations—(1) for minority groups, (2) to perform special tasks, (3) for specialists, and (4) for different authority levels—have multiplied.

COMPANY UNIONS, WHERE THE ELITE MEET TO EAT[1]

The earliest professional associations in the United States were formed in the middle of the eighteenth century, at a time when many craft workers in the towns were still organized in guilds, relics of the medieval tradition. The early medical and bar societies were local in jurisdiction; by the end of the century they controlled apprenticeship and admission to the profession. Licensing to teach in the eighteenth and early nineteenth centuries was done, if it was done at all, by church authorities, since many of the schools were affiliated with churches. Men interested in science also began to organize in the eighteenth century, though they were generally amateurs rather than vocational practitioners in a specialized scientific field.

Some organizing of professionals went on in the early nineteenth century. However, until mid-century, professional organizations were few, ephemeral, and not very powerful.

At mid-century the major wave of professional organization began, becoming most pronounced in the 1870's and 1880's and reaching a plateau by the end of the century. New local associations appeared for many professions, and state and national associations emerged for the first time. So extensive was the new growth that even a partial list of the new organizations reads like a chapter of "begats" from the Old Testament (see Appendix).

Formation of local trade unions began earlier (sometimes several decades earlier) than the formation of professional associations. When the latter came along, their patterns of organizational growth often resembled the patterns for trade unions with local associations coming first, followed by national organizations created from the top by a few people, without close ties to the scattered local associations, succeeded by state organizations. Local and state organizations were often autonomous.

Academic associations were organized first at the national level, and often did not form local chapters until much later, if at all. Engineers' and architects' societies were national, with local subsidiary chapters. Among the professions only the engineers formed city councils comparable to the city councils of trade unions. In contrast, the trade unions as such occasionally formed political parties (such as the Workman's Party in California in 1877), which professional associations in America have never done.

Professional organizations at all geographical levels were often founded and led by those people in the profession who held responsible governmental positions (and often, too, held responsible positions in the educational institutions that trained students for their professions).

The attempts by state government officials to organize professional associations and to prod the professionals into governing themselves are reminiscent of the attempts of the crown and Parliament to bolster guild organization and guild self-government in the fifteenth and sixteenth centuries: self-government at the king's command.

From the beginning, the nonacademic professions had normal workaday links with state governmental activity: The laws that helped to determine the conditions of public health affected doctors; The public schools employed teachers and administrators. Lawyers practiced before state courts and interpreted state laws for their clients. And architects and engineers designed public roads, bridges, and buildings.

The men in government supervising or overseeing such activities needed channels of communication to make their work more effective. Therefore, in most states departments of education furnished the leadership for the education associations. Some state superintendents obtained public financial support for teacher associations and their journals, but this varied depending upon which political party was in power. School administrators and superintendents (sometimes the state superintendent of schools) also served as officers and leaders in teacher organizations. Judges often dominated state and local bar associations. Army officers and city engineers often controlled architects' and engineers' associations. The California State Medical Society reorganized in 1870 at the request of the newly created state board of health; an executive officer of that board was its first president.

A handful of men founded many of the national organizations; their membership remained small for a number of years. The American Institute of Architects was founded by only twelve men, the American Association of Public Accountants by ten, the American Chemical Society by thirty-five, the original National Teachers Association by forty-three, and the American Bar Association by seventy-three. In 1880 fewer than the necessary quorum of fifteen attended the six meetings of the American Chemical Society. Membership in state professional organizations constituted only a small proportion of the total number of people practicing the profession.

Limited membership of professional associations at all geographical levels was partially due to their deliberately exclusive character. Although all of the associations wished to have enough members to operate successfully and to substantiate a claim to represent the whole profession, most were organizations of the "elite" who wished to "elevate" their respective professions and felt they could do so only if they confined association membership to the "better" members of the profession.

Often they existed purely for fellowship and the interchange of technical information, or they served as informal clearinghouses for the promotion and organization of work among the "better" members of the profession. This was particularly true in architects', lawyers', and some engineers' associations. The American Bar Association wanted to keep its membership small so as not to crowd its stylish banquet rooms at New York's Saratoga Springs. The Chicago and San Francisco bar associations conducted their business at twelve-course dinners. The Association of the Bar of the City of New York took social status markedly into account in screening applicants for membership.

Having other bases for their positions of eminence, the members apparently were satisfied to use their professional association (when they used it at all) primarily as a place for relaxation and informal communication with men of their own kind.

This orientation often led to the exclusion of non-Caucasians and women. On the other hand, the associations did at times admit to fellowship prestigious laymen of related occupations and interests. University and college administrators and professors were prominent leaders of teachers' associations. Pacific Coast architects' and engineers' associations included among their members military, mechanical, mining, gas, electrical, and sanitary engineers; architects; assayers; metallurgists; chemists; and manufacturers.

Within the limits of this elitist and social orientation, the associations attempted much that they were to accomplish at a later date. They established professional libraries. They were actively concerned with problems of professional education and with professional standards: the combat of quackery, the establishment of licensing, the pronouncement of ethical codes and some attempt at enforcement. By establishing standards and channels of communication that transcended local boundaries, they provided means through which professionals could move about and retain their professional standing. Bar committees studied the administration of justice. Bar associations endorsed candidates for judgeships. Teachers' associations helped to promote the cause of public education. The medical societies served as channels of communication for boards of health and some medical associations drew up fee schedules. All were trying by one means or another to "lift the standards of the profession."

But they did not achieve much success. The techniques of organization were not well developed, and the habit of organization had not taken firm hold. Like many trade-union associations in the nineteenth century, the early state and local professional associations were often ephemeral, disappearing in bad times.

Often professional associations that were national in name and pretensions were really local in membership. Although representatives of eighteen states attended the organization meeting of the American Bar Association in 1878, many of its members in the early years were southern lawyers accustomed to vacationing at Saratoga Springs, the resort town where the early meetings were held. The American Chemical Society was composed mostly of New York City chemists. In 1896 the distribution of the forty-five members of the American Institute of Certified Public Accountants was as follows: New York, thirty-seven; Massachusetts, three; California, two; and Georgia, Illinois, and New Jersey, one each. State associations, too, were often more "state" in name than in fact.*

For the national associations, as for state associations in large states, the small membership was in part the result of transportation difficulties. The airplane had not yet been invented; the nation had not yet recovered from the disruptions of the Civil War; and the Apaches had only recently been quelled in the West. Annual conven-

---

* Some state professional associations have at some point eliminated the word "state" from their names. Variations in usage in the text reflect these changes.

tions were moved about, so that the people in various regions would have a chance to attend and to join. Still, inadequate transportation limited attendance, and professional men in rural areas accessible only by horse and buggy were suspicious of "city slickers," even in their own profession.

Sometimes members of a profession who moved in geographical and social orbits different from those of the organization's leaders responded by forming rival national or state associations of their own, an easy step, since the office of a national or state association was generally located in the home of the secretary, and the staff— other than the officers themselves—consisted of wives and children or whoever else might be conscripted to do the necessary routine paperwork. The two sons of the secretary of the National Education Association "at an early age were broken in on office work, proof-reading, addressing envelopes, and licking stamps for a voluminous correspondence," and the only typewriter for the association was the secretary's personal machine.[2]

Other conditions of that time made it difficult either to organize the rank and file of the profession or to have much impact upon them. Most teachers worked for a few months a year at low wages in one-room schools. In the 1850's and early 1860's city teachers often obtained their jobs through brokers, who in turn capitalized on political influence or even bribery, or through the patronage of an elected school superintendent or school board members, who in turn were pressured by political bosses. Standards for hiring often were not high. Professional associations were primarily for teachers in public schools, which were just beginning to be considered a necessity. Most of them were elementary schools. In 1850 only about sixty public high schools existed. Proprietary (usually sectarian) schools and parochial schools carried the balance of the educational burden. Even in 1890, when the day of the academy was waning, there were still many more academies than public high schools. Proprietor-teachers or teachers in Catholic schools did not make good candidates for a professional organization.

Medicine divided itself into several schools of thought (regulars, homeopaths, eclectics, physio-medics, botanico-medics, and others), none very scientific and all bitterly competitive. Quackery was commonplace. Even reputable physicians still resorted to such methods as bloodletting.

Many lawyers, engineers, and architects were more involved in speculative or business enterprises than in the practice of their own profession. Professional methods and attitudes and the idea of lifelong dedication to one profession had not become entrenched among practitioners of the profession. A man might well try his hand at two or more professions, and doctors in the new western states often did not settle down in one place but moved about restlessly.

It was small wonder that professional associations did not exercise a firm control over professional practice, but it is significant that they tried to set a "good example."

PRACTICAL PROFESSIONALISM

For the professions the nineteenth century was a time of evolving vocational self-consciousness, manifested mostly by the elite of each profession, who had little control over the rank and file. Between 1890 and 1910 (1920 or even later for some professions) national and state associations changed in mood, structure, and goals. After a transition period in the 1890's the older professions of medicine, law, and teaching, and the newer ones, such as librarianship, accounting, and new or previously unorganized professions related to medicine, abandoned their elitist approach at the state and local levels, regrouping into guilds more exclusively vocational in membership and more broadly inclusive of members of the profession. The new associations attempted more disciplined control over their members to preserve the ideal of professional individualism vis-à-vis state government. Many of the national associations, considering their membership base inadequate, needing more members in order to do more effective work, made standards for admission to the association gradually less restrictive, until finally anyone licensed to practice or who had worked in the profession could belong. At the same time, the associations became more militant and practical in their attempts to raise the standards for admission to the profession.

Many national associations, in relation to state and local associations, and many state associations, in relation to local or regional associations within the state, underwent a period of reorganization in structure similar to the change in the 1880's from the old unitary Knights of Labor to the new confederative American Federation of Labor. The professional organizations reorganized along federal lines, instituting a representative system of government. The national associations provided for delegates from state associations, perhaps also from local associations, and possibly also delegates at large from the states. This not only gave the associations a more legitimate claim to represent the whole profession nationally but also enabled them to recruit new members more effectively at the grass roots. It facilitated the national associations' work that had to be implemented at the state and local levels. The state associations made similar revisions in relation to local associations.

The structural changes were in part the result of improvements in general transportation and communication facilities. A network of railroads now spanned the United States, automobiles were coming into use, and mail services had expanded. State associations were numerous enough to make feasible a national assembly of state delegates.

All of these changes in attitude and structure on the part of the associations of fee-basis professionals represented an attempt to conserve or restore, under the new urban, industrial conditions, the prestige, authority, and independence that the more well-established professional had enjoyed in the village or small-town society of the nineteenth century.

Because of the organizational revolution in business, labor, and other fields, and in particular because of the rise of the corporation, doctors and lawyers felt that they would have to organize more effectively or become mere employees, lose their clients and patients to corporations, or at the very least be forced to accept fees and conditions imposed by third-party intermediaries.

For doctors the threat of corporate practice of medicine appeared as early as the 1890's. After the turn of the century rapidly growing business institutions—trust companies, banks, land title companies, casualty insurance companies, and so forth—were invading the traditional provinces of the bar, using salaried lawyers to perform legal services for the public. Many attorneys feared that they would become merely clerks, identified more closely with the businesses that employed them than with their fellow professionals. Perhaps someday all attorneys would be employees.[3]

Those who did not become employees—the great majority of the legal and medical professions—were worried that the corporations would take away clients or patients, or alter the conditions of practice so that they would no longer be able to maintain the traditional fiduciary relationship with the people who came to them for help. Lawyers who worked for or counseled the corporate competitors found themselves in conflict with those who did not. When the latter tried to bring pressure on those who lent their names to corporate lay competitors, they encountered indifferent resistance or the plaintive response that a lawyer had to earn his living somehow.

In any case, both doctors and lawyers felt a loss of independence in relation to their patients or their clients. The corporate client grew in size and power, and the lawyer keenly felt this disparity. Doctors complained, but found it hard to do anything about low fees for life-insurance examinations. By the 1890's some corporations began to install medical-care plans for their employees, and mutual benefit societies sought to provide medical care for their members at a fixed price. The medical societies objected vehemently.

The spoils system, with its egalitarian implications, operated in public education as it did in public government. Teaching posts became sources of patronage for local elected superintendents, elected school boards, senators, governors, city officials, and politicians in general. A turnover after an election might mean that a highly qualified and conscientious teacher would be replaced by someone with more political pull. Sometimes teachers would be replaced annually so that patronage could be dispersed to a maximum number of people;

often they had to submit to an annual oral examination administered by laymen. Whereas doctors and lawyers resisted bureaucratization, teachers—being already on salary—wanted more of it, but their motives were similar.

The increasing number of professionals and the greater size and complexity, hence anonymity, of cities meant that the old, informal methods of reaching consensus about professional behavior and of putting group pressure on the professional were no longer effective. The professions now believed it was not enough to maintain their organizations as honor or social societies for the elite. Although in some of the older cities well-established bar associations clung to their elitist orientation, in many areas, by the 1890's, the bar was becoming as eager to maintain control over all lawyers as a reputable sorority is concerned about the conduct of its members, and for the same reason, metaphorically speaking: the reputation of the group depended upon the reputation of each individual. To enhance their control over the profession, bar organizations would have to abandon their exclusive attitude and open their doors to, and even recruit, all members of the profession.

After the turn of the century the professions of law and medicine had less control than in previous decades through official admission and disciplinary procedure. Increases in the number of applicants for admission to the bar in many states strained the resources of the courts that handled admissions. Serious disciplinary cases were handled in a decentralized, often haphazard, fashion by the courts. Because of protracted rivalry between schools of medicine, the practice of permitting state medical societies to appoint the members of state boards of medical examiners declined.[4]

The professionals wanted, in effect, more control over their own work. They felt that their status and power depended on their ability to control the quality and number of persons admitted to the profession and to maintain discipline. The professional wanted to create an abstract standard, enforced by his peers or by the state if necessary, that would guide and hence stand between the individual professional and those who might otherwise have arbitrary power over him.

Lawyers and teachers, in particular, desired more control over the total circumstances surrounding their profession. Since much of lawyers' work was done in court, they were naturally concerned about the nature of the judges. Since judges were frequently elected to office on a partisan ticket, they were apt to be closely linked with other candidates on the ticket and with the men behind the scenes who selected partisan candidates. In cities where workingmen were numerous and labor was politically powerful, middle-class lawyers often found themselves ineffective in political matters. Before the automobile, when railroads provided the main thoroughfare, these interests often controlled transportation and politics and government; in many states even the judicial branch. The judges elected did not always meet the standards of able members of the bar. Revitalized local bar associations could and did endorse judicial candidates, raise campaign money, and distribute literature to the voters. To strengthen the bar's voice in the selection of judges, in some states it could and did contribute to campaigns to make elections for judicial office nonpartisan.

Teachers, too, wanted to influence the future of their profession. The tide toward public education was running. Rapid increases in population meant many more schools and the public had accepted the concept of universal free, even compulsory, education. Much of the framework for public education was established at the state level, and professional educators were not the only voices to which legislators might be responsive. More effective lobbying was one of the primary motivations behind the reorganization of state teacher associations.[5]

The forms of professional organization in existence in the 1890's were inadequate to meet all these needs. Only a small fraction of each profession belonged to its organizations, and few members attended meetings.[6] Educational associations had little practical orientation.[7] In some states lawyers had no state organization; the state organizations of other professions were poorly coordinated with local and regional associations.

Coordinated organization at the state level was essential for professions that wanted to act as pressure groups. It would not do for different segments of the profession to work at cross purposes when seeking or attempting to block legislation; there had to be statewide consensus about goals. Yet, legislators, coming from all parts of a state, responded most to their own local constituents. The profession could exert pressure most effectively in the legislature if it pursued agreed-upon goals in a decentralized way. Statewide associations, working in tandem with local societies, would make possible unity of purpose and decentralization of method. Related to these efforts was the fact that national associations were interested in more thoroughgoing state organization, since most public laws affecting the profession were passed at the state level.

All signs pointed to the need for more comprehensive, cohesive, directed, vigorous, practical organizations, and so, in the quarter century between 1890 and 1915, led by only a few people, the professions shook off their inertia, remarshaled their forces, took a strong defensive position in favor of professionalism, and aggressively created or sought from government the tools that would enable them to entrench their new position and eventually to expand it.

Reorganization sometimes came first at the national level and then states followed. Sometimes national organizations were formed or reorganized after a state had led the way. The American Medical Association was federalized in 1901, having considered or experimented with quasi-federal plans since its beginning. The American Dental Association federalized in 1913. Between 1890 and 1910 many state education associations reorganized, merging rival associations, establishing permanent headquarters. Although many state associations had had journals in the nineteenth century, they had been ephemeral, and not until after 1910 did they achieve a sound financial footing.[8] The National Education Association reorganized in 1920 as a federation of state and local associations, with a representative assembly of delegates from the constituent units, and began publishing its own journal.

Reorganization of the bar stretched out over many years. State associations could send delegates to the American Bar Association in its early years, but in the first ten years not more than five came each year. A former ABA president tried to organize a federated association in 1887, but could not make it last. A long period ensued with the ABA at status quo, but with change in state and local associations. In 1901 the San Francisco Bar Association adopted a revised constitution, abolishing the former fifty-dollar initiation fee, greatly reducing dues, and providing for new standing committees. A membership drive, particularly for younger members, was begun. In New York City in 1908 the County Lawyers Association was formed, which opened its doors to any lawyer who had been admitted to the bar (a reaction to the New York City association's rigid elitism). Many state associations that had been organized originally in the 1870's and 1880's reorganized around the turn of the century. In some states where statewide bar associations had been unsuccessful, new and stable state associations were formed. The ABA tried an unofficial conference of bar delegates in 1916 and finally reorganized in 1936.

Many of the pressures and motivations that compelled the reorganization of some impelled other groups that had just begun to think of themselves as professional to organize. Organization was a way of crystallizing a nascent sense of identity.

By the 1930's professional organizations were firmly established. They had brought together independent professionals, many of whom dispensed their services on a custom craft basis, and created associations as independent of the corporate industrial hierarchies as medieval guilds had been independent of the feudal order.

NEW RELATIONSHIPS TO THE STATE

The professional organizations' ties with government became looser in the early years of the twentieth century. Few state superintendents of schools now served as presidents of the educational associations, as many had earlier when, as one historian has said of the advisory council created by the California State Teachers Association in 1891:

In the provision that the State Superintendent was to be ex-officio chairman of the Council it will be seen with what difficulty teachers entertained the idea of a self-directed organization. That the organization and the activities and purposes should be theirs, independent of an official overhead control, implied an experience which was all too meager. Reorganization of the association both evidenced and furthered a "consciousness of kind" among the teachers, and although teacher organizations still looked to local superintendents and administrators for leadership, they now acted upon the state rather than passively receiving the imprint of state officials' thinking.[9]

Doctors, too, now had weaker ties with government. At one time their organizations had directly chosen the members of medical licensing boards; the governor now exercised the power of appointment in an increasing number of states.

The balance of relationship with the state had changed: from being in part creatures of state government, the associations were mobilizing independently to influence state government from the outside. That the organizations were becoming more private showed their growing strength. The old associations were to the state what a company union is to its company; the new associations, like trade unions after the mid-1930's, demonstrated more independence and self-direction.

Professions began, nevertheless, to turn to government for more help. To be a profession meant to present a reliable, uniform face to the public; collectively, to have the public's confidence and respect. Experience had shown that the stray sheep of the profession were not to be won over by precept and example. There had to be better screening at the outset and some method of disciplining, when necessary, those who were already in. To accomplish such aims the professions had to borrow the sanctions of the state. They turned to state action willingly, not reluctantly, because they could not control purely through private sanctions either their own members—working independently for fees or for many scattered employers—or their rivals and competitors, who were equally dispersed. It was they who sought to have licensing laws and examining boards—laws that they drafted and boards whose members they helped to select and whose work they scrutinized. One of the primary aims of professional reorganization was to help create a licensing board where none existed or—where one already did—to tighten the profession's liaison with the board and to bolster its effectiveness. The greatest single spurt in the creation of new licensing boards in states across the country came between 1911 and 1915.[10]

The new professional associations were legally private, and nearly all, except the lawyers, were content that this was so. In many states private association was not enough for the legal profession. Particularly in the new western states, all the pressures that compelled more vigorous local bar-association activity and that brought about state organization were still present and partially unmet despite local bar associations and the formation of a state association.

Bar-association membership remained small long after those of other professional associations had begun to swell. In certain older city bar associations a policy of deliberate exclusiveness still prevailed, but in other—often western—states, and notably California, the small membership was a source of discontent to leaders of the bar.

Standards for admission to the bar continued to be low; the old machinery for discipline proved even more unwieldy and inadequate as new people moved in great numbers to the cities and the courts found themselves preoccupied with other work. Bar-association endorsement of judicial candidates did not always mean success at the polls. In the 1912 elections in San Francisco the local bar association sent notice of its endorsements to every voter, and all its candidates for the Superior Court were elected. In other years, however, the bar was less successful. One San Francisco attorney wryly complained in 1915:

We were told at the time of the election last year that it was enough to defeat a judicial candidate to have the San Francisco Bar Association endorse him.[11]

To battle against corruption in the courts had been one of the main aims of early bar associations. The Association of the Bar of the

City of New York had, in the course of its fight against the Tweed Ring, helped to bring about the impeachment of two judges and the resignation of a third. Immediately before and after the turn of the century the Chicago Bar Association managed to curtail jury bribing and to establish a new municipal court in place of corrupt courts. Yet bar efforts did not always succeed.

The California bar discovered that it was impotent to disbar judges who were guilty of accepting bribes to dismiss criminal action pending before them. The San Francisco Bar Association succeeded in effecting the recall of the judges but not in persuading the Supreme Court to disbar them. When an associate justice of the California Supreme Court was charged with accepting a bribe of more than $400,000, the editor who made the charges refused to testify before the association's investigating committee. The bar found itself tarred with the brush of corruption in the courts, corruption that threatened to demoralize (derationalize) the practice of law, and at the same time the bar was helpless to remedy the situation.

The organized bar had another cause for alarm, between 1910 and 1920, in the growth of administrative tribunals with quasi-judicial powers and in legislative proposals to put all power to make rules concerning the courts into the hands of legislatures. Some lawyers felt that the bar did not have sufficient power to ensure high standards for judges and the administration of justice and was therefore helpless to prevent public criticism and possible public pressure to change the whole traditional legal system.[12] Still another problem was the fact that independent lawyers were less and less able to cope with the problem of the practice of law by lay corporations.[13]

One possible solution, followed in some states, was to retain the purely voluntary character of bar associations, while creating a state examining board to provide centralized, consistent administration of admission to the bar; to give the state bar association legal power to recognize county bar associations, which in turn would investigate professional misconduct and could call upon the courts to subpoena witnesses; and to find some effective method, through the use of public law, of prohibiting laymen from practicing law.

In many states the idea ultimately prevailed that the state itself should create a self-governing bar organization, with compulsory membership, to which, following English precedents, certain powers over members of the profession could be delegated.[14] A Model State Bar Act was published in the *Journal of the American Judicature Society* in December 1918.[15] The American Bar Association's Conference of Bar Association Delegates in 1920 published a revised model act.[16] This spurred the formation of the North Dakota State Bar in 1921, the Alabama State Bar in 1923, and State Bars* in New Mexico and Idaho in 1925, and in California in 1927. Many other states soon followed.[17]

One California legislator opposed the State Bar bill in 1927 because "it would soon be followed by demands for self-governing accountants, barbers, dentists, doctors, nurses, optometrists, pharmacists, and real estate men." Others argued that it would be an opening wedge for the establishment of state syndicalism. Proponents countered that this was not a precedent for other professions, that the State Bar Acts did not incorporate or give legal powers to an existing professional association; nor did they create one. All lawyers were officers of the court and as such were already a body politic, and the State Bar Acts gave to this body politic in each state certain self-governing powers, subject to Supreme Court approval and review. State Bars were generally set up as public corporations, functioning as an arm of the judiciary. In some states, in the 1930's and after, State Bars were formed solely by rule of court.

The special status of lawyers as officers of the court did, in fact, make State Bars less a precedent for other professions than they might otherwise have been. Teacher organizations sometimes obtained legislation permitting payroll deductions for teacher-association dues (something like the checkoff for union dues). An answer to a National Education Association questionnaire in 1958 from 1,040 local teacher associations showed that 25.9 percent of them had payroll-deduction plans.[18] Otherwise, professional associations retained their

---

* When "State Bar" is capitalized, the phrase refers to an official quasi-public organization of lawyers; "state bar" simply means all the lawyers in a state.

legal status as private, voluntary associations, although unofficially some eventually became quasi-public. Even the State Bars, in their nonregulatory activities, often functioned like a private, voluntary association. In California the State Bar Act left intact the existing system of private, voluntary local bar associations. Virginia, North Carolina, and West Virginia have had both State Bars and statewide private, voluntary associations.

The new relationship between the professions and the state did not constitute syndicalism; the case was rather that the private associations borrowed state power to achieve their own ends. Paradoxically, the professions sought to use the state to achieve greater autonomy for themselves vis-à-vis nongovernmental pressures, and sometimes they even used government to protect themselves from government, as when teachers sought tenure laws to remove or mitigate insecurities attending the use of teaching posts as patronage by school superintendents or school-board officials.

The new attitude of professional associations toward the uses of public government was not only a reaction to the maturing of the industrial revolution but also both a cause and a symptom of structural changes in public government itself. In the last quarter of the nineteenth century, in many areas, certain business interests (particularly railroad interests) had gained almost a monopoly power over political parties and hence over legislatures, the executive branch, and the judiciary. In that same period a pluralism of power was building up in the socioeconomic sphere; farmers and labor, as well as the professions, had organized more effectively. The pressure of these many new groups wanting access undoubtedly played a major role in the 1910 revolt in Congress against the power of the Speaker and his controlling clique, a revolt that resulted in a diffusion of power and of access points in Congress.

In the states middle-class pressure for access to governmental power aided the Progressive movement. Since the major political parties were captives of other economic interests, the Progressives introduced measures to minimize partisanship in state and local elections. On the other hand, they favored rapid expansion of the number of governmental administrative agencies—an expansion that reflected and facilitated the pressure of more private groups for access to government. Political scientists are wont to say that the California Progressives weakened political parties, and that the weakness of political parties then paved the way for the strength of pressure groups and for close links between special interests and the state. They fail to consider that before Progressives captured power in California in 1910, many professional licensing boards already existed and the professions had by then reorganized to act as more effective pressure groups. Changes in the socioeconomic structure brought about changes in the structure of public government, which then permitted a reinforcement of these socioeconomic changes.[19]

TWENTIETH-CENTURY ELABORATIONS ON THE GUILD THEME

The new developments in organizations that were essentially elaborations upon the guild theme were (1) special organizations either within or outside the main associations, on the basis of race, sex, religion, age, or ideology; and (2) the spread of local associations at the base and the creation of special-purpose commissions and foundations at the top, which enabled the associations to work more effectively.

Minority Groups

Special professional organizations based on race, sex, religion, age, or ideology sometimes affiliated with the main professional associations, but never seriously challenged the power or the guild ethic of the main associations. They were generally formed by the main associations themselves, or they were organized by the minorities to fill a gap left by the indifference of the larger group.

In the early years, when individuals could belong to the national associations directly, Negro professionals sometimes did belong to them. But since white Protestant middle-aged males were in the majority, or dominated the leadership, of most professional associations, others began to form supplemental or subsidiary organizations of their own. After the Civil War, in most southern states Negro professionals formed their own professional associations in response to their exclusion from the white associations. Local and state societies were also organized by Negro doctors, dentists, pharmacists, and nurses.

If the new form of organization meant that only one state association per state was recognized, several state associations could not send delegates to a national assembly. Therefore Negroes could participate in the National Education Association both as individuals and as delegates from all-Negro and mixed *local* associations, but not from state associations. The American Medical Association refused to accredit separate Negro state associations. As one solution of their difficulties, Negro professionals formed national associations of their own. Membership was not confined to the South. By 1962 the National Medical Association of Negro physicians had fifty state and seventy-two local associations; the National Dental Association listed twenty-eight state and ninety local societies; and there were fifty-one local chapters of the National Bar Association.[20] Other Negro organizations were the National Association of Teachers in Colored Schools, renamed the American Teachers Association in 1939; the National Medical Association, begun in the nineteenth century; the National Association of Colored Graduate Nurses, organized in 1908 and disbanded in 1951; the National Dental Association; and the National Bar Association.

Even in a state so far removed from the Old South as California, Negroes often found themselves treated as a special group within their profession. Until 1878 the practice of law in California was limited to *white* males. The Los Angeles Bar Association, with many members from southern states, refused to admit Negroes until 1950. Although the main state professional associations usually recognized special associations or conferences based on sex, Negro organizations were usually outside the pale of official notice.[21]

Women were such a minority in many professions that their problems were in some ways similar to those of Negro professionals. Even when women constituted a substantial proportion of a profession, they sometimes had difficulty in winning due attention from the main professional association. Membership in the first national teacher association was confined to men only, although the board of directors could make women teachers honorary members. It took nine years for the association to get around to admitting women on the same footing as men. The American Medical Association did not accept its first woman delegate until 1876. Because women were excluded from the American Bar Association until 1918, in 1899 they had formed their own organization, the National Association of Women Lawyers. Women journalists, excluded for years from the National Press Club in Washington, D. C., formed their own club. In response to similar problems of original exclusion, or simply to find fellowship with their peers, women in various other professions formed special organizations.

Like patterns appeared at the state level. The first state to admit women to practice law was Iowa in 1869, and it was 1878 before they could practice law in California. The earliest local bar associations and the first state medical society and education association in California excluded women. Education and medical associations soon changed this policy, but it was well into the twentieth century before women were accepted by some local bar associations. The South Dakota State Bar Association admitted its first woman member in 1915. The Association of the Bar of the City of New York did not admit women until 1937. The Los Angeles Bar Association delayed admittance for a long time, on the grounds that women could never practice law on a par with men. As late as the 1940's, the University of Washington's new law school contained only men's washrooms, none for women having been built, on the premise that there would be no women in the law school. Women professionals responded to this kind of exclusion either by joining national women's professional associations or by forming local clubs of their own. Where the ratio between the sexes was reversed, as in the American Nurses Association, the association sponsored special conferences for men, and there was a special section for male nurses during World War II.

For professions that were still predominantly male right after World War II, auxiliaries to the professional associations were organized for wives at the national, state, and local levels. Sometimes the auxiliaries included wives and female members of the profession —which indicates the ambiguous professional status of the latter.

Separate professional associations for Catholics were not so much a response to prejudice against Catholics in the main associations but rather a matter of choice. The National Catholic Education Association dates from 1904, the Catholic Hospital Association from 1915, and the Catholic Library Association from 1921; these were all mainly organizations of institutions rather than individuals. Catholics often belonged to their special professional associations and to the general associations as well. The Church provided spiritual advisers and supplemental organizations for Catholic laymen in professions concerned with spiritual and ethical values of particular concern to the Church. In the archdiocese of San Francisco, at mid-twentieth century, the Church sponsored the Association of Catholic Nurses, a Catholic guild of pharmacists, St. Thomas More societies for lawyers, and others. Catholic training institutions sometimes formed associations or sponsored meetings for their graduates in the professions.[22]

Lutherans, too, have sometimes formed their own associations of professionals, with state chapters. Jewish lawyers in Chicago have their own bar association.

Unlike the associations based on race, sex, or religion, those based on student status, age, or retired status generally were formed under the auspices of the major associations. Many associations provided special membership in the main association for students or retired professionals. State organizations varied in their treatment of students preparing for the profession. Some simply left the students to organize themselves if they cared to. Others, such as teachers, took the initiative in organizing a student association, offered some subsidization, and provided for official liaison between representatives of the student association or its chapters and the governing body of the main association. Such professions as the academic disciplines and architecture admitted students to the main association as student or associate members, in the case of architects partly because "student" status might be prolonged for a period of many years while the would-be architect worked as a draftsman.

Sometimes an association considered it needed a special organization of young professionals under its auspices. After approximately a decade in which local junior bar groups were being formed, the American Bar Association created, as one of its sections in 1934, the Junior Bar Conference for lawyers up to the age of thirty-six, inspiring the local and state bar associations to develop organizations for lawyers under thirty-six.

While still in professional school many students joined honorary professional sororities and fraternities and continued in later years to attend their meetings. Professional schools also formed alumni associations. Such organizations were closer to the parent academic institutions than to the main organizations of the profession, but it was not uncommon for them to hold breakfast, luncheon, or dinner meetings at the time the state professional association held its annual convention. Full-time faculty members and deans of professional schools tended to join with their peers on a national basis.

Particularly since the 1930's separate professional organizations have occasionally been formed on the basis of ideology. The National Lawyers Guild, founded in the late 1930's and concerned primarily with social legislation and civil liberties, is one example. Splinter medical groups have arisen because of differences of opinion in the AMA. Two such associations, in opposite camps, appeared in 1943: the Association of American Physicians and Surgeons, which seemed to be *against* everything—the income tax, compulsory social security, federal aid to education (including medical education), and any form of union shop; and the Physicians Forum, which was *for* national health insurance and the improvement and wider distribution of medical care.[23] Ideological differences inspired certain special state organizations.

Local Associations

The twentieth century has seen a steady and at times a phenomenal increase in the number of local professional societies, particularly in the years of prosperity and population growth after World War II. By the mid-1950's there were approximately 2,000 county medical associations in the United States.[24] In 1958 there were 6,632 local teacher clubs affiliated with the NEA, with many more clubs that were still unaffiliated.[25]

Most professions relied on local associations to fill the need for continual fellowship and communication, which could not be met by an annual convention of the state and national organizations. The larger local associations were involved in many activities; they published journals, employed staffs, and sometimes built headquarters buildings, all of which mirrored or even rivaled in ambition the activities and facilities of state associations.

But architects, engineers, and academicians continued for several decades in organizational patterns that were oriented more to the national association. Local chapters for architects and engineers, sometimes with intermediate state councils, multiplied in the boom years after World War II. State organizations for architects and engineers began to operate more as legislative pressure groups. In California, organizations primarily of faculty members of the state and junior college systems also had a pressure-group orientation.

Those academic disciplines that were no longer purely academic but contained goodly numbers of practitioners who served the public (*e.g.,* psychologists and economists) formed state associations similar in nature to the state associations of older fee-basis professions, and other academic associations formed regional and local subdivisions.

Special-Purpose Organizations

The professional associations themselves formed foundations, councils, commissions, and institutes for special purposes, such as accrediting, research and education, public relations, or coordination of charitable activities or group service plans. Such special organizations were often separate from the main association, so that donations could be tax-deductible, or so the activities of different professions or of professionals and lay groups could be coordinated. Organizations as well as individuals could belong.[26]

When the functions included education or research, a public relations function (of a sophisticated sort) was frequently implicit, and the special foundation sought to broaden the profession's base in the community. The earlier narrow vocational concentration of the older professions had now made them strong enough to widen their activities. They could work with laymen to achieve scientific or social advances, as they had attempted to do in the late nineteenth century without the social position or the organizational apparatus capable of converting good intentions into actualities.

Most of these special organizations were adjuncts of a professional association that concerned itself with the practical interests of the profession. When the situation was reversed—when the professional association was used entirely or primarily for the exchange of technical information—then the profession sometimes needed a supplementary association to further the cause of the professional worker in more direct and practical ways. In response to this kind of need various academic associations formed the separate American Association of University Professors in 1914 and the American Institute of Chemists was formed separate from the American Chemical Society.

Other special-purpose organizations have been concerned with charity or with other means of aiding the poor (e.g., the National Legal Aid and Defender Association, founded in 1923). To coordinate local physicians' group prepayment plans, the National Association of Blue Shield Plans was organized in 1946. Special societies concerned with the history of each profession have been formed. None of these organizational developments challenged the hegemony of the main associations.

By mid-twentieth century each main vocational group had its own association, at every geographical level, with special associations for minorities. An organizational revolution had occurred among the professions.

CHAPTER 2

Freedom Through Conformity

One of the paradoxes of American life is that when Americans talk about freedom for the individual, they generally band together into organizations to do it. Why does this paradox exist—for example, in the professions? Freedom in a complex, interdependent economy comes *through* organizations. Without an organization to define and sustain his areas of freedom, the average individual professional would often not be able to be free. The paradox is not a real paradox at all.

Professions go through stages of evolution, from the time the persons performing certain functions become self-conscious about their occupational identity, discover others in like position, and begin to exchange ideas and information about their work, until the occupation is given a name and a formal vocational association is established. The association then helps to continue the task of defining and developing the occupation.

Latently and partially in the beginning, and more thoroughly and directly after they have arrived at the "bread-and-butter" stage, professional associations try to achieve professional cohesion (implying some homogeneity) and gain *control* over the profession, to make the profession's work more uniform and predictable and to check excessive intraprofessional competition. Professionals desire peer-group control, rather than public, client, or employer control, not only over the

53

profession but also over the conditions and the standards of the profession's work. Cohesion is necessary to attain control; control is necessary to attain cohesion. Through control the profession attempts to gain individual and collective freedom and security or, expressed another way, individual freedom and security *through* collective freedom and security. The professional association and its impersonal code stand as a buffer between the individual and those who might otherwise dictate to him.

At the same time that the professional association attempts to differentiate and separate the profession from the rest of the work system and the community, it also helps to integrate them. It sustains the position of the profession and defines the role of the individual professional in the modern, complex, interdependent socioeconomic system in which the performance of each vocational part must be reasonably predictable. One important aspect of the professional ethic in the twentieth century is an emphasis on dedication to truth, justice, or some other abstraction that helps to justify the profession's special position of authority and to reinforce it by reassuring the public about the profession's goals and boundaries. Utilization of public government and independent professional schools to perform functions the profession formerly performed for itself indicates more tangible reliance upon outside sanction. By working through these institutions, which presumably represent the consensus of the community, the professions obtain the community's seal of approval, and win high recognition of their legitimacy and rank. Just as the professions win a measure of freedom for individual professionals by subjecting them to the regulation of the group, so the whole profession gains a measure of freedom for itself by accepting some community control.

The professional association is often a vehicle for achieving collective status. It tries to gain prestige and status for the profession, bringing esteem to the individual practitioner. If this esteem is reflected in higher remuneration, while giving to the profession at the same time the reputation of rendering service rather than seeking profit, so much the better for the practitioner.

PATROLLING THE ENTRANCE GATE

Education

In the past 150 years, preparation for the applied professions has moved from apprenticeship (direct control by individual members of the professions, sometimes supervision by a professional guild), to training in schools run by practitioners, to professional training in colleges and universities.

For generations British attorneys and solicitors learned their trade by apprenticeship regulated by statute. Barristers were trained at the Inns of Court, which the bar established and ran. After the political upheavals of the Puritan Revolution and the advent of printed books, the quality of training offered by the Inns declined and students had the option of preparing at the universities, but in 1852 the Inns organized a Joint Council to offer lecture courses and to oversee the education of would-be barristers who were preparing either in the universities or by apprenticeship. The Law Society of solicitors and attorneys performed similar functions.[1] The apprenticeship system of legal education was imported into the United States and continued down to the twentieth century. Proprietary schools and then university law schools gradually developed as alternative places of preparation.

Medical education had a similar history of training by apprenticeship, followed by the formation of proprietary schools, then university schools—but the schools came earlier and there were many more of them. Medical schools were established in Pennsylvania as early as 1765. By 1900 the United States had 367 medical schools; many did not survive. Dental education followed the same patterns. Two dental colleges were established in Baltimore in 1840 and in Cincinnati in 1845.

Early teacher training, when it existed in any systematic form, was handled largely by private academies. Confronted with great hostility and opposition, the first state normal school opened in Massachusetts in 1839, foreshadowing the future in teacher training.

The tradition of training by apprenticeship lasted longer for nurses than for most other professions. Establishment of more systematic training programs did not begin until the 1870's. Between 1873 and 1880 fifteen nurses' training schools were established, often in the face of physicians' opposition. By 1950 hospitals owned and operated more than 85 percent of the country's nursing schools.[2]

Early legal, medical, and dental professional associations encouraged the establishment of schools for professional education, proprietary or otherwise. More recently, the associations of new professions or of professions that have not had wide public recognition have helped to established special schools (in some cases hospitals). Chiropodists and osteopaths have founded and operated their own medical schools. There are special schools for nurse anesthetists, for the teaching of hypnotism to medical men, and for the teaching of various other special or new skills in the medical field, founded and/or supervised by special professional associations.

Many of the professions (notably medicine, dentistry, law, and psychology) have at some middle point been plagued by proprietary schools that would not conform to uniform standards and that virtually sold degrees. This practice created a wide disparity in the preparation of individuals in the profession, which in turn worked to the detriment of the collective image and particularly to the detriment of persons having had training of high quality. At the turn of the century in San Francisco, eight groups of physicians and surgeons set up separate schools of medicine, and in the poorer schools students acted as cappers and steerers to bring in patients for their teachers. As late as 1956 a University of California psychologist asserted that, for psychology,

There are diploma mills which grant "phony Ph.D.'s" to anyone for a fee. A phony degree can be acquired in three months or less instead of the eight years required by the University and other accredited institutions. There are some 30 diploma mills in Los Angeles where one can get a Ph.D. in six weeks for $500.[3]

As a profession matures it strives to eliminate proprietary schools and to concentrate professional education in well-established colleges and universities, but the profession's status-seeking does not stop at that point.

The kinds of colleges or universities that do the training, the amount of training they offer, and the degree of jurisdiction given those who supervise and teach in the field are all taken as indexes of the profession's status. For this reason the professional associations have all campaigned for more and better professional training under university or college auspices. The apogee is reached when the profession can point to a separate college offering both undergraduate and graduate training or just graduate training within an educational institution of major rank. To have any formal course offered in the colleges is a step up. If a graduate degree or several courses in a "major" are offered (*e.g.,* in accounting)—especially if the courses are administered by a department devoted to the subject (*e.g.,* a department of city planning)—this is an advance. The next step is to have a "school" (*e.g.,* the School of Social Welfare, the School of Medicine). Sometimes a school within a highly prestigious university may be better than a separate, independent college (*e.g.,* for law or education); this is surpassed by a college within the university (*e.g.,* a college of engineering).

Medical professions have been concerned not only with preparation for their own profession but also with the training of those who work for them and under them. Dentists have helped to establish courses for dental hygienists. Although doctors and dentists want their subordinates to be well trained, they do not appear to want training to limit supply or to interfere with established authority relationships.

Pressure on the part of professional associations to eliminate training by apprenticeship and to foster training through universities has by no means resulted in their losing control over professional training, despite the increasing tendency of universities to man professional schools with full-time faculties rather than with practitioners or part-time practitioners, as was formerly generally the case. One of the major functions of twentieth-century professional associations has been to exercise control over professional education through a variety of devices.

Giving money has been one tried-and-true method. The American Medical Association, opposing federal aid to education, established its own foundation in 1950 to collect funds for medical schools. In 1962 the AMA journal reported that 55,688 physicians had given $1,303,161.10 to medical schools through the AMA's Education and Research Foundation and another $3,428,413.09 in direct contributions.[4]

The National Education Association and the National League for Nursing have used another method, that of offering consultation services, standardized examinations, and research information to schools training for the profession. Some professional associations have conducted or have persuaded others to conduct extensive surveys of the state of education for the profession and of projected educational needs for the future.

Although the professional organizations encourage and guide programs in the better schools and investigate and publicize conditions in the poorer schools, it has not been their custom to rely on these tactics alone. Sometimes working with associations of professional schools, they have turned to accreditation as another measure. One of the most effective programs has been that of the medical profession. At the time the American Medical Association was founded in 1847, a man could get an M.D. after a short apprenticeship and less than six months in college. By the turn of the century some medical schools required a high-school diploma as a prerequisite, and medical training took four years. In 1910 a landmark study of medical education, published by Abraham Flexner and Dr. N. P. Colwell, induced the AMA and other organizations representing the profession to set up a system of accreditation, which included not only professional schools but also hospital internship programs.[5]

Sometimes professionals dependent on the good will of other professionals for work (*e.g.,* dental laboratory technicians) have sought to have their professional courses accredited by the professionals on which they are dependent (*e.g.,* dentists). Because of cooperation between professional school organizations and professional associations in accrediting, many professions (medicine and

dentistry in particular) influence the size of classes, curricula, and
the choice of the kind of faculty.

Accrediting has also been a powerful weapon to enforce continually higher educational standards. Disaccreditation is the kiss of death
for any medical college or hospital internship program. Partially
because of accrediting, of the 444 medical schools ever established
in the United States, about 20 percent, only eighty-six, were still in
operation by 1962.[6]

Private accrediting activities would be far less effective if it were
not for public laws recognizing and enforcing the private standards.
Many professions have persuaded their state legislatures to write into
state licensing laws requirements that professional education be in an
accredited school or college, or give some form of special advantage
to those with preparation in such institutions. By 1939, for example,
twenty-three states required graduation from an ABA-approved law
school.[7] By 1952 twenty-nine state boards of medical examiners required that medical schools be approved by both the American Medical Association and the American Association of Medical Colleges
(whose lists were identical), nineteen required approval by the AMA
alone, and only three maintained their own lists. States have rarely
accredited hospitals not approved by the AMA. Even when state
boards have done their own accrediting, they have usually paid close
attention to the professional association's recommendations.[8]

An outstanding example of delegation of public authority to a vocational group occurred in 1937 when the California legislature delegated to the State Bar the power to accredit the state's law schools
each year on the basis of the percentage of their graduates who passed
the bar examination. Students in unaccredited schools would have to
pass a preliminary bar-administered examination at the end of the first
year before going on and would have to study for four years instead
of three. Several of California's poorest law schools subsequently disappeared.[9]

Professional associations exert control over curricula, too, by direct
or indirect power over examination for admittance to the profession and by establishing standards for the certification of specialists.

Control of professional organizations over college and university training for their profession has become so strong that one graduate school dean, at least, was moved to cry out in print, "Who's in Charge Here?"[10]

The professions are thus integrated into and have the seal of approval of the community and, at the same time, have a high degree of control over their own fate. They are not all equal, however, in this respect, nor are they static. The great universities are becoming, as public governments have long been, arenas in which contending outside forces battle for prestige and status.

Admission

Changes in the locus of responsibility for admission to the profession have been similar to changes in responsibility for education. In medieval England and in America in the late eighteenth and early nineteenth centuries, membership in a craft or profession came only after due apprenticeship and after examination, often administered by the master practitioners in the chosen field. Beginning with Massachusetts in 1781, every then-existing state but Pennsylvania, North Carolina, and Virginia had by the early part of the nineteenth century delegated to the state and/or local medical associations the power to examine would-be practitioners and grant certificates for the practice of medicine. A New York State law in 1806 gave county medical societies the power to examine and license and made the New York State medical society a board of appeals. In some areas bar associations had similar powers. Some of the new western states imitated this practice.

In the pre-Civil War days in America, however, formal standards for professional work were few and loose, and group control was almost nonexistent. Practice of a profession was a right, not a privilege. The client or patient had to assume responsibility for assessing the merits of the professional who served him.

Then came a revival of the idea that practice of a profession was a privilege, not a right, and that the public was entitled to protection.

The chief proponents of this new idea were themselves members of the professions, and it was they who saw to it that formal requirements for admission to the professions were written into state law.

State medical licensing preceded the Civil War. After the war some states began to license dentists, and New Hampshire set up the first state board of bar examiners. State licensing of accountants began in 1896, and architects and engineers were licensed shortly after the turn of the century. The first nurses' registration acts passed in North Carolina, New York, New Jersey, Virginia, and Maryland in 1903. Since then vocational licensing has become very widespread. By 1952 nearly seventy-five occupations were licensed in the United States. There were more than twelve hundred occupational licensing laws, an average of twenty-five per state.[11] The nature of licensing, however, has not always been the same. Requirements and practices have differed from profession to profession.

Sometimes a relatively unpowerful profession tries to raise standards through persuasion of employers. When a profession is not yet homogeneous or does not have sufficient power to get a state licensing bill passed, often the professional association itself gives an examination and issues certificates. Certification of specialists within a profession is usually done by boards set up by the profession itself, but sometimes a group of technical workers prefer to be certified by the association representing the professionals under whom they work or upon whom they are dependent for referrals.

The next step toward acquiring control over a profession is certifying by the state of all those with a certain level of professional training and attainment, while not precluding others from using the title or trying to gain employment in the field—a procedure often followed when the profession includes people performing many functions. The elite of the profession want some way of distinguishing themselves from the others, and they have often thought of certification as the first step toward more stringent licensing. In many states, for example, nurses were registered for years before they were licensed. This has also been a first step for psychologists, social workers, and landscape architects.

When the profession cannot agree on an enforceable definition of its work, for example, social workers and psychologists, mandatory licensing of all those who wish to use a certain *title*—although it is the title rather than the right to do the work that has been licensed— represents a further level of control. Another level of control is reflected in licensing as a requisite for all who wish to engage only in certain spheres of a profession (*e.g.,* teaching in the public schools, with no licensing required for teaching in the private schools). A profession often moves through several stages of self-consciousness, beginning with certification and finally achieving complete, mandatory licensing.

By the 1960's in many states osteopaths, medical doctors, dentists, dental hygienists (in twenty-nine states), chiropodists (in forty-four states), veterinarians, optometrists, pharmacists, nurses, midwives (in fifteen states), medical laboratory technicians, chiropractors, civil engineers, and architects were licensed by state boards, although licensing in some cases did not preclude unlicensed persons from engaging in related work. As of 1952, three states still licensed homeopaths; nine, naturopaths; seven, opticians; four, psychologists; and nine, librarians.[12]

State licensing has almost always been originally sought by the profession itself, usually speaking through a professional association. As E. C. Hughes said, through licensing "competence becomes an attribute of the profession as a whole, rather than of individuals as such." The public is protected, but the profession is also protected "by the fiction that all licensed professionals are competent and ethical until found otherwise by their peers."[13] Many professions feel that licensing gave them recognition, status, and dignity, as well as protection and control. A group higher in the pecking order of professional work sometimes desires licensing of the group under it if licensing will mean more control over that group.

Licensing laws are not the whole answer because such laws vary in their placement of the significant power to decide what kinds of persons should be given the license. For some professions (notably teaching and, in a few cases, law) a certificate or license is issued to anyone of good moral character who has completed the specified education in approved schools or colleges. No further examination is given. The schools or colleges are permitted to make the important decisions about who is fit to practice the profession.

Although standards for admission to the bar have often been set by state supreme courts, ordinarily the legal power to establish standards rests in state legislatures, which sometimes leave an area of discretion for licensing boards. Since existing practitioners are usually protected by a "grandfather clause," leaders of most professional organizations normally look with favor upon or lobby actively for raising admittance standards, just as they strive to upgrade education. National professional associations publish standards of education that they think ought to be prerequisites for licensing. The pressure for higher standards frequently meets legislative resistance.

Where there is public licensing, passing an examination and, in addition, completing educational requirements are normally required. Professions that do not have state licensing boards may administer examinations before issuing certificates. Traditionally, the courts have handled examination for admission to the bar, at first orally and later often with a supplementary written examination. Because this practice became a burden for the courts and in addition led to lack of uniformity in admission standards, the American Bar Association recommended in the 1890's that state supreme courts appoint boards of bar examiners, a recommendation also made by the Association of American Law Schools at the turn of the century. By 1920 more than half the states had complied. With the advent of the State Bar movement some State Bars took over responsibility for administering examinations. Otherwise the primary responsibility for examining rests with the public boards. Some boards keep that responsibility entirely in their own hands; others rely on representatives of the professional association to help prepare and grade examinations. Although not so much yet as for accreditation, the public boards are beginning to rely increasingly on the work of the national professional associations in preparing or even administering examinations.[14]

Through accreditation and licensing, professional associations have been able indirectly to reduce the numbers of persons who might otherwise enter the profession. The initial effect of accrediting medical schools was to cut in half the size of graduating classes. In the 1930's the Council of the American Medical Association and the American Association of Medical Colleges quite frankly pressured medical schools to reduce their enrollments. Since then the American Medical Association has given only limited support to measures to expand enrollment in medical schools.[15]

In the guild spirit of hostility to itinerants, the professional associations are not particularly hospitable to foreign-trained professionals wishing to emigrate to and practice in the United States.[16] With respect to facilitating migration of American professionals from state to state, the national and state professional associations sometimes work at cross purposes, national associations working toward more uniformity in standards and licensing procedures and state associations of some professions erecting barricades against the in-migration of out-of-state professionals.[17] State laws and policies of the state licensing boards almost always reflect the attitudes of the state professional associations.

FRATERNITY, FRATERNITY

Professional associations, of course, are not the only agencies through which professional identity and cohesion are created and sustained. The cohesion of the professional community probably depends to a considerable extent upon the processes and influences that cause a person to define himself in terms of his role as professional. Too little is known yet about these processes and influences for us to make any generalizations here. Certainly the least of the influences have been the courses or lectures on professional ethics given to students in training, though most professions seem to feel that some kind of indoctrination is needed.[18] Yet it is certain that the fledgling lawyer, doctor, architect, nurse, or engineer enters his profession with an image of the profession.

Although members of a profession probably influence one another more through daily contact than through the less frequent professional-organization meetings, nevertheless the associations do offer opportunity for fellowship, and through this fellowship members come to identify with their vocational community. Local associations hold weekly or monthly luncheon, dinner, or evening meetings. Some local associations maintain comfortable club quarters. By going to the larger state or national conventions at plush hotels, at resorts, or even (for architects) outside the mainland of the United States, members of the profession can indulge in the favorite American sport of combining business with pleasure. As one newspaper reporter said, American Medical Association conventions are opportunities for physicians to "hoist a few and have a little fun." When the railroads gave lower rates to teachers traveling to National Education Association conventions in the late nineteenth century, NEA membership boomed. The number of weddings growing out of these meetings is vivid evidence of the utility of conventions in producing professional cohesion.[19]

The "Welfare" Group

One of the main characteristics, in the medieval tradition, of twentieth-century American government has been the trend toward a "welfare" state—toward public concern about the halt and the poor. Here again is a seeming paradox, for business corporation executives and members of some professions have protested loudly against this public-welfare orientation at the same time that their own organizations have duplicated that orientation in miniature. The professional associations publish journals and provide their members with services, such as insurance and welfare programs, legal advice, group travel plans, job placement and counseling, and credit unions, as inducement for membership and as ways of binding the profession together.

By 1955 there were an estimated nine hundred teacher credit unions. The NEA has helped state and local teacher associations through research information and consulting services on retirement plans. The California State Teachers Association has hired actuaries on retainer to clarify retirement problems for individual teachers. The state association and the larger regional sections hired attorneys on retainer to help individual members with their professional problems.

Most national academic associations have operated as job marts, formerly in a casual way, more recently in an open and systematic manner. The American Medical Association and some state medical associations have a physicians' placement service. Beginning in the 1880's, local medical societies organized nurses' registries so that they could recruit private-duty nurses as needed. Nurses' organizations gradually took over this function. The American Nurses Association established in 1945 a wholly owned nonprofit subsidiary, the Professional Counseling and Placement Service, Inc. State associations, with California the first, followed suit.

None of the associations has had a monopoly on the brokerage of employment. None has the influence of the carpenters' union or the craft unions of other skilled workers over placement of their members. And certainly none has had the degree of control enjoyed by those skilled craftsmen in the printing trades who hire their own replacements without conferring with the employer. Placement is an adjunct, not a main part, of professional-association activities; it is because they have so little control over placement that most nonacademic professions rely so heavily on licensing to give them a measure of control over their profession.

Other services by national associations include publishing directories of members of the profession, bibliographical guides to professional literature, and, for physicians and surgeons, handbooks on drugs and diseases. The national associations of other professions, for example, teachers, do research and publish information on comparative salaries and supply and demand for professional workers.[20]

The associations have made minor efforts to look after the more needy members of the profession. All of these actions have been in the mutual-aid tradition of the medieval craft guilds, although in quantity and scope sometimes they have been gestures rather than major efforts. They do, in some way, help bind the profession together.

The Ethics of Noncompetition

Twentieth-century codes of professional ethics, unlike earlier ones, are another unifying force. Nineteenth-century ethics were primarily concerned with the relationship between the individual and those he served. The professional organizations, beginning in the 1870's, gave a new emphasis, in the form of professional ethics, to behavior that would make the profession more cohesive while preserving the autonomy of the individual professional.

To reinforce homogeneity growing out of more uniform training and out of licensing laws, and whatever sense of community resulted from fellowship and the services offered through the professional associations, the professions have enacted rules relating to ethics that allow the profession simultaneously to retain power and to present a collective image of "dignity and honor."[21] Unity requires that competition be curtailed.

Among these rules a cardinal principle has been "Thou shalt not compete unduly with thy fellow professionals." The rules pertaining to advertising are quite specific: no using of black lettering in telephone books to distinguish one's name from the others, no large signs on or near office doors, no firm name on Christmas cards. Professional articles or statements to the press must not involve personal or business advertising.

Business is not to be solicited directly, though in the case of some professions, such as architecture, it may be solicited with restraint. Some professions frown on competitive bidding and have rules governing competition for jobs, just as industries have tried to curtail "excessive" competition or even to rig markets. Undercutting, in bidding or pricing, the going professional rate is frowned on; this is equivalent to what businesses and some professions, such as pharmacy, mean by "fair trade," and similar motivations and effects are reflected in trade-union attempts to minimize wage differentials.

In the past several decades teacher-association codes of ethics have proscribed underbidding for a job or applying for a job before a vacancy. The National Education Association's Classroom Teachers'

Department took a stand against merit ratings as a basis for determining salaries. Teachers' unions have even attempted to cut down the salary differentials between younger and more experienced teachers.

In the same spirit efforts have been made to put a floor under professional fees by the publication of fee schedules or relative value guides. For more than a century local medical societies and bar associations have been publishing fee schedules. In 1956 the California Medical Association began publishing, as an optional guide, studies of the relative values of different kinds of services. There has been no strong attempt generally to enforce fee schedules and certainly no attempt to prevent fees from going higher than the schedules. In 1961–62 the American Bar Association Committee on Professional Ethics held for the first time that a lawyer's charging below a minimum fee schedule "may be evidence of unethical conduct." Group policies on fees, including setting fee schedules, sometimes appear to be aimed at "more, more . . ."—as in the case of the unionized professions and at least one specialist medical association, one of whose leaders frankly proclaimed that the association was created to help get higher fees for its members. However, the implicit aim has been to equalize wages, fees, or salaries for persons within a functional category. In recent years bar and medical associations have even tried to curtail excessive fees, reflecting to a remarkable extent the medieval concept of the just price.

Codes of ethics have attempted to curtail intraprofessional competition in several other ways. The codes of CPA societies have declared it unethical for one accountant to steal another's employees without first giving him notice. When one professional refers a patient or client to another member of the profession for help on a special problem, the latter is not supposed to try to keep the patient or client thereafter for his own. Lawyers are not to attempt to exert personal influence on a judge or jury. In the interests of solidarity, most professions have placed careful restrictions on specialization or announcement of specialization to the public.

Culture and Heroes

In the absence of extensive detailed empirical studies, it is difficult to determine just how effective the professional associations have been in permeating the consciousness of all members of the profession and welding the profession into a unified vocational community. Probably their success is only partial at best. In Chicago and New York there are wide class differences within the bar, for example, reinforced by and reinforcing ethnic-religious differences, primarily between Protestants and Jews. There is some evidence to indicate, however, that in states where there is greater homogeneity within the profession, and for some professionals in the older cities, too, the association serves cultural as well as vocational needs of the members.

Of significance is the fact that most professional associations have their histories and their heroes, phenomena providing a rich field for further exploration by social scientists. The "histories" prepared by the history committees of professional associations have usually been either dry annals or narratives of the organization's "accomplishments" or biographies of members of the profession. Since history committees are usually manned by senior members of the profession, the preference for biography may reflect their own unconscious yearning for immortality, but due note should be taken of the functions of history and symbolic biography in buttressing group identity, a function comparable to that which national histories and political biographies serve for the larger state. The professional association's heroes are not necessarily the same as those of the profession at large. Usually the founder of the profession or an early conspicuous leader and the founder of the organization are commemorated—honor thy father and thy mother!

In naming one of its members "Dentist of the Century" in 1959, the California State Dental Association published a revealing explanation:

Our professional organizations operate as small worlds or cultures of their own. We develop our methods of conduct and ethical behavior. We have our own language or jargon. We set certain values and establish our own authorities, and evolve certain typical procedures. In this process we invariably develop what might be called stereotypes or images of what we believe our typical professional person should be.

They chose a "dynamic, not static," man, who was one of the first to recognize the need for research, scientific journalism, and the professional organization, and to lead others in the same direction.[22] Heroes are both evidence of and agents for the solidarity and collective striving of the group.

Public Relations: How to Attain Support Without Interference

Control over education and entrance into the profession, professional fellowship and belongingness, are valuable for their own sake, but the professional associations also wish to protect and advance the profession's position in relation to outsiders. The association promotes or "sells" the profession to the public and protects the profession from lay interference and criticism.

National associations started hiring specific staff persons to be in charge of public relations in the 1940's. Many state professional associations have also hired professional public relations counsel, usually first on retainer and then on salary when his services are deemed indispensable.[23] That formal concern with public relations is primarily an urban phenomenon is indicated by the fact that California's larger local teachers' clubs have been concerned with public relations, but the smaller clubs and rural ones have not.[24]

It is not easy to mold or alter a public image, since it largely reflects the public's reaction to thousands of individual contacts, or is the combined product of many portraits in motion pictures, plays, novels, magazine stories, and the newspapers. The images conveyed through cultural media undoubtedly influence certain personality types to enter the profession and may even affect professional men's behavior, so that the image—true or not to begin with—helps to create the fact. Not all the professions are in the same position. Lawyers, with such notable exceptions as the mythical Perry Mason, have been often portrayed in a negative light. The public image of doctors is by now so inflated in a positive direction that the disparity between the image and the reality has sent many a patient away dissatisfied. Social workers, librarians, and teachers have longed for more "prestige" in their public portrayals and often have expressed their concern vigorously to television networks, for example, when their roles have been presented in ways they consider inaccurate or demeaning. Professional associations have occasionally protested or acclaimed particular portraits of the profession, but they have little direct control.

The "days" and "weeks"—Law Day, Engineers Week, Public Schools Week, health weeks of all kinds—officially proclaimed by the President or by a state governor have been useful in publically legitimizing the professions, as well as in making them prominent. The professional organizations have accompanied these weeks with appropriate ceremony and ritual and have welcomed commemorative postage stamps. Just as corporations and trade unions have erected handsome buildings to impress their image upon the public, so have some professional associations sought the public relations advantage of handsome buildings to house libraries, meeting rooms, and offices for staffs of up to eight hundred or more persons. Businesses and trade unions have given conspicuously to charity and have supported civic activities, and professional associations have urged their members to engage in community affairs—just as medieval guilds once volunteered their members for community service.

The professions have tried to sell themselves in more direct ways. Professional associations have operated speakers' bureaus, distributed news articles, and sponsored radio and television broadcasts about the work of their profession. Teacher associations have set up local discussion groups of teachers and laymen. Professional associations have cultivated the press by awarding newspapers and journalists for outstanding reporting about schools, the law, medicine. In 1923 the American Medical Association began publishing *Hygeia,* a health magazine for laymen (renamed *Today's Health*).

To help recruit potential members of the profession from among the more desirable young people, many professional associations have sponsored scholarships and provided speakers and printed material about the profession to the schools and youth agencies.

Some of the professional organizations' activities help to bring in more business for the profession. Lawyers', doctors', and CPA associations prepare pamphlets for public distribution on "How to Select an Attorney," "How to Select a Doctor," "How to Select an Auditor." Architects' associations set up, in effect, dignified advertising exhibits that convey to the public the values of architectural services.

Medical associations have directed most of their public relations activities toward defending the profession against legislative and other governmental actions; that is, the association does for the individual professional what he cannot do alone. Homogeneity and group cohesion are necessary for this association function. To be "free"— that is, to advance and protect his interests—the professional must give up some freedom to the group.

Some public relations efforts attempt to create a set of predictable expectations for the relationship between the professional and his client, pupil, or patient. Most of the activity focusing on the more sensitive relational problems comes under the heading of "professional ethics," which has often been defensive rather than positive. Along with educational qualifications and licensing, ethical precepts, publicly stated and conspicuously enforced, attempt to reassure the public about the merits of the profession as a whole and in this way help to protect the individual professional. The aim has been to gain acceptance for peer-group rather than lay standards for professional behavior and peer-group enforcement.

Specific ethical rules—to define the professional's role in relation to his patient, pupil, or client, to enumerate predictable expectations, and to give the user of professional services reasonable assurance that he can trust the professional—back up vaguer claims to trustworthiness. Expressed another way, the rules that once created and defined a fiduciary relationship are now the basis upon which the professional claims to be interested in service rather than in profit and hence worthy of the community's trust and respect.

Since CPA's have to remain independent of their clients in order to be neutral in the technical process of auditing, a CPA must not accept a contingent fee or have a financial interest in a client's business, nor should he get too high a percentage of his work from one client. The attorney must not take on new cases when a conflict of interest would result. Since a man cannot serve two masters and gain the unreserved trust of each, the problem of conflict of interest has arisen in all the professions, and all have had rules exhorting their members to avoid such problematic situations. Teachers have often worked as book salesmen in the summer to supplement meager incomes. Their associations have maintained that they ought not to sell within their own community and should not exploit their status as teachers to gain entry into homes. If they sell books, they should not do so as members of the teaching profession. A music teacher who accepts a kickback for recommending particular retailers of instruments or who accepts pay for tutoring a member of his class;[25] an architect who receives money for specifying certain materials; and a doctor who accepts a rebate on the drugs and appliances he prescribes even more seriously violate the fiduciary principle.

At the time of writing, the codes of medical societies did not prohibit doctors from owning stock in drug companies or owning pharmacies, rest homes, and the like, provided there was no "exploitation of the patient." At its midsummer meeting in 1962 the American Medical Association adopted its Judicial Council's report on the ownership of pharmacies and pharmaceutical companies by physicians. The council held that such ownership was not unethical per se, but should be judged in terms of whether as a result the physician's patients were exploited, received inferior medical care, had to pay more for drugs, or were prescribed unnecessary or inadequate drugs, and whether ownership was a subterfuge for rebates. The council suggested that physicians and pharmacists establish codes defining the nature and extent of cooperation. In 1962 an executive of the California Pharmaceutical Association announced that physicians owned 254 pharmacies in the state, and in 1963 the state legislature passed a bill to curtail such ownership.[26] As the socioeconomic system has changed, conflicts of interest have presented some of the thorniest ethical problems of the twentieth century, not only for the professions but also for other vocational groups. The issue has touched trade-union officials who own stock in a corporation with which they are bargaining as a representative of the workers, corporation executives who own stock in competing corporations, and governmental officials in a variety of situations.

To preserve the fiduciary principle, most professions have had rules against fee splitting—a particularly sensitive point for surgeons or other specialists whose patients or clients come primarily through referral. The codes have stated that each professional should bill the patient or client separately, with no rebate agreements between professionals. Lawyers are not to commingle clients' funds with their own.

Efforts to reinforce the notion of trustworthiness involve simultaneously individual professionals and the profession as a whole. In the elitist era of the nineteenth century, professional-association leaders did not attempt to justify the whole profession but chose to distinguish themselves from amateurs and quacks. More recently professional associations have tried to preserve a solid front vis-à-vis the public in general and those who buy or receive services in particular. Consequently most professions have had rules against criticizing members of the profession in front of a lay person. The medical profession has been the most concerned about maintaining a united front, even to the point of discouraging doctors from testifying against one another in malpractice suits. Violating the code amounts to an appeal to lay rather than peer-group judgments—in opposition to the foremost *raison d'être* of the professional associations and of professionalism.

Associations of the fee-basis professions (*e.g.*, the bar) either have refused to entertain officially any charges that a member of the profession is incompetent once he has been duly admitted to the profession or (*e.g.*, some medical societies) have defended the member against such accusations. Bar associations in the past usually were unwilling to intervene when a client accused a lawyer of overcharging. American lawyers have practiced under financial conditions

quite different from those in England, where fees have been subject
to review by the courts and where contingent fees have not been allowed.[27] In the United States a contingent fee might frequently be
from one-third to one-half of the total amount recovered. Only a few
types of lawyers' fees, such as those for probate, have been fixed by
statute.[28]

The tendency of professional associations in recent years has been
to try to forestall public discontent by keeping members in line.
Attempts have been made to establish both a floor—statutory or
otherwise—for salaries or fees and some kind of ceiling—even though
a vague and unenforceable one—to protect the profession from the
wrath of overcharged patients and clients. Since most patients' complaints are about fees, county medical societies have set up mediation
screening committees.

The American Bar Association's code of ethics changed "no
lawyer should follow bar association schedules of minimum fees as
his sole guide in determining the amount of his fee" to read, "In
fixing fees, lawyers should avoid charges which overestimate their
advice and services as well as those which undervalue them." A
California bar leader who had a very high income from the practice
of law warned in 1959 that "exorbitant fees charged by some attorneys are damaging the entire legal profession and could lead to
some form of outside regulation or interference."[29] In 1961 the
California bar studied the possibility of establishing a ceiling on
contingent fees.

Recently—again in the tradition of medieval groups, which were
responsible for their members' debts—bar associations have begun
to establish clients' security funds, so that the profession could re-
imburse the client when an unethical attorney had misused the client's
money. By 1961 sixteen state associations and many local bar associations had established such funds. Only three of the states (Arizona,
New Mexico, and Washington) had State Bars.[30]

In the realm of ethics, as in other professional-association activities,
the aim is not only to define and protect the role of the professional
in relation to laymen but also to forge unifying links between the

profession and the rest of the community. The professions have protected themselves by stressing their duty to the public good or to some abstract ideal. During the nineteenth century an attorney was to swear "never to reject, for any consideration personal to himself, the cause of the defenseless or the oppressed," which was many years later interpreted to mean that attorneys should not be chastised for defending persons accused of "communistic practices," since the system of law held that every person had a right to defense. In civil cases, on the other hand, the lawyer swore to act as counsel in only those actions, proceedings, or defenses that he considered legal or just. His duty to the dignity and solemnity of the law required that he maintain due respect for the courts and judicial officers and that he preserve proper decorum in the courtroom.[31]

Twentieth-century bar associations have stressed the idea that lawyers are officers of the court. It has been a useful concept, lending to lawyers the dignity of being agents of "justice," just as doctors have benefited in status from their link with the awesome forces of life and death, college professors from theirs with "truth," and the ministry from theirs as interpreters of divine will.

Professionals stress their duty to the public, the state, or some transcendent ideal to justify the claim to special status. The professions have often pointed out, with some merit in their argument, that they needed prestige and trust in order to function properly. Of course professionals have not always lived up to their high standards. A reasonable degree of conformity to published codes of ethics buys both public approval and some freedom for professionals.

Twentieth-century laws governing the licensing of professionals have frequently stated two conditions for granting a license to practice: (1) that the professional be someone who has not been convicted of a felony or misdemeanor involving moral turpitude; and (2) that the professional swear to uphold the constitution of the state and not to engage in subversive activities.

The courts have defined turpitude as an act contrary to the fundamental moral precepts of the community, something intrinsically bad, not an accidental act but one with full intent or so grossly careless that it is equivalent.[32] The courts have ruled that murder, robbery, larceny, extortion, and fraud are clearly within the meaning of the term when applied to lawyers. Violating a narcotics act might be considered moral turpitude, but breaking a law governing the use and distribution of alcoholic beverages in some cases might not. For an attorney, the phrase has normally been applied only to grave offenses that bear on his moral fitness to practice law. Community standards determine its precise definition for all professions. In short, the courts have said that a member of a profession must abide by the social standards of his place and time. The professions would not have it otherwise, for they have been dependent on public good will and acceptance.

Some professions, for example, law and social work, have fostered statutes that would exclude from admittance persons who advocate or knowingly belong to organizations that advocate overthrowing the government by force and violence. Practicing a profession has frequently been contingent upon acceptance of the established political system or at least willingness to change the system only by peaceful and gradual means. Again, this has been a way of protecting the whole profession against possible public reprisal for the political practices of any member of the profession.

The state has generally considered practicing a profession a privilege that it can take away for gross violations of the community's political as well as moral norms. Professional associations have gone beyond this point and pressured their members toward a high degree of conformity to prevailing social codes and public opinion. The California State Dental Association code of ethics has stated that a dentist must avoid "any conduct which leads to a lowering of esteem of the profession." The California Teachers Association manual on ethics has condemned teachers who drive recklessly, fail to vote, step to the "front of the line standing before a popcorn machine," ridicule matrimony, or limit out-of-school activities to socializing at a local tavern. This profession, even more than the others, has been highly sensitive to any public disapproval.

The professions have not made these concessions unilaterally.

Because lawyers need freedom to defend unpopular clients, many members of the bar, even during the peak of American anti-Communist sentiment in the late 1940's and early 1950's, have been unwilling to impose discipline upon fellow lawyers for activity that might be interpreted as indicative of subversive leanings, as long as outright advocacy of violent overthrow of the government is not involved. In the late 1950's and early 1960's, when race relations were becoming explosive in the South, bar associations faced a related dilemma of how to protect a lawyer's right to defend Negroes charged with breaking segregation laws.

Teachers have had to defend their right to teach controversial subjects. The California association's Public Relations Advisory Panel concluded in 1954 that school boards and administrators had the duty "to make it unmistakably clear that examination of controversial issues by students is an important and necessary part of the American educational process." Again, as for lawyers, not all members of the profession have conceded the need for this freedom.

The same can be said about librarians vis-à-vis book censorship. The professional association has had to shore up the wavering courage of librarians on the job, who, one researcher has reported, tend to "remove or hide books they considered controversial."[33]

Medical men, who have power over life itself, have long had to defend their freedom to probe into the mysteries of the body, when religious men would have it otherwise, and to take what they consider necessary medical risks. It is to the interests both of the profession and of society that a delicate balance between freedom and conformity be maintained.

Channeling Advancement of the Craft "Mystery"

Professions seek balance in another area of their activity: influence over the discovery and dissemination of new professional knowledge, an influence that is used to encourage new discovery and education and to check new ideas or knowledge that would threaten the well-being of the profession or radically disrupt its sense of identity. The profession wants and needs to have some peer-group control over the discovery and spread of new professional knowledge. Through this control it protects itself and the public against quackery and facilitates the spread of new discoveries once they have been approved. However, this control also implies a measure of restriction, a resistance to new ideas or techniques that might unseat old chieftains or require a radical shift in orientation or jurisdiction.

Through their magazines and journals, scientific and technical conferences and meetings, continuing education programs, and the informal social interchange at association meetings, the collective "mind" of the profession is molded, skills and techniques are developed and transmitted, the limits of the intellectual scope of the profession's knowledge are established, and the avenues in which knowledge might advance are marked out.

Having communication as one of their original purposes, many associations have established and maintained a library for members' use and for the exchange of technical information. The American Medical Association, with its courses, conferences, and scientific journals, has been described as "a great postgraduate school for doctors trying to keep abreast of the incredible pace of modern drugs and medicine"; the exhibits at its conventions have been called "the biggest and brightest medical 'sideshow' on earth." Nine of the AMA scientific sections of specialists have published their own journals, and more than half of the AMA's yearly allocations have gone to scientific activities.[34] At American Bar Association meetings nationally renowned laymen and lawyers have provided up-to-date information on law, government, and economic development. The National Education Association's research division, which began with a one-man staff in 1922, had grown to a staff of fifty by 1957. In 1955 alone, the NEA and its commissions, committees, departments, and divisions published 20 monthly magazines, 181 bulletins, 36 yearbooks and other books, and 1,070 miscellaneous publications. Most academic, engineering, and scientific associations have been primarily media for the exchange of technical information; so have many of the specialist associations of the fee-basis professions, such as the American College of Physicians and the Aero-Medical Association.[35]

Since the 1940's many professional associations have sponsored formal continuing education programs for their members.[36] Medical leaders in the late 1950's were discussing ways to make mandatory physicians' participation in continuing education programs. Two suggestions were that membership association be contingent upon such participation, or that renewal of license depend on it or on passing new examinations.[37]

Professional associations have done a great deal to bring new knowledge into the public domain. Professionals are supposed to share professional discoveries with their peers. A doctor or dentist may patent surgical instruments, appliances, and medicines, and may copyright publications, methods, and procedures, but he cannot do this in a way that retards or inhibits research or restricts the benefits of the protected material.

Intriguing questions to which we do not yet have answers include: Where and how does new knowledge arise, where does innovation occur, and have the professional associations been equally hospitable to all new ideas and approaches? Do some persons find access to professional journals on scientific and technical matters easier than others do, and what causes the difference? Do conferences highlight certain approaches at the expense of others? How are associations used in intraprofessional competition between different schools of thought? What have been the relative influences of teachers, practitioners, and those who are primarily researchers on the advancement of the profession's skills and knowledge, and how do the patterns of communication between these groups affect the nature of the knowledge communicated?

The legal and many academic professions, through the use of footnotes and other forms of acknowledgment, continually refer back to prior knowledge and to the main conceptual frames of reference that tie the profession together. Much of what is said in the name of truth unconsciously serves the psychic and sociological needs of the professional group—renders it cohesive, gives it continuity and community—so that new knowledge that would radically disrupt existing patterns may have a difficult time making itself known, may even have to build around itself a new profession and new professional organizations. In the academic world, where once there was only philosophy, now there are history, political science, sociology, anthropology, psychology, and more to come.

The associations are not the only influence, of course, on the shape and direction of advancement of professional knowledge. The needs of the whole social system make themselves felt. As long as societies need national cohesion and a sense of purposive continuity, nationalistic history is taught. As the socioeconomic-political system becomes rationalized, social sciences searching for general laws on a more contemporary plane evolve. Breakthroughs in engineering seem to occur when the whole system is ready for them, or else they are ignored. The role of professional associations in all of this is not yet understood. Certainly more studies are needed of the relationships between the nature and uses of knowledge and inter- and intra-organizational power.

Clearly there is a close correlation between a vocational group's position in the socioeconomic system and the organizational forms and group ethics necessary to sustain or advance that position. Contemporary neo-medievalism did not arise accidentally; the contemporary guild system was not the result of conspiracy. The modern economic system, with its anonymity and interdependence, could not function if there were no institutions to define occupational boundaries, rights, and obligations. From a social standpoint the problem has been how to keep those boundaries, once they are defined, from becoming so rigid that they preclude necessary adaptation to changing technology, changing social organization, and changing consumer needs and demands.

CHAPTER 3

The Work Revolution
and the Consumer Revolution

Two revolutions have been occurring in the twentieth century in relation to professional services: one continuing (now *within* the profession) to split the work system into interdependent work roles later reintegrated, through new organizations, for the conduct of professional work; the other revolution affecting consumption of professional services, now larger percentages of the public benefit on a more continuing, rather than an episodic, basis, with new methods for distributing these services. The changes in the organization of professional work and in the system of distributing professional services are comparable to, if not precisely the same as, the changes in industrial production in the first half of the nineteenth century: toward more specialized vertical and horizontal division of labor; many more professionals working together as a unit, rather than independently; special organization of authority layers within different kinds of work institutions; and the interjection of intermediaries between the professional and the consumers of his services, with more mass consumption and with departures from the fee-for-service method of payment.

The work and consumer revolutions have interacted. The structure of government and the lawmaking and law-enforcing processes affecting the professions have become much more complicated than they once were. The question is no longer merely one of distinctions and interactions, differentiations and integrations, between the professions and the larger community and its institutions; also to be considered are the interrelations between different elements of a profession and between the profession and intermediate institutions that organize work and consumption.

SPECIALIZATION

The growth of specialization has resulted in a proliferation of specialist organizations within the main professions. Specialization having begun earliest and having gone furthest among medical doctors,[1] there soon were numerous national specialized medical organizations. Often two or more associations competed for the same field. When national organizations were created, they were usually soon followed, but sometimes preceded, by local and state chapters primarily concerned with technical subjects.

Prior to the constitutional convention of 1849, New York lawyers had been divided into two categories, each practicing in a different type of court. In 1921 a Carnegie report on legal education suggested that American lawyers revert to this kind of categorization, a system similar to that in England. Most bar associations, however, favored a single profession and frowned on any specialization labels. Although all lawyers continued to belong to a single profession, specialization did arise and with it additional organizations, although specialist attorneys also belonged to the general bar association.[2]

Specialization for chemists, as another example, was reflected early in special associations: the American Leather Chemists Association, 1903; the American Institute of Chemical Engineers, 1908; the American Oil Chemists Association, 1909; the American Society of Brewing Chemists, 1945.

Beginning in the nineteenth century in the case of medicine and engineering, and becoming noticeable in the 1920's for lawyers and educators, three new trends affected professional organizations.

First, men who held special positions of authority within a given vocation began to form separate organizations still keeping their ties with the main body of the profession. Although the various education professions or layers of authority within the field of education have tended to belong to the main teacher associations, they have also formed supplemental associations. The National Association of School Superintendents dates from 1865. The National Association of Secondary School Principals began in 1916, as did the National Association of Deans of Women. The National Association of Elementary School Principals began in 1921. Similar organizations have appeared at the state level, with or without affiliation with a corresponding national association.[3] The bar has divided on the basis of authority and function, with national and state associations for judges, law professors, district attorneys and county counsel, public defenders, hearing officers and referees, attorneys general, and other government lawyers.

Second, the growth of a complex, industrialized civilization has required new professions to perform new kinds of work or to perform aspects of work formerly within the jurisdiction of older professions. These new professions have formed organizations of their own and function more or less on a horizontal plane, in terms of authority and status, with the older professions. The division of medicine into separate schools of thought has been declining. The American Institute of Homeopathy, founded in 1844, is a dwindling association. In the 1950's the American Medical Association and the American Osteopathic Association conferred about possible amalgamation. On the other hand, the division of the healing arts into such separate professions as dentistry, chiropody, veterinary medicine, pharmacy, optometry, began early and has continued, with each having its own national association. Engineering, too, has seen the definition and growth of numerous independent professions or branches of old professions. Engineers in the fields of safety, heating and ventilating, refrigeration, power, illumination, lubrication, and electronics and many other new engineering groups have all formed their own national organizations. Newer academic disciplines—sociology, anthropology, psychology—have resulted in new associations. New professions began to be self-conscious in the post-World War II era: public relations men formed the Public Relations Society of America; management consultants formed an organization, as did market researchers, physical therapists, occupational therapists, dietitians. Many of these new associations have been facing, and responding in similar ways to, the same kinds of problems the older professions faced seventy years ago.

When the professions do not meet new public needs, either because the consumer market is an unfamiliar or unlucrative one, because there are not enough professionals, or even because consumers do not want to pay high prices, sometimes new professions or lay vocational groups arise to fill the gap: for example, lay marriage counseling; designing of small buildings by professional designers rather than architects; giving of health services by chiropractors rather than physicians; supervising of artificial insemination of animals by lay practitioners rather than doctors of veterinary medicine; claims adjusting and representation before administrative boards and lower courts by laymen rather than attorneys.

Sometimes state licensing, which recognizes and isolates an elite professional group, opens the door to the formation of new professions to do the "grubbier" or peripheral work in the same field. And, of course, new vocational groups usually form their own associations.

In many fields there is a third trend: a vertical division, concomitant with the new division of labor on a horizontal plane, leading to the creation of new specialists on the basis of function, often parts of a work team in which some kinds of professionals are subordinate in authority. Members of the new layers of authority subordinate to physicians in the work team have formed their own professional organizations. To a lesser degree, similar vertical as well as horizontal organization has been occurring in dentistry; *e.g.,* the American Dental Hygienists Association, formed in 1923. Vertical division of labor has not been extensive in teaching and library work, but there has been much discussion of the need for categories of less well-trained workers to relieve the teacher or librarian of routine work.

As an indication of the growth of both horizontal and vertical division of labor in medicine, Herman M. and Anne R. Somers have compiled the following table listing health-service occupations in the United States for 1955:[4]

Professional, Technical, and Kindred Workers

Chemists	3,000	Pharmacists	111,000
Chiropractors	24,000	Physicians and surgeons	225,000
Dentists	98,000	Psychologists	4,000
Dietitians and nutritionists	22,000	Rehabilitation counselors	2,000
Engineers, sanitary and others	5,000	Social workers	11,000
Health program specialists	3,000	Statisticians and actuaries	2,000
Librarians, medical	7,000	Technicians	
Natural scientists		Medical laboratory	50,000
(*e.g.*, biophysicists)	4,000	Dental and dental	
Nurses, professional	430,000	hygienists	26,000
Nurses, student professional	113,000	X-ray	50,000
Optometrists	17,000	Therapists	24,000
Osteopathic physicians	12,000	Veterinarians	17,000

All Other Workers

Assistants, physician's office	75,000	Hospital and medical	
Assistants, dentist's office	55,000	program	9,000
Attendants, hospital and		Medical-records personnel	15,000
institution	337,000	Midwives	15,000
Managers and officials		Opticians	1,000
Health-department		Practical nurses	175,000
sanitarians	8,000		

With vertical and horizontal division of labor, difficult problems have arisen of coordination, teamwork, and relative spheres of jurisdiction and authority. A *Medical Economics* poll of 1,094 specialists found that 91 percent of them worried over jurisdictional disputes with their colleagues.[5] Because of this discord professional associations actively guard the professions' interests vis-à-vis potentially competitive or collaborative groups.

Sometimes members of different professions work together on a common problem, such as lawyers and doctors in malpractice suits, or lawyers and representatives of various professions who serve as expert witnesses, or lawyers and doctors and social workers on adoptions, or lawyers and accountants on business problems. Professional associations help to define their respective roles. One effect of the growth in the size of public structures and the development of a more complex building technology is that architects have to work with other professionals as a team: soil and site, structural, electrical, and mechanical (heating and plumbing) engineers. Architects themselves have urged the adoption of the concept of an aesthetic team that would include landscape architects, interior designers, sometimes painters and sculptors. Wherever two or more professions overlap, there have been jurisdictional disputes and questions of authority relationships. Who shall be the coordinator? Who does the synthesis for the client or patient? The associations try to establish general principles to govern the work relationships involved.

When the problem has not been one of collaboration, but rather competition for work between established professions and new vocational groups, sometimes the former groups have tolerated "encroachments"; sometimes they have reached jurisdictional agreements with the competing groups; more often, they have used a variety of devices to combat the encroachment.

CONSUMER DEMAND

Among the most important of the forces with which many professions must contend, in part a byproduct of their success, has been the growth of consumer demand for professional services; whereas once it came from only a few, that demand is now widespread. This has in turn changed the way professional services are dispensed and paid for—radically changed the structure of private institutions related to professional work and the role of public government.

Over a thousand-year period the modes of dispensing professional services may, in a sense, have gone full cycle, with public government coming to occupy a position somewhat analogous to that of the medieval Church. When the Roman Catholic Church held sway over the whole of Western Christendom, it monopolized education, the purpose of which was the training and indoctrinating of the clergy, not the laity.

With the advent of Protestantism and denominationalism within Protestantism, the various sects divided control over education. Denominational colleges were still primarily training schools for the clergy, but elementary education for the laity was sponsored by the Church—partially because stress on the individual's direct access to the Bible had been an ideological weapon in the class war between the upper middle class and the clergy of the Catholic and Anglican establishments, and also because now denominations were competitive and needed to indoctrinate their members and win outside adherents. If Church and State were closely united, as they were in New England, public schools were established. In regions where many denominations competed, each had its own parochial system. In parts of the South, where the Church of England was strong, and demonstrated its customary indifference to lay education (being an established church, without the compelling need to recruit new adherents), well-to-do people provided private schools for their own offspring and contributed to the poor through their church and the charity schools. Denominational competition via the establishment of institutions of higher learning continued unabated throughout nineteenth-century America. In the early part of the century these colleges were still presided over, and classes were taught, by clergy.[6]

In some phases of the medieval period, the Church administered the position of medicine, social work, science, and engineering. The Church also had its own law and lawyers. As in education, the Catholic Church and Protestant denominations continued to play a substantial role as employers of professionals or as intermediaries in the dispensation of professional services, while parallel professional services were being offered more and more on a secular basis.

Large numbers of secular professionals in nineteenth-century America worked as individuals on a fee-for-service basis, serving a relatively small percent of the public.

Changes in the nature of the consuming public in the twentieth century have led to changes in the methods of dispensing services. Population growth alone has greatly enlarged the number of potential consumers, and medicine helped to produce and then has been affected by the lengthening life-span, with more than four times as many persons over sixty-five in the United States in 1960 than in 1900. The percentage of old people was steadily increasing. Since the old are sick more often than the young, this condition has also increased the demand for medical services.[7] Urbanization and industrialization have brought more illnesses and accidents, more social and legal problems. By 1960 approximately 85 percent of the American people lived in the large metropolitan areas. Accessibility to services has further stimulated demand. So has a steadily increasing per-capita income with more money available for services. By 1959 approximately 40 percent of all family units were in the after-tax income bracket of $4,000 to $7,500 a year, compared with 20 percent in 1929 (using figures adjusted to take relative purchasing power into account); and 22 percent had after-tax incomes of over $7,500, compared with 9 percent in 1929.[8] Services formerly considered luxuries can now be purchased. The lengthening and spread of public education has tended to raise the level of expectations. In quality as well as quantity, Americans have been demanding more from professionals. And those with low income have begun to feel that regardless of ability to pay, they are entitled to some kinds of professional services as a matter of right.

The professional associations necessarily have taken some interest in the problem of services for people who cannot pay. For several centuries secular fee-basis professionals held the view that charity problems would be handled by the largesse of individual professionals. At one time "professional" nursing, under the aegis of charitable organizations, was almost wholly an act of mercy. Even today much social work is largely of this nature. It was once the concept and practice that doctors would handle a percentage of charity cases, that lawyers would volunteer to help widows and orphans on a personal basis, and that courts would assign attorneys to defend without pay indigent persons accused of crime. Sometimes medical societies maintained referral lists of doctors who would care for indigent or part-pay patients.

The codes of fee-basis professions, notably in medicine and the law, mildly exhorted members to give gratuitous services to deserving cases, but the mandate was not a strong one. For doctors this meant that the burden of charity, when it was assumed at all, was on the conscientious or tenderhearted, not on all members of the profession. Except for the successful lawyer with extraordinary philanthropic leanings, the task of defending the indigent accused of crime fell to the neophyte attorney. Such internship brought him experience, but his mistakes might cost the otherwise defenseless client his freedom, possibly his life.

Private philanthropic organizations constituted a second solution to the problem of caring for the indigent; for example, the nineteenth-century poorhouses and charity schools. Twentieth-century free legal aid has not been very comprehensive. Although there were 236 legal-aid offices in the United States by 1962, the National Legal Aid and Defender Association reported that nine large metropolitan areas had no organized legal services for the poor.[9]

Since private philanthropy has not been an adequate solution for all those who need professional, medical, or social services, a third approach is the provision of direct government aid to the indigent at public expense. Early in the nineteenth century public funds began to subsidize schools formerly maintained for the poor by private charity. In the twentieth century it has become common practice to treat indigent persons free at county hospitals. The services of social workers have also been available increasingly through government rather than private charity.

As a result of agitation beginning in the late nineteenth century, some cities have established public defenders to take the cases of indigent persons accused of crime. However, the idea of a public defender has spread slowly. By 1949 there were only twenty-eight public-defender offices in the United States. In 1962 more than half of the existing 110 defender offices were in California and Illinois, and 35 states and the federal courts had no defender system. Purists among lawyers argue that loyalty to the government that employs him and unconscious fraternal sympathy with the public prosecutor may temper the defender's zeal in protecting the rights of indigent persons accused of crime, but no practical alternative has been offered. In 1960 the office in Alameda County, California, had applications from approximately 60 percent of all persons charged with a felony in the county. (Not all of them proved to be indigent and therefore eligible.) About 500,000 people were served by defender offices in the United States as a whole. The public defenders handled very few civil cases, and so failed to solve the whole problem.[10]

Neither bar nor medical associations have played a strong role as intermediaries for the care of the needy, though there have been precedents for such a role. In 1940 the State of Washington provided by statute that county funds could be appropriated for legal aid and that the State Bar was to have supervisory powers over all legal-aid bureaus. War came the next year, and the statute remained on the books but did not go into effect. It was generally conceded that such a plan would work only with an official State Bar, not through private bar associations.[11]

Lawyers, doctors, and dentists grumbled at welfare cases handled at public expense, but they usually conceded that private charity did not work. A compromise plan has compensated private practitioners out of public funds. By 1950 less than half the counties in the United States paid counsel for indigent persons accused of major crimes, as was done in the smaller communities in states which had public defenders in the cities. When in 1961 the Kerr-Mills bill to provide federal funds for administration of medical care for the needy aged was being debated, organized medicine did not oppose the bill, but saw to it that under the bill private practitioners rather than county hospital residents would give physical examinations. In 1934 the California Medical Association persuaded the Los Angeles County Hospital to abandon clinics for out-patients in favor of private doctors, the fee to be paid by the county. The dental association in California lobbied for a law that would permit county welfare patients to be treated by private dentists.

The problem of costs for professional services extends, of course, far beyond care for the indigent. In the nineteenth century the tax-supported pauper school gave way to the concept of universally available free public schools, so that in the twentieth century publicly supported education all the way through college has been treated as a right rather than a privilege. Low- and middle-income people are beginning to think of medical care, too, as a right; and at the very least they want professional services at a reasonable cost, with some way of spacing payments or socializing the risks of high costs in crisis situations.

Behind some of the pressure for changed methods of payment have been changes in the need for services, the modern tendency being away from use only episodically and/or in time of crisis and toward continual use of services, with consumers sometimes seeking preventive services to avoid a crisis later.

According to Somers and Somers:

At the beginning of the century, the three leading causes of death were influenza and pneumonia, tuberculosis, and diarrhea and enteritis—all acute infectious diseases which affect primarily the young. By 1950, the three leading causes of death were diseases of the heart, cancer, and vascular lesions of the brain—chronic degenerative diseases associated primarily with older age groups and characterized by insidious inception, long duration and a high proportion of residual disability. . . . It appears clear that a progressively larger proportion of the nation's total demand for medical services will relate to the growing problem areas—chronic and mental illness. The corollary of this shift is an increasing need for long-term preventive, rehabilitative, semi-custodial, and medical social services in contrast to the great current emphasis on treatment of acute illness.[12]

The vast increase in government regulation has affected the practice of law, at both the state and federal levels. The federal income tax, beginning in 1913, has become one of the most devious and powerful tools of social control, touching everything from the birth rate to opera. Whereas once a peaceful citizen could be born, live, work, and die with a minimum of direct contact with law and government, interpretation of governmental rules and regulations has now become a necessary part of nearly every enterprise. All of this, plus the increased complexity of human relationships, has made preventive law more important; that is, seeing a lawyer routinely in matters of contract, property, or business arrangements. The interpretation of federal income tax laws has provided business for lawyers and accountants at least once a year.

A similar continuity of consumption has characterized salaried professions. Constant and rapid additions to scientific and technological knowledge have necessitated stressing continuing adult education rather than education concentrated in childhood and abruptly terminated during the teens. Industries use engineering and scientific researchers on a year-round, full-time basis, rather than only occasionally to develop new products.

Trade unions and industry have demonstrated growing concern to provide medical care for employees and union members. In the last quarter of the nineteenth century, railroads and mining and lumbering companies operating in remote and unsettled areas instituted medical facilities for their employees. In the first three decades of the twentieth century a few other industries continued and/or modified this precedent. Although by 1930 health-service plans sponsored either by employers, unions, or both covered only 2 percent of the labor force,[13] since World War II, unions and employers have assisted in extensive provision of health-service coverage for employees. For employers, this trend grew out of the new application of the old concept that a "contented cow gives more milk." When the wage-stabilization program of World War II curtailed union bargaining on wages and hours but permitted it for fringe benefits, union interest in medical care increased greatly. One way of providing care, of course, was simply to hire company doctors, possibly with workers contributing to costs of care in ratio to use. More frequently employers and unions have served merely as intermediaries, utilizing various forms of outside group plans, which either pre-existed or arose to meet this new demand along with rising demands of other individuals and groups. Most of these new plans have been based on the principle either of prepayment for services or of socialization of risk.

Employers, particularly multi-employer groups, have preferred cash-indemnity insurance for employees as involving the least red tape. Some unions, notably the teamsters' and building trades' unions, have also chosen this system. One answer to the new needs and demands has been the expansion of commercial health insurance for individuals and, after 1911, for groups. Although doctors' and dentists' associations have occasionally grumbled about insurance companies as intermediaries or failed to cooperate with various voluntary health-insurance plans, they have not actively combated private insurance and have even praised it in preference to more objectionable forms of prepayment. They have attempted to develop and enforce standards for health-insurance coverage and administration, especially when representatives of a group have negotiated with private-insurance carriers for coverage for all members of the group.

Following a scheme worked out by a professor at Baylor University in 1929, Blue Cross mutual (nonprofit) hospital-insurance plans became widespread in the 1930's, with the approval of the American Hospital Association and at first the opposition and then eventually the approval of the American Medical Association. The advent of Blue Cross mutual insurance plans stimulated regular commercial-insurance carriers to further promotion of their own programs.

Medical associations have objected vociferously to the development of closed-panel organizations operating on the basis of prepayment for services rather than the insurance principle, with partial or total restrictions on the patient's freedom to choose his own physician and with the physicians often working on salary rather than for a fee. Some organizations actually have been health centers owned and administered by trade unions for the benefit of particular groups of workers. Others, open to use by the community, have been controlled by unions, employers, or other organizations; by cooperatively organized consumers; or by participating physicians. The International Ladies' Garment Workers' Union established the first union health center in New York City in 1913. One of the first health cooperatives, which are usually found in rural areas, was the Community Hospital Clinic that the Farmers Union Hospital Association set up in Oklahoma in 1929. Group Health Insurance of New York is an example of a group plan jointly sponsored by doctors and consumers.

As an alternative to closed-panel groups, as well as to forestall government compulsory insurance, various medical organizations have established plans of their own. The county medical societies in Washington and Oregon provided a precedent for this as early as 1917. The Washington State Medical Association set up in 1933 the State Medical Bureau (later called Washington Physicians' Service) to coordinate the county bureaus. By 1957 there were seventy-three medical-association Blue Shield plans in the United States, Canada, Puerto Rico, and Hawaii.[14]

In the late 1950's, with both business and trade unions nationalizing at a rapid pace, Blue Shield programs had to be coordinated so that plans could be sold on a national basis when this was required. Hence the formation of the National Association of Blue Shield Plans, which was forced to surmount doctors' strong preference for local autonomy. Many physicians continued to object to the Blue Shield approach, too.[15] In California the Physicians' Service accounted for a fraction of prepayment coverage, and, beginning in 1954, some of California's physicians started county programs with some control in the hands of the medical profession but with less scope than the state association's program.[16]

The New York City Central Labor Council foreshadowed still another approach to group insurance. The council announced in September 1959 that it was considering buying its own hospital chain and operating an insurance system to compete with the Blue Cross and Blue Shield programs.[17]

Dental programs have followed the same patterns as medical ones, only on a smaller scale and about twenty years behind. Trade unions had established medical-care plans during and after World War II, and, looking around for new uses for their growing welfare funds, began in the late 1950's to develop plans for prepaid dental services. One of the first solutions was the closed panel of dentists to provide dental services on a prepaid basis. Despite the objections of organized dentists, these groups have prospered. From time to time there have been threats to expel members from the dental association, but the organization has rarely carried them out. By 1960 dental-service corporations were operating in California, Washington, Oregon, New York, and Rhode Island.[18]

The professional associations' service corporations were designed to retain control over medical work conditions, but the corporations have halted neither the growth of closed panels nor the pressures toward tax support of all medical care.

Combined prepayment and insurance programs have helped to meet an enormous demand for medical services. In 1940 fewer than 10 percent of Americans had any hospital insurance, only 4 percent had some surgical coverage, and slightly over 2 percent had any form of nonsurgical medical insurance. By the end of 1957 the percentages were roughly 71, 64, and 42, respectively.[19] By 1962 the Health Insurance Institute estimated that 140 million Americans had some form of health insurance.[20]

In contrast, other professions have been experimenting with acting as intermediary between the patient and the professional. The Alameda-Contra Costa County Optometric Association established in 1955 the California Vision Services as a nonprofit corporation. In July 1956 the CVS signed group contracts with two labor unions for prepaid vision care. The organization secured official sponsorship in February 1957 of the California Optometric Service.

Lawyers' associations have offered no prepayment plans, but have operated referral services, with lists of attorneys for counsel at nominal cost. Lawyers could participate or not, as they chose. The Los Angeles Bar Association established the first of these services in 1938. The American Bar Association's Referral Service Directory showed, in 1961, 4 plans in operation in Illinois, 7 in Michigan, 14 in New York, 11 in Ohio, and 16 in Pennsylvania. California had 41—13 in Los Angeles county and 11 in the Bay area. After initial misgivings bar associations advertised their reference services though advertising by individual lawyers continued to be taboo. Because organized bar activities were no threat to professionalism, recognized bar associations could do what private groups were not permitted to do. The Los Angeles Bar Association took another pioneer step by adding a criminal defense lawyers' service in 1954.[21] Accident-insurance policies usually provide for coverage of attorney's fees, at least a partial equivalent for lawyers of medical insurance for doctors.

It is possible that group prepayment may become an important factor in the dispensing of legal services, as for medical care. Legal services have been on occasion dispensed through lay intermediaries; and bar associations, like medical associations in similar situations, have objected. The Brotherhood of Railroad Trainmen has operated a legal-aid bureau to recommend certain attorneys to union members, the attorneys to work for a 20-percent contingent fee and to pay one-fourth of that for the support of the bureau. At one time California banks and trust companies advertised free legal services (*e.g.,* drafting wills and trust agreements) to attract potential customers. They gave legal advice, foreclosed trust deeds as agents for third parties, and presented reports to the probate courts through lay agents. Collection agencies advertised legal services and prepared their own cases for trial. Automobile clubs have deposited bail for members in automobile accident cases and sometimes defended them in court. Individual trade unions sometimes have an attorney on retainer to look after members' legal problems. Business corporations, too, occasionally supply to employees the counsel of the "company lawyers." And sometimes state professional associations, such as the California Teachers Association, have employed an attorney to aid members.

At the time of writing there were no statistics from which to assess the impact of departures from the fee-for-service basis of dispensing lawyers' services.

Government began to enter the field of education in the nineteenth century, so that use of private schools became a choice rather than a necessity and the great majority of schoolteachers became public employees. The medical profession in America in the mid-twentieth century feared that some equivalent change might occur in medicine, as had already happened in England under the National Health

Service Act passed by Parliament in 1946 and put into effect by the first postwar Labour government in 1948.[22]

In architecture, social work, and law, too, new consumer demands for services sometimes have been made to and through public government, often implying increased government activity in fields formerly left to the initiative of private professionals. Whether the third-party intermediary is a private insurance company, a trade union or business corporation, a group plan, or the public government itself, the old patterns of individualistic fee-for-service practice are shifting, and professional associations are compelled to reassess their ethic, their role, and their relations with public government.

NEW ORGANIZATIONS FOR PROFESSIONAL WORK

Consumer demands and needs have not, of course, been the only pressures for change. Technological advances, the bulk of new knowledge, the availability of capital, socioeconomic changes that have made large-scale undertakings more feasible as well as necessary— these and other factors have altered the old ways of dispensing services. Whatever the causes, all of the contemporary pressures for change seemed to point in the same direction: away from the guild model of an independent practitioner who directly serves those who consume his services, and who is regulated primarily by his peers, and toward the collectivization of professional work. To serve greatly increased demand, to provide continuity of service over longer spans of time, to permit coordination of workers, to allow work on projects of larger size, to make possible greater use of expensive equipment, to centralize and perhaps automate administration of clerical work, to correlate professional work with other kinds of service—for all of these purposes it has become more feasible to administer prepayment for services on a large scale through a third party, to bring larger numbers of professional workers into a going organization as salaried adjuncts. This has led to modifications in the old establishments in which professionals have worked—universities, school systems, hospitals, business corporations, government agencies.

Changes in the modes of compensating a given profession have tended, in the course of time, to move in the following sequence:

1. Individual, independent performance of work in exchange for fees from individual patients or clients or on the basis of limited grants of money under contract.

2. Individual performance of work, but on terms negotiated with an intermediary and with the intermediary continuing to perform some administrative functions relating to the professional and those he served. The intermediary might be the professional worker's own professional association or a subsidiary, a private organization or corporation, or public government.

3. Salaried work, under circumstances in which either the professional worker and/or members of his own profession in the work establishment determine a substantial amount of policy or laymen determine policy. Another possibility is a professional being hired to serve only his employer or to serve customers, patients, students, or clients.

With no intermediary, the professional might share quarters, equipment, and clerical and administrative staff with other members of his profession acting either as partners or as associates. Each might have his own patients or clients and collect his own fees. Or the group might share income as well as responsibility for patients and clients.

When there are one or more intermediaries, a professional might work in his own office, or share quarters and possibly income with others of his profession, or work for a salary in a closed-panel clinic. Another variation is setting up an establishment in which some professionals are on fee basis and pay a salary to other professionals— with or without intermediaries between the group as a whole and the patients or clients they serve.

The number of large offices has been growing, using intermediaries or not. Among the largest independent American architectural firms in 1962, one employed as many as 171 architects and another had 125 engineers; 300 draftsmen might be working in the same establishment.[23] Large urban law offices might bring together 100 or more partners, junior partners, and lawyer employees.

This tendency toward group practice has helped to revive the old possibility of corporate practice, which the professional associations strongly resisted for so long. In the 1890's, when a medical "union" was formed in San Francisco, the state medical society threatened to expel any of its members who cooperated, and professional antipathy toward corporate practice continued to be strong in the first three decades of the twentieth century. In the 1950's and 1960's, when federal tax laws granted many advantages to corporations, the professions began to reconsider their former stand. Incorporation, however, would tend to encourage the growth of group practice, and the patient or client might come to think of the corporation rather than the individual professional as the one responsible for his care; many more professionals might become employees rather than principals —conditions that contemporary guilds had been primarily created to avoid. Despite these objections, many states did pass laws permitting incorporation for some professions. But incorporation looked less tempting after new Internal Revenue Service rules indicated that professional corporations would have corporate tax advantages only if they had *all* the attributes of a corporation.[24]

The growth of group practice has forced the professional associations to reconsider not only what the relationship of the group or clinic should be to the professional association but also—if codes of ethics are to be consistent—what norms should guide the relationships of individual members of a large clinic to one another.

Professional associations have had to review, too, their role vis-à-vis the work establishments administered by laymen in which professionals work, whether on salary or for a fee.

William Kornhauser has noted some meaningful facts and figures on the relative growth in the number of professionals who work on salary rather than on a fee-for-service basis. Even in 1870, there were only half as many self-employed as salaried professionals. Between 1900 and 1950, excluding teachers, journalists, and clergymen, the main salaried professionals increased more than ten times, whereas the labor force only doubled and the total professional force quadrupled.[25]

The institutions in which these salaried professionals work have become more secularized. The proportion of public to parochial schools and colleges has steadily risen. More and more social work is done under secular auspices. Although there are still many nonsecular hospitals in the United States—in 1957 Catholics were maintaining 884 hospitals; in 1955 there were 75 Methodist hospitals; there are Jewish hospitals and hospitals of other Protestant denominations—their proportion to the total number has been declining.[26] Since professional employees of institutions having religious ties often also belong to special associations, this secularizing trend means that larger numbers of professionals might increasingly identify more closely with the main body of the profession.

A more interdependent division of labor has brought specialized professional workers together in larger projects requiring more capital equipment and providing services to the ultimate—often distant—consumer in more impersonal ways. Engineering and science have already moved far in this direction. In the early 1960's approximately 3,500 professional, technical, and clerical workers were assembled under one roof at Livermore, California, engaged in work on scientific problems related to atomic warfare. Similar aggregations of professional research workers can be found in large business and industrial corporations and in some universities and hospitals. Agencies of government employ numerous and diversified professionals, too. Since many of the older professional organizations were built around the concept of the worker as an individual craftsman, often on a fee-for-service basis, the new conditions of work and interprofessional relationships have brought forth new kinds of organizational responses.

Unlike doctors in European hospitals, in which authority flows from the administrative top, many private physicians in American hospitals have maintained their private offices outside and used the hospital for their private patients, in addition to donating care to the indigents in the wards. In this kind of institution members of the medical staff are assured of professional autonomy and authority over their own work. However, increased hospital costs and a constantly increasing ratio of nonmedical to medical personnel in hospitals (about 7 to 1 in 1961–2) have tended to diminish the authority of private physicians who use the hospital on a part-time basis or at least have made the exercise of authority more complicated. The hospital, rather than the physician, has usually paid nonmedical personnel. The growing practice of staffing hospitals with salaried medical men[27] has raised new questions about the place of the medical staff in hospital policy-making and the authority of the individual physician in relation to the services he performs. Inevitably it has raised questions about the role of medical societies vis-à-vis hospital administrations. If physicians are salaried, these questions are comparable in nature to those about the academic associations' relations to college and university administrations.

As one-room schoolhouses have given way to multi-storied schools in unified school districts, larger numbers of administrators and administrative staff people have worked under the direction of each superintendent and many more teachers work under one roof. New problems have arisen consequently both as to the relationships of teachers to one another and to administrative personnel. A still more complicated pattern of relationships is introduced when the school or hospital or even a law clinic is an adjunct to an educational institution and is used for training purposes.

Many professional associations were originally established by persons holding responsible administrative positions in the establishments in which professionals worked, so that often there was no clear-cut distinction between the needs of the establishments and the needs of the professionals who worked there. Later the work institutions often formed separate organizations.

As the professions have been dividing on the basis of levels of authority there has been an additional tendency for the various echelons of employees in hospitals, industry, and government to establish vocational associations specifically of their own. There are special associations for industrial physicians, nurses, and other professionals working in industry. The American College of Hospital Administrators was founded in 1933, and hospital employees are now represented by, among others, the American Society of Hospital Pharmacists, the American Association of Medical Record Librarians, special associations of hospital nurses, and the American Association of Hospital Accountants.[28]

One of the manifestations of the tendency to separate professionals according to authority has been the growth of unionization, which in effect separates administrators from the organization of professionals whose work is administered. The Chicago Teachers Federation, founded in 1897, joined labor's Chicago Trades Federation in 1902. Between 1902 and 1916 twenty teachers' groups in ten different states affiliated with the American Federation of Labor, and the American Federation of Teachers was founded in 1916 to provide national integration of local teacher unions.[29]

In 1952 engineering and scientific unions formed an independent national federation, the Engineers and Scientists of America. By 1960 the ESA had approximately 10,500 dues-paying members, mostly in the large aircraft and electrical industries. Fewer than 7,500 engineers and scientists in 1960 belonged to unions affiliated with the AFL-CIO. During World War II the American Chemical Society and the American Society of Civil Engineers helped form collective bargaining groups independent of organized labor, but because they were allowed to die or were continued on an ineffective basis, genuine collective bargaining was difficult to enforce. Professional societies have objected, in particular, to industrial unions combining professionals with other kinds of workers. One company-wide bargaining group is the Engineers and Scientists of California, which began in the late 1940's and had about 1,500 members in 1962, all employees of the Pacific Gas and Electric Company.[30]

Some nurses have joined hospital workers' unions. In 1953 twenty-two of thirty-four librarians at the University of Southern California made headlines when they designated an AFL Office Employees International Union as their bargaining agent. In New York City, between World War II and the early 1960's, lawyers, psychologists, doctors, and dentists established unions. Professional associations—

often led by administrators, men with a vested interest in individual independence, and sometimes employers of other professionals— quite naturally have done all they could to discourage or control unionization.[31] Changes in the conditions of professional work, however, indicate that someday the professional associations may be as unlike the professional guilds of the first half of the twentieth century as the trade unions of the 1840's were unlike the eighteenth-century craft guilds. Their relationship with government will inevitably alter.

Until recently the established professional organizations have been conservative in nature. They resist changes in their environment and change themselves reluctantly and only when environmental forces have made readjustment imperative.

The total situation for professional work is changing so rapidly, and the variables producing change are so many and so complicated, that it is impossible to say with certainty what the future will be. However, some things are manifest: the one-room schoolhouse has given way to consolidated schools in which there is grade-level or subject-matter specialization. The one-horse doctor, who did all the medical jobs for miles around, has been succeeded by doctor specialists in clinics. "Medical care is changing from a private relationship between two individuals into . . . a great network of specialized institutions."[32] The work of the versatile country lawyer is now handled by urban law factories. Everywhere one looks there is more organization—at each geographical level within a professional association, for each category within a profession, for previously unorganized vocational groups, organizations representing consumers, organizations representing the institutions in which professionals work, organizations of organizations, and organizations of the people who work for organizations. The twentieth century has seen a revolution in the dispensing of professional services in America comparable to the industrial revolution in the nineteenth century.

As Somers and Somers have pointed out, "There is generally a minority that welcomes the opportunities and the imperatives of new knowledge and new circumstances, and a majority that struggles to resist or delay alteration of the familiar. In medical care, as in other spheres of activity, the scientific and technological revolutions and their far-flung implications have not yet been organizationally assimilated."[33] The same could be said of every other field in which professionals work.

The medieval craft guilds, despite the aid of government, were powerless to halt the new industrialization outside their walls, and eventually found themselves superseded by trade unions. In all their battles and negotiations over rights and relationships, the professional associations have continued to keep in mind the ideal of an independent practitioner serving individual clients or patients or working in a context that acknowledges his autonomy and judgment. However, as the nature of professional employment is changing, sooner or later the nature of professional associations may have to change, too.

Whatever the future may bring, for the past 150 years in the United States, there has been a gradual differentiation and widely accepted articulation of an increasingly large number of work roles, at the same time as these clearly distinguished parts have been more and more closely integrated into the whole interdependent economic system. The appearance of major professional associations to define and protect the roles of professionals in relation to the public and to other economic groups has been one manifestation of this process; the development of many special groupings within each profession has been another. Interrelated with all of this has been an evolution of new forms and processes of government.

PART **III**

~

*The Continuum
of Government*

CHAPTER 4

Professional Associations
as Governments

Some professional associations, as has been previously stated, are a kind of private government. Like American public governments, professional associations have conducted programs and offered services that might otherwise have been done through more private enterprise or not done at all (*e.g.*, educational programs, group "welfare" programs for members of the association, research, counseling and placement). They, too, but to a considerably lesser extent, regulate the behavior of their members—their "citizens." They represent the interests of their constituency in relationships with other groups, or "governments." Some professional associations have also developed into preliminary arenas of public government, in which a large part of the most important public law affecting the profession is first formulated.

Two major facts about professional associations, both as private governments and as preliminary arenas of public lawmaking, stand out: (1) the initial structuring of the association and the development and change of its structure are determined by the socioeconomic-political context into which the association fits, as well as by a

109

dynamic within the association itself; and (2) the structure of the association alters with the passage of time in ways that, despite variations in detail, appear to be similar for the different professional associations, and these changes in turn alter relations with public government.

THE FORMAL STRUCTURE OF PROFESSIONAL ASSOCIATIONS

The internal structures of formal organizations having a quasi-governmental nature vary according to the nature of their members, the socioeconomic-political positions of members, the purpose of the organization, and, sometimes, how long it has been in existence. Organizations tend to fall into one of three rough structural categories adumbrated by Max Weber: the stable, hierarchical pyramid; the guild; or, for want of a better word, the sect.[1]

The first category includes the Roman Catholic Church, some of the Protestant churches organized along episcopal lines, most large twentieth-century business corporations, and in fact most large stable organizations whose officials need special experience and training and that are therefore bureaucratic rather than democratic. Some of the large, well-financed, older professional associations that have very large permanent staffs begin to resemble this form of organization. In fact, professional associations were often created to define and protect the rights of professionals either within or against this kind of organization. The ordering of employees or functionaries may become hierarchical and bureaucratic while the organization is still theoretically or in some other aspect an association of equal or autonomous individuals, as in the case of a large, stable business corporation still perceived, in part, as a company of stockholders.

Professional associations have usually fallen into the second category, which includes such seemingly diverse associations as the medieval craft and professional guilds, the joint-stock trading companies and Puritan congregational churches of the sixteenth and seventeenth centuries, and many craft unions until the 1930's. Members of these associations are approximately equal in attainments and social status. They have been admitted by the other members on the basis of special qualifications that all the other members also possess, and theoretically they have an equal share in framing the association's policies.

Just as there is a close correlation between socioeconomic position and ethic, there is also a close correlation between socioeconomic position and political forms and philosophy. It is interesting to follow the emergence of liberal, democratic ideas and practices step by step, from the self-governing guilds, through joint-stock companies operating along Lockean lines, through dual covenants and congregational organizations of Puritan churches down to the time of the American Revolution, when the state was conceived as having been created by a compact among presumably property-holding and presumably equal individuals. Nineteenth-century craft unions and modern professional associations show traces of this tradition. It might even be said that the history of the guild type of organization, the history of liberal, democratic ideas, and the history of middle-class struggles or defenses against men in the top power positions in pyramidal organizations and in hierarchical social situations are often the same. In other words, what Puritan ideas were to the Anglican church, the political theories of the seventeenth century were to the monarchy; what the medieval guild was to the feudal lord, and the craft union of skilled workmen has been to the employer, the modern professional association is in a modified way to school or university, hospital, or corporation administrators. The guild and its concomitant internal political structure and ideas are the power weapons of the middle class.

A third type (although of course not the only other type) of organizational structure involves really less an organization than a movement led by charismatic and demagogic personalities, egalitarian or defensively elitist in doctrine, emotional in tone. This kind of movement often begins as a rebellion against a status quo dominated by pyramidal and guild organizations—just as the religious sects in the United States were formed to satisfy emotional, social, and religious needs not served by the more established churches of the seventeenth and eighteenth centuries. Some nineteenth-century labor organizations and political parties have been of this type, even when pyramidal on paper. Liberal democracy tends to be too formalistic and too individualistic to please the members of sects. They want a sense of emotional unity and the vicarious feeling of power that a strong leader can give. With the possible exception of some of the nineteenth-century medical cults, professional associations have not fallen into this category.

Twentieth-century professional associations are fundamentally guilds in form as well as in function. Their internal governments have taken over some of the patterns of business corporations, and because they cover wide geographic areas in an age of far-reaching communication and rapid transportation, they have imitated some aspects of the American federal system of government.[2]

Officers of professional associations are more like business corporation officers than like public administrative officials. Except for the executive secretary, they are normally elected for brief terms, either by the board of directors from among its members, as in a business corporation, or by the delegate assembly, or occasionally through mailed ballot to the members.

The boards of directors (or boards of governors or executive councils) that make detailed policy are directly comparable to the boards of business corporations, though they might also be compared to the British cabinet or even in some cases, according to Oliver Garceau,[3] to the central executive committee of Soviet Russia. An association may have two or three executive-administrative bodies: a council or board, an executive committee, and a board of trustees. The particularly powerful executive boards of national associations virtually run the organization, because the assembly of members or their representatives meets so briefly and infrequently (at most twice a year) and because delegates to the assembly are far-flung. The meetings of many boards, both state and national, are by express rule or custom not open to nonboard members of the association. Clearly Montesquieu's doctrine of separation of powers, which had so much influence on American public government, has not significantly affected the government of American professional associations. The boards of directors operate in part like a legislative upper house, but they also function as the executive and possibly the judicial branches of the association.[4] In these respects the governmental structure of professional associations is similar not only to corporate government but also to American colonial government, which bore many resemblances to the government of joint-stock trading companies.

The structure of professional associations is like the structure of American public government in that, for example, the professional associations have written constitutions, though only limited judicial review. They have representative government, universal suffrage for all members, secret ballot, parliamentary procedures. Local units elect representatives to a delegated legislature at the state level, and the state in some fashion sends delegates to a national legislature. Their legislatures, which are often larger than American public legislatures but meet for briefer durations, resemble public legislatures in some of their forms and procedures.[5] There are similar problems in determining the basis and manner of apportionment of representation; many of the private legislatures have speakers and standing and interim committees like those of public legislatures; state delegates to the national private legislatures caucus as state delegations do in the federal House of Representatives; and "program" comes down from above to private legislatures, as it does from the executive branch to public legislatures.

In the large national associations, such as the National Education Association, the American Bar Association, and the American Medical Association, the delegate assembly usually elects the president, for he is the public representative in national affairs for the whole, presumably nationally united, profession. The president of the association not only has presiding and administrative duties but also is spokesman for the profession before public legislatures and the public at large. Though much power is formally vested in the president, the office is regarded as honorary and presidents are expected to stay within established patterns. Association presidents, like mayors in cities operating under a council and professional-manager plan, are primarily for ceremonial purposes.

CHANGE AND PARADOX

The internal development of many American professional associations in the twentieth century parallels similar developments in American public government in three major ways.

Decentralization and Centralization

1. *There have been gradually more regulatory and service activities at all geographic levels, more independent activity on the part of units at all levels, and at the same time more national integration.* In short, more government at the national level has not necessarily meant less local government, but rather more government at all levels.

Like many other phenomena in twentieth-century America, professional associations have been undergoing processes of both magnification and miniaturization; that is, the whole has got bigger while the parts have become more clearly articulated, differentiated, and integrated into the whole. The number of associations at the local and state levels has increased, and many of them are vigorous and opinionated vis-à-vis the national association. On the other hand, methods of integrating the associations at various levels have become more effective, and broad forces are at work that tend to increase the importance of national unity and of the national associations.

Seen from the national perspective, the associations tend to fall into three categories: those that are unitary, whose membership is directly in the national association and whose local chapters are subsidiary units of the national group; those in which local, state, and national associations are tied together in various degrees and modes of federation; and those in which the various geographic units go their separate ways. Whichever way they begin, associations tend to gravitate to the federative mode of organization.

Very often unitary organizations do not have strong governing powers over their own members. They rely on persuasion and influence to accomplish their goals and are not, in any complete sense, private governments.[6] Professions whose local, state, and national associations are partially independent of one another tend to have more disciplinary power over their members than do those whose local chapters are subsidiary units of a national association.[7]

The long-range tendency, both in organizations that begin as unitary and in those that begin in a disjointed fashion, is toward the pattern the general medical associations now follow, an integrated organization with each level having its own major function. This form of organization appears to be the most effective for control over membership. Physicians in all but a few states join the American Medical Association and their state medical association by being admitted first to a county medical society. Until AMA dues were made separate in 1950, joining a local component automatically meant membership in the AMA.[8] The governing structure of these organizations is pyramidal: the local units elect delegates to the state association's house of delegates, which elects delegates to the national house. The local units are chartered by the state associations, and the constitutions at each level must not conflict with the constitution of the level above. The state and local associations work with and through their national association in matters of professional education, public education, and federal legislation. At best, national integration is still only partial, though it is increasing, and one of the strongest deterrents to complete integration is the continuing decentralization in American public government.

Decision-making in professional associations is divided geographically somewhat as it is in American public government, but for many associations decisions made at the national level apply only to the internal affairs and public program of the national association or to the profession's federal legislative program. State associations, through their own representative bodies, make most of their own decisions.[9] Most of the rules and policies that directly affect members are enacted at the state level.

Normally state and local units determine the procedure for selecting their delegates. Persons selected customarily have been major leaders within the state and local associations; the national assembly is an assemblage of state and local leaders. Men come to the presidency of national associations typically through a long chain of organizational service, local, state, and national.

Two classic problems like those arising under the United States Constitution—the problem of who shall interpret jurisdictional issues, and then enforce a decision, between associations at different geographic levels, and the problem of whether the national body has direct jurisdiction over individuals or must work only indirectly through state and local units—have not been resolved in professional associations in the same manner as they have in American public government. There is no clear-cut federalism, with its brilliant conception of dual jurisdiction, in professional associations. The concept of judicial review has been only imperfectly developed.

The American Medical Association has the most well-articulated and integrated judicial system, but—as in American public government—the issue of states' rights constantly looms. One problem has been an absence of effective sanctions against recalcitrant units. Expulsion is always possible, but as Garceau has said, "A voluntary association cannot afford to contribute too lavishly to its own dismemberment."[10] Excommunication is sometimes used when the heretic was going anyway!

Like the American federal government, the national professional associations have resorted to the carrot (more than the stick), the national conference, the deploying of contact men, and propaganda as techniques for bringing about more uniformity and conformity among their component units.

Whatever the pulls in the opposite direction, there has been a gradual tendency, as in American public government, toward more national uniformity and centralization of decision-making. The national associations have promoted uniformity from the beginning; their efforts have been more successful partially because of improved communication, undoubtedly also because of changed mobility patterns among their members. For some salaried professionals who are in short supply (*e.g.,* nurses, teachers, engineers), movement about the country is easy and common. Uniformity in state practices both eases mobility and results from it. Some fee-basis professionals—architects and engineers, lawyers, accountants—of high rank within their profession regularly offer their services on a national or even an international basis while maintaining an office or offices in fixed locations. They, too, find uniformity an advantage. Centralization of decision-making has also come about because of increased activities by the American federal government in areas affecting the professions. In these respects professional associations are like trade unions, in which centralization and departure from local autonomy have been inevitable by-products of the nationalization or regionalization of business.

Centralization has important internal political implications for professional associations, for, as in American public government, the broader the geographic jurisdiction of the governing body, the higher the educational and occupational prestige level of the governors and the greater their lifelong commitment to organizational politics. Centralization means that more and more decisions will be made by urbanites occupying positions of authority within the professions; by specialists within the profession rather than generalists; and by people remote from the day-to-day problems of the average practitioner. And this leads to the second point about internal development.

Democracy, Bureaucracy, and Oligarchy

2. *The problems are becoming more technical, complex, and interconnected, requiring more expertise on the part of policy-makers; more bureaucratization of staff means that many important decisions are made by a few administrators at the top; yet there is also more internal democracy*—more universal suffrage, higher participation, more communication between leaders and members.

Evidence of More Democracy

Most professional associations include higher percentages of the profession as members than formerly. In 1912 the AMA represented only 50.6 percent of all physicians in the United States; the percentage rose to 65.1 in 1929, declined again to 60.8 in the depression year of 1935, and increased again to 66.8 by 1940. In 1957 it was estimated that 90 percent of all private practitioners in the country belonged to the AMA. The ABA's membership rose from a total of only 3.2 percent of the lawyers in the United States in 1910, to 9.2 percent in 1920, to an estimated 46.2 percent in 1960.

The same trends have been apparent in state associations. In 1907 only 14.7 percent of the teachers in the United States were members of state teacher associations; by 1916, 34.1 percent; and by January 1923 membership had jumped to 61.5 percent. Associations in southern states showed the least increase in membership.[11]

For most professional associations, although some have more rigorous admittance standards than others, the rise in the percentage of the total profession represented has been due in part to a deliberate change in policy from more to less exclusiveness. During the ABA's first quarter century, five years had to elapse after a lawyer's admission to the bar before he could be a member of the ABA. This was then changed to three years; and in 1928 any lawyer in good standing was eligible for membership, though a member could still be excluded by negative votes from four members of the association's board of governors. Not until 1912 did the ABA aggressively attempt to increase its membership; the NEA did not seek a broader membership base until 1917.[12]

Voluntary nonmembers often include the very young and the very old; the very poor; men working on salary (*e.g.,* in the armed services, for various branches of government, for industry, teaching in professional schools), where the profession consists primarily of fee-basis practitioners; people working in rural areas; and people who are in a marked minority by reason of race, religion, or sex.

But there were many involuntary nonmembers. In the early years the medical societies excluded men who subscribed to unorthodox methods of practice. Medical societies, bar associations, and even some teacher associations did not accept women; eventually all let down the bars. And race has long been a basis for exclusion, though

TABLE 1

NUMBER OF DOCTORS IN THE UNITED STATES AND IN THE
AMERICAN MEDICAL ASSOCIATION[13]

Year	Doctors in U.S.	Doctors in AMA	Percent in AMA
1912	137,199	69,402	50.6%
1913	137,199	70,274	52.7
1914	142,332	75,820	51.8
1915	142,332	75,637	53.1
1916	144,368	77,962	54.0
1917	145,338	81,207	55.9
1918	145,338	79,867	54.8
1919	145,364	82,288	56.5
1920	145,364	82,994	57.0
1921	145,608	84,542	58.0
1922	145,608	85,522	60.8
1923	145,966	88,070	60.3
1924	145,966	90,056	61.7
1925	147,066	90,128	61.3
1926	147,066	91,190	62.0
1927	147,291	93,337	63.3
1928	149,626	95,830	64.0
1929	149,521	97,452	65.1
1930	152,503	98,187	64.3
1931	152,633	98,898	64.7
1932	156,440	98,436	62.9
1933	156,487	95,996	61.3
1934	156,440	96,701	61.8
1935	161,359	98,137	60.8
1936	161,339	100,591	62.3
1937	165,163	103,755	62.8
1938	165,163	107,724	65.2
1939	173,879	112,210	64.5
1940	173,879	116,266	66.8

in recent years the professional associations have begun to desegregate.

The American Medical Association has refused to accredit its Negro counterpart as a constituent society, but the national teachers' and nurses' associations have taken steps to integrate Negroes more thoroughly into the association. In 1947 a joint committee of the

National Education Association and the (Negro) American Teachers Association recommended that Negroes be fully integrated into the NEA; in 1948 the NEA welcomed Negro delegates from three states that also sent white delegates. The American Nurses Association at its convention in 1946 voted unanimously to recommend to state associations that they integrate as soon as possible. Tennessee, the first to comply, was followed shortly by sixteen other states. The ANA made special provisions for direct membership of Negro nurses still barred from their state associations. By 1962 all the nurses' state associations were integrated.

At the state level racial exclusion is still practiced, even in states outside the South. As late as 1953 a bill was introduced in the California state legislature, but did not pass, to attempt to require the State Bar board of governors to adopt a rule prohibiting the recognition of any bar association that denied membership on the basis of race, creed, color, or national ancestry. The majority of the county medical societies in the South still exclude Negro doctors.[14]

In the Cold War years after World War II most associations also excluded persons who advocated the overthrow of the government by force. In 1941 the American Federation of Teachers reported it had uprooted the Communists in its ranks. In 1949 the NEA passed a resolution, with only 5 out of 3,000 voting no and with almost no debate, barring Communists from membership.[15]

Medical associations have also excluded or attempted to exclude applicants who participated in closed-panel prepayment plans, but the courts have declared that it is unlawful to deny membership on this basis.[16] But except for political subversives, the tendency has been more and more to admit categories of persons formerly excluded. Indeed, the trend of public law appears to be the same for professional associations as for trade unions: to prohibit arbitrary exclusion or possibly any exclusion at all and—in the case of the State Bars—even to uphold compulsory membership. If membership were the only criterion, it could be said that now, far more than ever before, the professional associations speak for the great preponderance of their profession.

TABLE 2

MEMBERSHIP IN THE AMERICAN BAR ASSOCIATION[17]

Year	Number of Members	Percent of Lawyers in U.S.[a]	Year	Number of Members	Percent of Lawyers in U.S.[a]
1878	289		1912	5,584	
1879	524		1913	8,033	
1880	552		1914	9,855	
1881	556		1915	9,609	
1882	571		1916	10,636	
1883	626		1917	10,884	
1884	671		1918	10,692	
1885	702		1919	10,825	
1886	704		1920	11,331	9.2%
1887	751		1921	14,111	
1888	752		1922	16,970	
1889	962		1923	19,554	
1890	943		1924	21,887	
1891	1,110		1925	23,524	
1892	1,062		1926	24,247	
1893	1,102		1927	25,719	
1894	1,144		1928	27,332	
1895	1,307		1929	27,411	
1896	1,393		1930	28,667	17.8
1897	1,489		1931	27,578	
1898	1,496		1932	29,795	
1899	1,541		1933	27,748	
1900	1,540	1.4%	1934	25,951	
1901	1,720		1935	27,178	
1902	1,718		1936	28,228	
1903	1,814		1937	29,452	
1904	2,000		1938	30,820	
1905	2,049		1939	31,680	
1906	2,606		1940	31,626	17.6
1907	3,074		1941	30,834	
1908	3,585		1942	30,601	
1909	3,716		1943	30,968	
1910	3,690	3.2	1944	?2,000	
1911	4,701		1945	34,134	19.0[b]

(Table 2 continued on p. 122)

(Table 2 continued from p. 121)

Year	Number of Members	Percent of Lawyers in U.S.[a]	Year	Number of Members	Percent of Lawyers in U.S.[a]
1946	36,484		1951	45,628	
1947	41,290		1952		
1948	41,262		1953		
1949	40,926		1954	52,624	
1950	42,121	22.8%	1955	55,101	
			1956	82,000[c]	
			1957		
			1958	89,887[d]	
			1959	94,872	
			1960	97,996	46.2%
			1961	101,520	
			1962	109,979	
			1963	113,466	

[a] Lawyers and judges in the United States according to U.S. Census: 1900, 108,000; 1910, 115,000; 1920, 123,000; 1930, 161,000; 1940, 182,000; 1950, 184,000; 1960, 212,000. Martindale-Hubbell figures are larger: 1951, 190,000; 1955, 251,514; 1960, 236,088; 1961, 257,403 (as reported by the ABA). *The Statistical Abstract* for 1962, using the Martindale-Hubbell directory, reports an even greater number of lawyers in the United States: 1951, 199,964; 1954, 241,514; 1957, 262,320; 1960, 285,933.

[b] Percent of lawyers in 1940.

[c] Approximately.

[d] As of December 31, 1957.

As a result of membership changes, persons of middling rank in the profession have more opportunity to hold leadership posts. At one time the National Education Association had as presidents such men as the presidents of Harvard, Columbia, and Stanford. During its first sixty years, administrators and professors overwhelmingly dominated the NEA, partially because offices tended to go to positions rather than to individuals—positions of authority and held by men. As a result of the revolt in 1910, a woman became president, but she was a superintendent, not a teacher. The first classroom-teacher president was chosen in 1928, but not until after administrator-versus-teacher pressures had been building up for a long time. Since then presidents more frequently have been classroom teachers.

The same is true in state associations. In 1918, 72 percent of the California Teachers Association's Council were administrators; by 1927, 68 percent; by 1942, 50 percent; and by 1962, only 22 percent.[18]

The new democratic spirit in education associations reflects not only a closing of the formerly wide gap in education and quality between the leaders and the run-of-the-mill members of the profession, and an increase in the percentage of the classroom teachers who belong, but also a change in philosophy. In the late nineteenth century councils of notables or elders governed national and state education associations. The NEA organized in 1880 a fifty-one-member council consisting of prominent educators and some college presidents. It was to be an elite group, with somewhat ambiguous constitutional authority, that would pass on its wisdom to those less wise. The oracular nature of the council was gradually diminished by additions to its size—until a limit of 200 was established in 1940—so that by the mid-1920's it no longer had its former distinctive quality, and in 1947 it was discarded altogether. The new empiricism in education and learning was partially responsible for its downfall; social science research methods replaced the dogma of the notables.[19]

Although boards of directors, particularly of national professional associations in which the membership is scattered and remote, exercise a high degree of discretion and power, historically the trend has been to try to make boards more democratic through shorter terms, greater limitation of the number of terms, and increases in the size of the board. Other tests of democracy yield mixed evidence. Although most associations appear to be dominated by "ruling cliques," there is enough turnover in office to permit the would-be office holder access.[20] Another test of democracy is whether there is factionalism within the organization and whether real contests for office occur. The authors of *The Worker Views His Union* maintain that leaders and active members of trade unions regard factionalism as necessary for local democracy. Factions, they say, keep close watch on one another, permit the development of rival centers of power,

TABLE 3

MEMBERSHIP IN THE NATIONAL EDUCATION ASSOCIATION [21] [a]

Year	Membership	Year	Membership	Year	Membership
1857	43	1892	3,360	1927	181,350
1858	75	1893		1928	193,145
1859		1894	5,915	1929	205,678
1860		1895	1,065	1930	216,188
1861		1896	1,579	1931	220,149
1862		1897	1,857	1932	207,418
1863	187	1898	1,963	1933	189,173
1864		1899	2,214	1934	187,645
1865	173	1900	2,332	1935	190,944
1866	126	1901	2,838	1936	165,448
1867		1902	3,215	1937	181,228
1868		1903	4,288	1938	195,605
1869		1904	4,541	1939	201,682
1870	170	1905	5,261	1940	203,429
1871		1906	5,168	1941	211,191
1872	292	1907	5,044	1942	217,943
1873	380	1908		1943	219,334
1874	345	1909	6,030	1944	271,847
1875	355	1910	6,909	1945	331,605
1876	214	1911	7,036	1946	340,973
1877	160	1912	7,865	1947	386,643
1878		1913	7,582	1948	441,127
1879	256	1914	7,063	1949	427,527
1880	354	1915	7,441	1950	453,797
1881	247	1916	7,878	1951	465,266
1882	290	1917	8,466	1952	490,968
1883	253	1918	10,104	1953	516,463
1884	2,729	1919		1954	561,708
1885	625	1920	52,850	1955	612,716
1886	1,197	1921	87,414	1956	659,190
1887	9,115	1922	118,032	1957	703,829
1888	7,216	1923	133,566	1958	616,707
1889	1,984	1924	138,856	1959	667,120
1890	5,474	1925	158,103	1960	713,994
1891	4,778	1926	170,053	1961	812,497

[a] Using U.S. Census figures on the number of teachers in the United States, NEA membership was .5% of all teachers in 1900; 1.1%, 1910; 7%, 1920; 20%, 1930; 18%, 1940; 38%, 1950; 42%, 1960.

keep members informed on issues, add interest to meetings and elections, help develop leadership ability independent of the administration, give members an opportunity to choose between competing programs and candidates, increase the importance of membership meetings as decision-making bodies, make officers discreet in their actions, and hold them accountable.[22]

Some professional associations practice factionalism privately and deplore it officially. Others encourage contests for office. Election of the first woman president in the National Education Association followed a year-long campaign of letter writing and vote soliciting by a militant women's group, who nominated their candidate from the floor in opposition to the nominating committee's choice—and won. More recently it has not been unknown for an election contest in the NEA to be waged for a year.[23]

The American Medical Association passed a resolution in 1902 that soliciting votes for office was not in keeping with the dignity of the medical profession and would be considered a disqualification for office. State associations may also forbid electioneering. However, it is not unusual for several candidates to run for president-elect and for elections to be preceded by considerable behind-the-scenes maneuvering. This does not necessarily mean that candidates represent different viewpoints. It is customary for men who rise to office in the AMA to have for years worked their way up gradually from county society office. Basic differences between opposing candidates are unlikely; elections for delegates to the AMA House are rarely contested. In Alabama the president has appointed the delegates. Only four out of twenty-four state societies, in the early 1950's, reported competition for AMA delegates' posts. The Kansas medical association is unusual in that it requires two nominees for each position.[24]

The AMA, strongly desirous of maintaining a united front to the public, deplores open disagreement. *The Journal of the American Medical Association* rarely prints opposing views; nor are most state journals controversial, the *New England Journal of Medicine* being a notable exception.[25]

TABLE 4

MEMBERSHIP OF SOME MAJOR NATIONAL
PROFESSIONAL ASSOCIATIONS, 1961[26]

American Institute of Architects	13,500
Society of American Registered Architects	3,000
Association of Women in Architecture	1,095
American Society of Landscape Architects	1,750
American Bar Association	97,000
Federal Bar Association	7,800
National Association of Claimants Counsel	7,600
American Patent Law Association	2,200
American College of Trial Lawyers	1,250
National Lawyers Guild	1,000
National Association of Women Lawyers	1,000
National Bar Association [Negro]	740
Federal Communications Bar Association	500
Association of Insurance Attorneys	325
Association of Immigration and Nationality Lawyers	250
Consular Law Society	100
Association of Customs Bar	47
American Chemical Society	91,000
American Institute of Chemists	2,900
American Oil Chemists Association	2,750
American Society of Biological Chemists	1,651
American Leather Chemists Association	932
American Society of Brewing Chemists	870
Society of Cosmetic Chemists	750
National Education Association	713,994
American Institute of Electrical Engineers	65,000
American Society of Civil Engineers	45,800
American Institute of Chemical Engineers	19,000
American Library Association	24,000
American Medical Association	176,000
American Society of Internal Medicine	6,500

(Table 4 continued on p. 127)

(Table 4 continued from p. 126)

National Medical Association [Negro]	5,000
Industrial Medicine Association	4,000
American Dental Association	94,696
American Veterinary Medicine Association	15,300
American Psychiatric Association	12,000
National Chiropractic Association	8,247
American Nurses Association	174,000
National Council of Catholic Nurses	20,000
American Association of Industrial Nurses	4,500
American Institute of Biological Science	85,000
National Association of Social Workers	27,000

Organized opposition to incumbent policy has developed in medical associations in California and New York, but overthrow of established leadership is rare.[27] Medical associations usually manage to maintain a united front, which may not mean that dissent is quelled, but rather that the majority of physicians agree with or are willing to go along with the stands their associations take. Surveys and polls of physicians indicate that this latter interpretation is correct. Even when dissident groups within the national AMA form over public policy issues, they do not attempt to capture the association's governmental machinery.[28]

Free debate is more commonplace and more accepted in bar-association circles, probably because lawyers are accustomed to opposing one another in their daily work and have well-established traditions permitting underlying fellowship and unity despite strong advocacy of opposing views. Controversy is their style of life.

With the possible exception of the medical associations, the absence of dissent appears to result from membership apathy as much as or more than from any effort to quell dissidence. Until 1936 only about 2,000 to 3,000 attorneys attended the annual ABA convention, less than 2 percent of American lawyers. An American Medical Association survey indicated that 60 out of the 64 societies with more than 300 members reported attendance of under 50 percent; 48 of 581 with fewer than 100 members reported less than 50 percent; whereas 111 of the smaller societies reported 90- to 100-percent attendance. The New York Medical Society considered 25-percent attendance at business meetings "good."[29]

Voting participation, particularly for nurses' associations, is often low, even when voting is by mail. In fact, some associations report that mail ballots result in cut-and-dried elections or give an edge to men who have been well publicized.[30] Since members are given the opportunity to vote and are permitted or even urged to put themselves forward for office, their indifference to these opportunities might imply a form of consent. If they disagree with the policies of the leaders, often they apparently do not disagree strongly enough to make their dissent known and felt. In any case, democracy in many associations—as measured by membership, participation, voting, and office holding—has increased over the past several decades.

Bureaucracy and Oligarchy

On the other hand, there is evidence of oligarchy and bureaucracy: long tenure in the more powerful positions; the path to high office at the national level normally through long service in offices at levels below; and positions of power tending to be held by persons of high (but not the highest) prestige and authority within the profession. Further, permanent staff members play an increasingly important role in making or guiding decisions.

Recent studies of the major associations for teachers and the leading fee-basis professions show that despite the democratization that has occurred, the leaders are still people who occupy positions of relatively high prestige and authority within the profession (administrators and professors), men rather than women except where women outnumber the men in overwhelming numbers, Caucasians rather than non-Caucasians, urban rather than rural, middle-aged rather than young men, persons who have some control over their own time (which means men from large law firms with big clients, surgeons, education administrators, and supervisors). They make an avocational career out of association politics, serving in offices at every level and throughout their lives. Often they have ample opportunity to communicate with one another outside the professional association because they belong to the same large law firm or practice in the same hospitals, because they frequent the same clubs or socialize (within a profession, not between professions) in the same places. Especially at the higher levels they have worn and do wear several hats—within the professional association at various geographic levels, by teaching as well as practicing or perhaps administering a professional school, by serving on public boards and advisory committees, and by holding office in other specialist professional associations or on the boards of special foundations. The higher the level of office, the more the professional schools from which the office holders have originated are the schools of high prestige.

In two careful statistical studies of leaders in education organizations—one for the United States as a whole and one for the Inland Empire region of the Northwest—two Stanford masters' candidates have shown that for the United States as a whole, "the vast majority of educators in elementary schools have little or no voice in their professional associations."[31] Whereas most of the members have been women working in rural communities and teaching at the elementary level, and not in administrative capacities, teacher organizations have been controlled mainly by men from cities with populations over 25,000, teaching at the high-school level, and in administrative capacities. The broader the geographic jurisdiction of the association, the more this tendency is revealed. Only in large urban associations have women classroom teachers had reasonably proportionate representation in leadership positions.

Garceau's studies of leadership posts in the AMA and selected state medical societies indicated a comparable pattern. He found that they were dominated by urban specialists who had well-established practices and could leave their patients to assistants or partners while they did medical-society work, or who had independent incomes or practices where the unit return was exceptionally high. He also noted a higher preponderance of professors than their proportion in the profession would warrant. The longer the tenure, the higher the proportion of professors and urban specialists; the more powerful and important the post, the higher the percentage of these men.[32] A more recent study has found that in 1949 there were 72,500 general practitioners, 55,000 specialists, and 23,000 in mixed categories, yet 90 percent of the AMA officers were usually specialists, all but one of the members of the 1954 board of trustees were specialists, and all presidents, vice presidents, and speakers since 1947. About half of all doctors in private practice in 1957 were family physicians, but only 35 members of the 192-member House of Delegates of the AMA were family doctors.[33] A study of the Massachusetts and Colorado houses showed the same balance in favor of urban areas and the same difference between long- and short-term men.[34]

There have been no such thorough studies of other professions, but a rough tabulation of members of the board of governors, officers, and committee chairmen of the California State Bar for the 1950's indicates a high proportion from two or three law firms in Los Angeles and five or six in San Francisco—large law firms with a high proportion of corporate clients. Although nurse administrators and professors constitute only a small percentage of all nurses, they hold most of the officer posts in nurses' associations. Dentists, too, tend to select specialists as state and local leaders, although in 1961 the ADA house had only 47 specialists, including 22 orthodontists, out of 416 members.

Since the number of specialists has been rising in proportion to general practitioners among physicians, dentists, and lawyers, it can be expected that their professional associations will have more rather than fewer specialists as leaders. As the association gets larger and its affairs become more complex, it requires more leaders who can spare the time. The president of the California State Bar reported in 1961 that it took the members of the board of governors about 6,000 man hours a year to serve; there were forty actual meeting days plus all the time required for preparation.

As the association grows older, larger, and wealthier—as most of the large ones have—it hires more and more staff people. For a long time professional associations resisted hiring professional public relations men and legislative advocates on the grounds that it was "unprofessional" or "undignified." Then, beginning tentatively in the 1930's and capitulating rapidly in the 1940's and 1950's, they did hire such men, as well as special legal counsel and research directors. In the 1950's some of them were also adding actuaries for their many insurance problems and special directors for radio and TV.

Staff members often wield considerable, though sometimes inconspicuous, power, and staffs are increasingly professionalized and bureaucratized. Many staff members do not belong to the profession they serve and, in fact, are in a specialist profession of their own or the National Association of Association Executives. As staffs grow in size and permanency they are given pensions and other benefits, resulting in a low turnover in the higher offices. If they move, it is apt to be from the professional association in one state to the association in another state. Ruler of the staff roost is a salaried executive secretary, whose job is not an easy one. During 1953 the executive secretary of the California Teachers Association attended 141 conferences, conventions, and committee meetings; made 72 speeches, necessitating more than 125,000 miles of travel and over 100 nights away from home; and directed the operations of headquarters. Under the executive secretary may be a deputy and several assistants, each in charge of a major aspect of the association's activities.

The power of executive secretaries varies, and this is undoubtedly due not simply to individual personalities but to differences in the nature of people drawn to a particular profession. The executive secretaries of bar associations tend to have less power than their counterparts in medical and teacher associations. In most associations, however, the executive secretary not only is chief administrator over a corps of subordinates but also serves as public relations man and legislative advocate for the association. He is the pivot wheel in the professional association and probably its most powerful individual, though nominally he takes his directions from other people. He is the expert among amateurs, for he usually holds his post a number of years, whereas association officers and board members come and go.

For years the American Medical Association was said to be the lengthened shadow of the editor of its journal, who was called the "czar of the medical world . . . the most dynamic, the most vocal, the most capable in terms of myth-making and business management."[35] The executive secretary of a state teacher association not only greatly influences everything that goes on within the association but also may be one of the greatest single influences upon public education in the state.

As problems become more technical and complex the amateur and transitory officers of associations more than ever must put their faith in staff men to map out programs and make the daily decisions. Staff men are to the professional associations what the civil service is to public government.

Although an egalitarian democracy is lacking within professional associations, there is no reason to presume that professional associations are less democratic than American public government, where voter turnout in local elections may also be low, where turnover in Congress is markedly below turnover in the houses of some professional associations, where a bureaucratized civil service has replaced the spoils system, where more and more decisions are made at the top by those in command of the necessary technical information, where not only is there more government at all levels but also the national government plays an increasingly important role, and where the median education and social rank of top national decision-makers are markedly above the median for voters at large. As in professional associations, in public governments there has been some increased democratization: suffrage has gradually been extended to those without property, to Negroes, and to women; political parties have been transformed from private to public associations; and open primaries augment the convention system of selecting candidates.[36]

With the advent of an interdependent division of labor, with the maturation of an economic organism whose frame of reference is increasingly national rather than local, there is greater articulation of the parts at the same time that they are more integrated into the whole —in the professional associations and in public government. Since it is a highly complex, rational system, the comprehension and consent of the participants are necessary if it is to function well. What is true of the economic system is also true of the political system, which interacts with it. And so we have the seeming paradoxes of centralization and decentralization, bureaucratic oligarchy and democracy.

Individualism and Community

3. *There is strong ideological stress on individual freedom, and yet at the same time more and more is done for the welfare of the citizen-member, more socialization of risk among members has developed, and more emphasis has been put on the member's duty to the association—the corporation "family" of the community.*

Since the paradoxes in the development of professional associations also appear in American public government and in other private organizations, it is reasonable to conclude that none of the traits is accidental, but rather that each is an integral part of the total development of the American socioeconomic-political system. The seemingly contradictory traits are different facets of a whole, necessary to one another.

THE VERTICAL INTEGRATION OF GOVERNMENT

The degree to which a profession is interested in some kind of formal regulation of itself outside of the institutions of work is a product of its power in the private socioeconomic sphere: the more vulnerable its position, the more it wants outside regulation. Professions vary greatly in the amount of regulation they seek.

Public Government Can Be Helpful

What do the associations use public government for?

It should be remembered that for most professionals public government is not simply an abstract sovereign or a detached public agency to which they relate as an ordinary citizen might relate. When public government is their employer, as it often is, relations are comparable to those of a private employer and employee. When public government is their client, as it is sometimes for architects, engineers, and accountants, the relationship is comparable to that with a private client. Public government subsidizes directly or indirectly the work of many professions. Lawyers and accountants are intermediaries between private citizens and public government. Where the profession neither serves the general public directly nor has a direct relationship to public government in its everyday work, but is instead employed by private organizations—such as independent or quasi-independent colleges and universities, large engineering corporations, and large research institutes, even if the financing comes from government—then that profession does not often turn to public government for aid in solving its problems. The most essential relationship of these professions is with the private employer, and to define itself, its work, and its rights vis-à-vis that employer, the profession relies on a national association, stressing the "mystery" of the profession's skills and knowledge, or it takes the course of unionization. The organized professions or segments of professions that serve the public or have an everyday work relationship with public government tend to depend heavily on government—primarily state government—to provide them with recognition, tools, and sanctions so that they can exercise control over the circumstances of their work. When they turn to public government, for most of them "control" and "work" are the key words. Although bar associations have broad legislative programs and some medical societies have tried to repeal the federal income tax, seldom (for some, never) are professional associations officially concerned with governmental actions on issues not related to their work or to work circumstances.

When professions seek governmental help, they do so with the following aims in mind: (1) to control preparation, entry, and practice; (2) to maximize favorable public opinion and so obtain guarantees of freedom on the job; (3) to rationalize work; (4) to maximize economic returns; and (5) to facilitate their work.

1. They want help in gaining control over preparation for and entry into their vocation, as well as control over those who are in the profession, when they do not have sufficient control over the job market to gain these ends by private means. Usually this is the case when they work for many dispersed employers or for individuals on a fee basis.

If a profession gains control over the qualifications, preparation, and examination of all those who enter the profession, it has taken the first major step toward more comprehensive control over its own work. Unless it can gain a private monopoly on the job market, which is difficult indeed when preparation for the profession is no longer solely by apprenticeship, the only way to control entry into its ranks is to borrow the coercive power of an organization that embraces the whole community—namely, the state. The professions do not want to, and in fact do not, stand in relation to the state as governed to those who govern. Rather, they go to the state for a seal of approval, for public recognition of their identity and merit.

Where they feel that their status is sufficiently high in the public eye, in relation to employers and in relation to competitive professions, they ask the state to delegate to them a good deal of self-governing power. To the degree that they feel insecure in their private position vis-à-vis the public, employers, or competitors, they are content to be delegated less power and have more regulation done by and in the name of state agencies, providing they are strong enough to get favorable regulatory laws in the first place. They prefer to have the state as a go-between where they are particularly vulnerable to attack, but they seldom give up the idea of self-government. Consequently there is a close tie between the state board or agency and those who are supposedly regulated. The associations seek from public government tools to help them organize more effectively; for example, statutory authorization of payroll deductions for teacher associations or recognition of the right of publicly employed professionals to form unions for collective bargaining. It is a question of balancing factors, counterbalancing the forces impinging upon them, using the state as a buffer, borrowing its power and dignity, to create as large a sphere of self-government as possible.

Statutory delegation to professional associations of the power to set and enforce rules of behavior, with the backing of the public law, constitutes the apogee of professional status. With their tenure rights and their rights to testify in cases of dismissal, teachers demonstrate that a measure of autonomy and self-government is possible even for vocations employed entirely by public government. Teachers and lawyers provide interesting examples of the fusion of private and public authority. Groups having such self-governing rights and freedoms protected by law have parallels in the medieval situation. The Anglo-American jury system is based on the principle that a man should be judged by his peers. In the stratified feudal social system this meant judgment by his equals, who were also familiar with the circumstances of the case. The State Bars' disciplinary system, one that teacher associations seek to establish, harks back to ancient ways, and other professions would willingly follow suit.

2. All of the professions want some measure of status—that is, prestige in the eyes of the public—and some measure of freedom on the job, and they believe that the two go together. They think maximizing favorable public opinion entails both controlling the nonconformists within the profession, who might jeopardize the reputation of the whole, and creating as large a sphere of autonomy and freedom for professional practice as society will allow. They strive for a balance between freedom and conformity, using the latter to gain the former. Consequently they seek governmental statutes and regulations that will guarantee their freedom or help neutralize public pressure that threatens to encroach on their freedom. Publicly enforced definitions of their freedom are, of course, more reliable than mere private claims. Public statutory declarations of conformity

to community norms are more convincing and conspicuous than private declarations.

Teachers want a share in decision-making in the school systems, and they want freedom in the classroom. Since administrators, parents, and the general public cannot be relied upon to grant this kind of freedom, teachers welcome state laws that define their rights. The teachers' union, which represents those teachers who feel the most constrained, places heavy stress on civil liberties of all kinds and seeks laws prohibiting discrimination on the basis of race, age, and sex.

Each of the professions wants its authority to be accepted and respected in its own sphere. To succeed, it has to reassure the public that it will not violate the fundamental standards of the community. The form this reassurance takes is writing into law provisions that persons who have been convicted of crimes involving moral turpitude relating to practice of the profession will not be admitted to practice or retain the right to practice. In other areas of special tension between the profession and the public, individual clients, or patients, a statutory law may clarify the situation. As long as public pressure for book censorship exists, librarians want state laws that will keep the local censors at bay but will also spell out censorship rules so that the librarian is not in too vulnerable a position.

A profession may also want from public government commemorative postage stamps and ceremonial weeks. Sometimes even a special public agency, bureau, or department, possibly with a cabinet post directly pertaining to the profession, is sought not only because it provides access and service but also because it symbolizes the profession's "arrival," legitimacy, and importance. It then wants as much control as possible over the agency's decisions; in this way it can control its own fate in the name of the community at large.

3. The professions employed by government want to rationalize the work process—make work uniform and predictable—and mitigate the more conspicuous instances of personal influence or chance that affect professional advancement. They are in the process of defining

rights and obligations in terms of vocational status. Their efforts in this direction are only partial and sometimes not articulate, but discernible nonetheless. Uniformity aids in controlling the profession; on the other hand, control is used to achieve more uniformity. Even though the group stresses individualism vis-à-vis outsiders, conformity is sought within the group. In this way the professional has a buffer between himself and those who might otherwise exercise arbitary jurisdiction over him.

Teachers, particularly, resort to state law—to regulate class loads and hours of work, to achieve a more uniform standard. The teachers' union has a strong leveling bent; it seeks to equalize salaries so that there is less differential between old and young. All teachers are interested in protecting themselves against arbitrary lay whim, and they rely on state tenure laws. As a result of their lobbying, New Jersey passed the first statewide tenure law in 1909; by 1957 thirty-three states had tenure laws, some not yet statewide in application.[37] Many state colleges and universities provide tenure for teachers. Civil service reform has similar aims, but does not stress peer-group determination of rights and obligations. The independent fee-basis professions lean in this direction when they feel they have more freedom to gain than to lose by this approach. They also want control over the circumstances surrounding their work. Unlike the trade unions of skilled craft workers, the professional associations turn to statutes and administrative rules, rather than private contract, either because the employer is government or because employers are too dispersed for the purpose of bargaining.

Since most professionals other than teachers are privately employed, the issue of tenure has been irrelevant or has not been a state matter. However, since the number of professionals employed by government is constantly increasing, the issue may become significant in the future; other professions may look to the teachers as a precedent.

4. The professions want to maximize their economic returns. If public government is employer, client, or subsidizer, the profession may seek larger appropriations to finance the projects in which members of the profession are employed. This is not always true. The

incomes of lawyers and tax accountants are deeply affected by the extent of governmental activity, since much of the profession's work is to aid clients in their relationships to public government, and yet both groups often espouse a laissez faire ideology. A few professions want both floors and, to some extent, ceilings on professional incomes in order to permit control and to safeguard against public discontent. They may turn to public government if the need seems urgent and if their private bargaining power or control over pricing of services is manifestly inadequate. Similarly, professions have sometimes turned to public government to establish minimum salaries or fees and have also sought governmental aid in matters of retirement and, for teachers, sick leave.

Public law profoundly influences the economics of demand for professional work and the salaries paid. Since teaching jobs depend on school financing, this has been a central concern of the National Education Association and state teacher associations.

5. Finally, the professions seek to use the tools and resources of public government to carry out their professional work. Despite what cynics may believe, the motivations of the professions are not entirely narrowly self-interested ones. All of the professions evince genuine interest in the end purpose of their work; and when public government plays a role affecting that end purpose, they take an interest in that government action.

Many professions are forced to be concerned with public government because it is through public government that other groups seek to alter the nature or terms of professional work. If a profession does seek regulation, in order to place a protective buffer zone of peer-group standards between the individual professional and the layman, then it generally finds that the internal sanctions of the professional association are not enough and that some kind of reinforcement from public government is necessary. In order to achieve that reinforcement, the association has to integrate its internal structure more closely and keep its members more cohesive—in short, it has to regulate in order to get regulation. And so the reciprocal relationship between private government and public government becomes ever more reciprocal. The more regulation there is at either level, the more there is at the other level, and the structure of government in both cases is affected accordingly.

How to Change Pressure Groups into a Place in Which Public Law Is Made

Since professional associations need the aid of public government, many of them have at some point fallen necessarily into the classification "pressure group"; but they have not been ephemeral pressure groups, and the phrase is not an accurate description of their present relationship to public government. They have evolved slowly, some of them for more than a century, as part of the maturing of the industrial revolution. Although they have been throughout this time in the process of realizing an idea (in the Hegelian sense), of developing their basic nature, which was present or latent all along, they have changed over the years. They have grown large, stable, organizationally skillful. Their ties with other segments of the community have become deeply rooted. Professional associations are now regarded as part of the institutional framework of the socio-economic-political system. To sustain and advance their position in relation to the ordering of work and authority in the whole socio-economic system, they have relied increasingly on public government. A secure position, once achieved, has in turn contributed immeasurably to their access to public government. Whereas once the older associations were the sounding boards of public officials, and later pressure groups clamoring in the lobbies, they have become so institutionalized as law-proposing mechanisms in their own fields that for most work issues they are no longer pressure groups but constitute instead preliminary arenas of public lawmaking.

Increases in Unity, General Resources, and Community Ties

Contributing to this process of institutionalization have been increases in membership, so that they have embraced larger and larger percentages of the whole profession; the establishment of representative assemblies; the permeation of organization into all geographic areas, with more effective integration of geographic units; more and better headquarters; closer ties with outside groups; and more skillful public relations.

A pressure group is one that does not have fully developed access to public government. Most professional associations are in such a position at one point in their development. Incompleteness of access is in part a result of lack of unity on legislative issues, which has characterized the early stages of most professional organizations in whatever decade those early stages have come. An editorial in the *Western Journal of Education* in 1905 stated: ". . . the Legislature assembles, and each school man with a hobby, and sometimes without one, but claiming to represent educational opinion, clamors for the ears of the lawmakers, and very bedlam is let loose, much to the discredit of the teachers."[38] In the early twentieth century lawyers' and doctors' associations complained strongly about internal divisions, the lack of consensus, and the weakness of the state professional associations. Under these circumstances the legislature was likely to be wary about adopting any program; it was apt to listen to professionals who were more involved in politics than in professional activities and who might even be hostile to the professional association and its leaders. Fifty years later social workers at a similar stage in their organizational development struggled with like problems. Sooner or later professional associations learn to remedy this situation by perfecting their internal organization.

As was previously stated, part of the process of perfecting internal organization includes improvement in liaison between national and state associations. This in turn implies improved liaison for lobbying purposes, although state and national associations do not always see eye to eye.

The acquisition of permanent headquarters has also bettered the associations' lobbying position, especially when the associations moved headquarters to Washington, D.C.—as the National Education Association did in 1917 and as many NEA departments have since done—

or when they established a branch office there—as the American Medical Association did in 1944—or when they established branch offices in state capitals.

Also of help have been the hiring of professional staffs (the NEA's first full-time executive secretary began work in 1898) and increases in staff size, sometimes to as many as eight hundred at the national level and to fifty or more at the state level. Increasing attention to research of all kinds has helped to build an image of authoritativeness; for example, the NEA's research division, begun in 1922, had expanded by 1934 to 140 staff people and nine divisions.[39]

Improvements in general communications have included establishing journals for national, state, sectional, and even local bodies (in 1957, 165,000 weekly copies of the AMA journal were distributed[40]); issuing bulletins, pamphlets, and other literature; conferences, workshops, itinerant field workers.

The nature and content of professional journals have changed; the original journals often meandered. The early California teachers' journal printed poetry, travel accounts, and whimsical essays. The nurses' magazine printed recipes under the heading of "dietetics," and there were "perennial complaints that it was dull, stupid, antiquated and moth-eaten."[41] After World War II the journals became businesslike bulletins, with down-to-earth reporting of legislative news and an approach to legislation advocating action. Programs at meetings and conferences, formerly vaguely inspirational talks and rituals, later included practical discussion of immediate action to solve specific professional problems.

Also useful have been public relations activities not necessarily centered around a legislative issue, but simply to establish the prestige of the profession. The National Education Association developed its press service in the early 1920's. In 1923 it began to take its message to the people via radio and sponsored a weekly program over the network of the National Broadcasting Company.[42]

An appeal to patriotism has been a standard tactic in the public relations efforts of professional associations. For example, Law Day, sponsored by the American Bar Association, is on May 1, the day the Soviet Union commemorates its revolution. The American legal system, and implicitly the American legal profession, are memorialized as being at the heart of the "American Way of Life." Engineers Week comes at the time of George Washington's birthday. This same kind of utilization of patriotism is apparent in the journals and official histories of professional associations when they discuss their public services. They repeatedly refer with pride to service given during wartime as warranting a special claim upon the American public's respect and gratitude.

Attempts to produce a long-range favorable climate of public opinion have included inducing colleges to offer special courses, stimulating the writing of textbooks with "suitable" information in them, and even subsidizing college professors; there are donations to civic, cultural, and charitable enterprises. Prescription drug companies and their charitable foundations were reported to have spent $25 million on public-service activities in 1961, amounting to 4.3 percent of their net taxable incomes, including $6.2 million to schools and to universities; $2.7 million to United Fund drives, local and national health and welfare agencies, and grants to hospitals; and $2.2 million to church and civic organizations and cultural activities.[43] Insofar as activities of this sort are designed to influence, when the time comes, attitudes toward legislative bills, they amount to bribing the whole society. Funds spent on direct lobbying of legislators are negligible by comparison.

As appeal to the public has permeated all activities and has ranged from the indirect to the very direct, so has the tactic of intergroup alliances. Many joint committees and collaborative efforts have no direct connection with legislation at all, but joint enterprises for other purposes build a secure base for alliances to support or defeat legislation when the occasion arises.

More Regular Lobbying and a More Realistic, Direct Approach to Power

As their tangible and intangible resources have grown, and their "base" in the community has broadened, the associations have gradually turned from a naïve and indirect to a realistic and direct approach to power, and they have turned from irregular, amateur lobbying to lobbying on a year-in, year-out, professionalized basis.

Sometimes an inexperienced organization begins with vague and high-flown legislative aims and then, after finding itself unsuccessful, narrows its focus to practical bread-and-butter issues and concentrates for a while on issues of licensing and control over its own members. Once the organization gains this kind of control, it must continue to prove its use and value to its members. Like a trade union, a professional association must be concretely effective if it hopes to retain its members' allegiance. The teachers' association must include in its legislative program requests, for example, for raising teachers' minimum wage, improved retirement benefits, clarification of rights to sick leave with pay.

Professional associations have gradually learned to become more efficient and realistic in shaping their legislative programs and in lobbying. In the early years many of the professional associations were headed by people who enjoyed positions of eminence in their own localities and who were as unwilling to talk explicitly in terms of power as they were to call a limb a leg. They made high-flown speeches and apparently expected this to be enough. During the first half of its existence the NEA did little lobbying. At that time, "lobbying by teachers or other professional groups was generally frowned on."[44] The AMA was for a long time—and the ABA is still occasionally—reluctant to admit that it engaged in lobbying at all.[45] In the period after World War II, these three associations have shown more willingness to talk more frankly about power.

To maximize their effectiveness, now that they are getting over their public shyness about the realities of power, the professional associations have begun to work in terms of early grass-roots participation in political campaigns and year-round cultivation of government officials. This has entailed a closer, though not as yet very complete, integration of the political activities of national and state associations.

The most active national organization in these respects is the AMA.

Upon recommendation of its Council on Legislative Activities, the AMA's board of trustees in June 1961 authorized the formation of the independent American Medical Political Action Committee AMPAC, with a former AMA president as head, to fight proposals to include medical care under social security. The committee was deliberately modeled after the AFL-CIO's Committee on Political Action. Its purposes were to help form state and local political committees and provide them with information, distribute records of parties and candidates, and aid voter registration drives and get-out-the-vote campaigns. Its board, which first met in August 1961, consisted of ten physicians and a representative of the AMA's Woman's Auxiliary. The AMA's board of trustees was to appoint members yearly. Resources were to be used to analyze local campaigns and focus support where it would be most fruitful. By 1962 forty-six states were involved, and the committee was publishing a legislative newsletter, the *Political Stethoscope*. In the 1962 elections AMPAC was bipartisan, giving support—chiefly financial—through district committees to candidates in primary and general elections on the basis of the candidate's sympathy to the cause, the probability of his being elected, and the answers to such questions as: What is his leadership potential? Is he a key member of a congressional committee? What would be the psychological by-products of his victory or defeat? Will his campaign affect another contest?[46]

State or local professional associations might actually endorse certain candidates in the primaries and general elections—usually incumbents who have already demonstrated they would vote "right" —or endorsement might be made by such independent interprofessional committees as the healing-arts committees. Some associations send out commendatory letters for certain candidates before the election, without making an outright endorsement. These letters usually go to members of the profession living in the district. Sometimes a campaign arm of the medical profession uses the letterheads of individual professionals for letters prepared and mailed to the voters from a central headquarters. Candidates may be asked to answer questionnaires on issues and their answers would then be distributed to members of the profession in the candidates' district.[47] Some campaign committees for the medical profession have organized members of the profession to do precinct work. Other professions may simply urge their members to participate in primary and general election campaigns. Lawyers need no urging!

As state professional associations have grown in expertise, they have learned to maintain contact with legislators on a year-round, year-in-year-out basis, and to do it as much as possible through people in the profession in the legislator's home district; medical societies work through the legislator's personal physician. They invite legislators and candidates to address their local chapters or their state conferences. At the local or regional level, they hold dinners or receptions for candidates. Their lobbyists, along with lobbyists for other groups, attend testimonial dinners given for the more influential legislators. Another tactic has been to give legislators special awards for outstanding work in, for example, education or medicine. Sometimes the candidates seek out the professional organizations, as well as vice versa, solicit funds from them, and advertise in their journals. Teacher associations urge teachers to invite candidates to local school functions and ask school officials to discuss legislative issues, well in advance of the legislative session, with candidates in their districts. The top staff people and lobbyists for state associations find ways to keep in contact with legislators when the legislature is not in session. Intersession contact has been made easier as state legislative interim committees have begun to meet in various parts of a state throughout the year.

An important element of the national associations' recent approach to lobbying has been the money at their disposal to finance year-to-year lobbying operations as well as special campaigns on specific issues. In its first decade the NEA was often financially embarrassed. In 1959–60 it had a budget of over $6 million.[48] To combat national health insurance the AMA imposed a levy of $25 per member in 1948–9. At first mandatory, later it was made voluntary. Its $1.1 million advertising campaign in 1950 was augmented by over $2 million worth of advertising contributed by other groups.

In 1949–50 the AMA spent more than any other group registered under the federal lobbying law: $1,326,078. In the first nine months of 1952 the AMA's reported expenditures—$309,514—for lobbying were second only to those of the National Association of Electric Companies.[49]

The state associations, like the national associations, have also been able to rely on greatly increased budgets, partially the result of increased membership and of increased dues per member. Besides, education and medical associations make additional levies on members for specific legislative battles.

Some of the associations have inspired committees to collect money—in ways that stay within the letter of the law—to contribute to candidates' campaign funds; the earlier the contribution, the more effective it is. According to an analysis of campaign-contribution reports, the regulated professions are "among the heavier contributors to legislative campaigns." The record of contributions traceable to professional associations indicates, however, that they have not given sums nearly so large as those donated by branches of organized labor to legislators or by businesses and industries to gubernatorial candidates.[50]

There is more complete integration of national and state associations in lobbying as well as in political activity. Many national associations originally promoted state licensing legislation and did not turn to federal legislative activities until later. They performed a staff or service function for local and state organizations or served as a communications center for members who had national orientation. The national associations have continued their interest in state legislation. The American Medical Association's Bureau of Legal Medicine and Legislation subscribes to a legislative reporting service, which gives details on every health bill introduced in each state. The AMA notifies state association officers of important bills and analyzes their merits.[51] Sometimes national associations mail proposed laws or information concerning pending legislation directly to state legislators or state agencies. The American Bar Association at one time sent copies of a brief against a proposed child-labor constitutional amendment to 3,000 legislators.[52] However, the Conference of Commissioners on Uniform State Laws, which the ABA helped to found, seldom calls on the ABA to help get proposed uniform laws passed in the states.[53] When a national association takes a position different from that of the state association, it may even sponsor lobbyists to the state legislature.

National organizations may also conduct interprofessional conferences at the national level to negotiate conflicts between professions over state legislation. For example, after psychologists, psychiatrists, and physicians clashed over New York State licensing bills, the conference committees set up by the American Psychological Association and the American Psychiatric Association issued a joint report in 1960.[54]

The national associations increasingly have had federal legislative programs, and state-national relations have become reciprocal. As national legislative battles have waxed and waned and waxed again, growing broader, deeper, and more intense with each cycle, education and medical associations have organized more for political and legislative action at every geographic level, their lobbying efforts operating from all levels. Some state medical societies sent their own lobbyists to Washington.

The National Education Association's Division of Legislative and Federal Relations maintains close liaison with chairmen and members of state-association committees on federal legislation. In the fall of 1955 the NEA sponsored state and regional conferences in twenty-seven states, culminating in a December conference in Chicago of all state and federal legislative leaders, to help evaluate the White House Conference on Education and to plan the 1956 federal legislative program.[55]

The ABA is least effective at coordinating state- and local-association activity with national-association activity on pending federal legislation, although the Washington office does send out the *Washington Letter* to over 4,000 bar officials.[56]

Accompanying these changes in tactics and in strength have been changes in the personnel who do the lobbying. When associations are relatively new, they go to the legislature on an *ad hoc* basis and lobbying is done by the paid executive secretary and/or interested leaders of the profession. If the newly selected legislative chairman is the lobbyist, or if reliance is solely on that year's officials, the faces will be unfamiliar to the legislators and the association's representatives will be novices in the intricacies of legislative persuasion. As Belle Zeller has pointed out, this is not very successful. Better results are obtained if the same person represents the association year after year, so that he metaphorically *is* the profession in the eyes of the legislators. This is possible when the executive secretary is the lobbyist, and many state medical societies still rely primarily on their paid executive secretaries for this function; of course much depends on the personality and character of the executive secretary. A second step for many associations is hiring a paid observer to be on the spot at all times, since the executive secretary has other business to attend to. Last, a paid lobbyist is hired, first on an *ad hoc* basis, eventually on a year-round basis, and sometimes with the assistance of other paid professionals. In the 1940's the AMA employed lobbyists, a public relations man, and an economist. Often the lobbyists are ex-legislators who formerly presented the association's bills.[57]

Hiring professionals to lobby leads to more, rather than less, member participation in lobbying because more attention is paid to mobilizing support. Staff members have played an especially strong role in national associations' lobbying because association members are so dispersed (*e.g.,* the AMA's Bureau of Medical Legislation and Economics and the NEA's Division of Legislative and Federal Relations). Committees representing members of the profession have become increasingly important. To some extent association members are made members of special legislative committees not because they are expected to do much lobbying or make important decisions, but as a device to arouse their interest, elicit their support, and demonstrate their support to the profession, the legislature, and the public.[58]

Some state associations have legislative action committees separate from the committees that screen legislative proposals; they are composed of people from each district, with, if possible, prior experience and contact with the legislature. They may ask that each local society have a legislative action committee and appoint a small committee at the state level for coordination and communication. Education associations work through school principals, who in turn urge the teachers under their jurisdiction to contact their legislators, or, in rural communities, they may seek the aid of prominent local citizens. Physicians may be asked to solicit the support of their patients. This machinery, usually much more impressive on paper than in practice, can be used to start a spate of phone calls, wires, and letters to congressmen—when the word is given by the national association—as well as to the state legislators for the state association's legislative program. Prominent nonstaff people are used as "fronts" to testify before public legislative committees and to make public addresses.

To foster member activity and maintain grass-roots pressure on legislators, associations have relied increasingly on special weekly or bi-monthly legislative newsletters and on speakers and literature sent out well in advance to local chapters to acquaint them with pending legislation. It takes money, expertise, and time to accomplish all of this, assets that usually only mature associations possess.

It takes time, too, for a lobbyist to develop full access to the legislature. The lobbyists representing less well-established associations are sometimes novices themselves, unaware of legislative intricacies. The lobbyist for any of the established professions in the larger states in the 1950's and 1960's was usually a highly educated, highly capable, highly respectable, highly paid man. He commanded respect not only as a person but also because the average legislator often did not have enough technical knowledge to make independent judgments about professional fields and hence had to rely on the lobbyist for information. Present in the halls of the legislature day after day, year after year, he sometimes came so close to the internal legislative power struggles that he might, behind the scenes, discreetly aid one person or another to win the speakership of the lower house, which often carried with it the power to appoint both legislators and bills to committees. Or he might become an intimate friend of the "dean" of the Senate. He might actually influence the choice of legislators for the committees most affecting the profession he represented. He might also develop for his clients a close, continual, and reliable relationship with several legislators.[59] When the wife of a long-time physicians' lobbyist for the California Medical Association died, in 1963, the occasion was noted with regret on the floor of the state assembly, one assemblyman suggesting that a floral tribute be sent as a token of gratitude for the care—presumably medical—the physician had given the legislators. Being "in" comes rather late in the evolution of a professional association's legislative expertise. Yet the wise association learns not to rely on it too much, for it depends on the personal relationships of a few people, whose tenure might be temporary. Legislators are replaced by new ones. Sometimes, as in 1958 in California, there is a marked shift in party alignment; or much of the legislature is new—one-third in California in 1963. The association's experienced lobbyists may find it hard to realign themselves with young, inexperienced legislators; or the lobbyist may be replaced. However, as drastic alterations in the California legislature's personnel have shown, as many as one-fourth or more of the legislators may be replaced and the established lobbyists will continue on, virtually unruffled. Associations and their interests are perennials; legislators come and go.

Self-Government Through the Public Legislature

Power begets power. Access expands access. Once the profession has the benefit of a public licensing board manned by people from the profession who serve on a part-time basis and who work hand in glove with the profession they regulate, the board serves as a symbol to the legislature of the profession's legitimacy, and it works, often discreetly, to present the profession's point of view on subsequent legislative proposals. An administrative agency primarily concerned with research, gathering statistics, and giving advice, which is manned by civil service personnel but has a jurisdiction related to only one profession or segment of a profession, may function similarly. The agency and the profession collaborate in developing technical legislative recommendations. The United States Office of Education has been staffed with specialists who have close ties with individual segments of the education profession. The tendency is for each of these specialists or groups of specialists to approach Congress as a representative of their part of the profession, rather than as representatives of the Office of Education as a whole.[60] Agencies that must deal with a profession having several partially conflicting subgroups back up the claims of the most elite groups.

Once bills are in the hopper, the whole process of legislation seems to favor the proposals or positions put forth by high-prestige organizations whose legislative advocates work on a year-round basis and are continually in attendance during the legislative session. They are intimately acquainted with the legislative terrain and have established points of access and influence far in advance. They know what legislators to select to carry their bills. They can pressure the bill's sponsor into acting on a bill that might otherwise lie inert. Always alert, they are present when decisions about a bill are made: in the preliminary stages, when a sponsor hears from interested parties and may amend the bill; when bills are assigned to committee; before and at standing committee hearings; at the time of floor debate in both houses; when clerical actions may affect timing; perhaps in conference committees; when the Chief Executive has the bill for signature; and at numerous unformalized points of decision-making in between. The structure of committees may be in their favor, since they are built around established and accepted subject areas. Also favorable are the unarticulated cultural presumptions that, for example, send a bill concerned with independent adoptions to a lawyer-manned judiciary committee rather than to a welfare-oriented social-welfare committee. The organizations are aided by the fact that their proposals may often be couched in technical language or require an expertise the legislators do not possess, so that the legislature may assent on faith. Since they usually have a vested interest in the status quo, they are also helped by the tendency of state legislatures to be passively receptive rather than actively creative in the formulation of new legislative proposals; by the natural deference to high-prestige professionals on the part of middle-class legislators; and by increasing legislative deference to or reliance upon the expert. In their defensive battles, they are also aided by, among other factors, the legislative tendency to take no action on controversial matters that have not reached major political proportions.

In short, when legislative proposals are narrow in scope and appear to apply only to the profession, the more well-established professions can often in effect write their own laws; what they want, they get. They do not enact law through the public legislature in a completely unilateral way. In the process of formulating its legislative program in the first place, the experienced association, taking into account the general political climate and the probable mood and temper of the legislature, modifies its proposals accordingly. Public officials usually participate in the association's proposal-formulating processes, sometimes as ex officio delegates to the association's legislative body. The association realizes that for continued effectiveness it must either keep its proposals narrowly technical or create an aura of impartial service to the commonweal—preferably both. The established association cannot afford to stress narrowly and manifestly self-interested legislation. A form of "public interest" permeates the lawmaking process even in its private stages. Taken all together, these facts in turn support the contention that such professional associations are truly preliminary arenas of public lawmaking. They are not outside pressure groups, but an integral part of the institutions through which public law is made. Whether the "public interest" is truly served by all of this is, of course, another matter.

THE CONTINUUM OF GOVERNMENT

What, then, is the relationship of professional associations to the structure of public government?

1. *Private governments.* To some extent some professional associa-

tions are autonomous private governments. Yet it is surprising how little purely internal control the professional associations exert over their members, as distinguished from control via, or in collaboration with, public government; even the lawyers who govern themselves via State Bars do so in the name of the state.

Members of the associations, of course, vote to install or accept internal services from the association or to embark on a particular program. But participation in such programs usually remains optional for individual members. Government implies something more than the pronouncement of group opinion, the reaching of informal consensus, or the giving of mutual aid. It implies enforcement, sanctions. Other than the structural, housekeeping rules for the operation of the organization itself, almost the only rules professional associations have enacted that are designed to guide the behavior of the members in their everyday work are those contained in the codes of ethics or rules of professional behavior. The small number of these that are formulated and enforced in a purely internal manner, without resort to public government, are the rules concerning advertising, solicitation, or public criticism of the profession; that is, rules designed to minimize internal competition and maximize professional cohesion. On most other matters the associations rely on state law to set the guidelines for professional behavior.

2. *Preliminary arenas of public lawmaking.* One of the commonly used models of American public government presumes that the process of legislation takes place primarily in the public legislature. Private organizations are viewed as pressure groups attempting to influence legislative decisions from the outside.

For most laws affecting the detailed work of professionals, this is not a fair picture of the facts. It is more accurate to say that the legislative process begins, among other places, with the formulation of legislative proposals within private organizations, that the process within organizations by which group consensus is reached is part of the broader process, that negotiations between groups on issues that have not yet reached the public arena are a further extension of the process, which culminates in public battles and the final legislative vote. This latter picture is more accurate in the light of the fact that private organizations, such as professional associations, are responsible for the initiation and much of the content of a high percentage of the legislation directly related to their work. It must be emphasized, however, that they serve as preliminary arenas for the formulation of public laws only in relation to *some* kinds of public issues, those having the closest and most narrow connection with the ordering of professional work.

3. *Agencies for the enforcement of private and public law.* Professional associations perform a governmental function in two administrative ways: in policing activities in their arena of work and in policing their own members. In both instances their collaboration with public government is such that it is difficult to tell where one begins and the other leaves off.

The AMA, for instance, as a private association tests and passes judgment on new drugs, medicines, dietary and other special-purpose foods, and therapeutic and diagnostic devices; but the AMA was also instrumental in getting public pure food and drug laws passed, at both federal and state levels, and it assists public administrative agencies in the work of enforcing the public laws.[61]

Only some of the associations attempt to enforce upon their membership either the organization's own internally articulated codes or the public law. Bar and medical associations are the most active in this respect. Nurses', architects', and engineers' associations often have no operative formal disciplinary machinery at all.[62]

When a profession is weakly organized, there is usually little internal or public control over the profession. Where organization is strong, there may be more internal control, but the association also relies heavily upon the sanctions of public government. A profession deems itself to be in the strongest position when its organization exercises control over its members, but does so by virtue of public delegation of authority with the sanctions of public government. If the phrase "private government" is taken to mean organizational autonomy in controlling its membership, then none of the associations is truly a private government.

The associations often make no clear distinction between internal rules and sanctions and those that are integrated with the public law. In some cases their application of private rule and public law is so mixed that it is difficult to segregate enforcement that refers only to internal rules; though for violations of the public law the penalties are often more severe, and the process of appeal and final enforcement of penalties takes place in public rather than in private agencies of government. Government, for the stronger professional associations, is a continuum, a matter of continual interaction and close integration between private and public governments. This does not mean that they are being closely regulated by an alien state, since they do in fact write much of the public law pertaining to their profession, as well as participate to a considerable extent in the task of enforcement. They borrow the sanctions and the legitimization of public government in order to accomplish their own ends. At the same time, the public government—in granting its seal of approval and lending its resources—does exact a price.

CHAPTER 5

Differentiating and Reintegrating Special Interests

The preceding discussion presents only part of the total picture, that seen from the standpoint of the major associations of the most prominent licensed professions. Even for those professions it does not take into account the two significant changes in the organization of professional work described earlier: (1) the evolution of many new professions, and divisions within old professions on the basis of authority and specialization; and (2) transformation of the institutional context in which professionals work. There have been, as a result, alterations in the modes of governing the profession, in relationships between the professional associations and work institutions, and in relationships with government. It is remarkable that these changes have followed roughly similar patterns, patterns that are analogous to some of the major changes in the nature of public government since approximately the sixteenth century.

With many deviations and exceptions the trends appear to be as follows: (1) a period when the elite make decisions informally, without necessarily articulating broad, abstract principles applicable to the whole body politic; (2) a period when different categories of interest within the body politic become more formally articulated; when eventually there is formalized combat over principles and power, a more open and militant process of adjusting interests (*e.g.*, between competing professional groups, through trade unions vis-à-vis an employing corporation or through political parties vis-à-vis the state); and a tendency to write the resulting "law" in general terms (in codes or rules, contracts, treaties, or statutes); (3) finally, a period when the differentiated and articulated parts of the system are more closely integrated into the whole while retaining their separate identity, with consensus reached through negotiation and bargaining, over relatively small details, between representatives of the several "interests," and with open combat on the basis of general principles introduced only by those outside the bargaining circle.

In the history of Anglo-American political institutions, the first period came prior to the full maturation, in the seventeenth century, of Parliament as a lawmaking body. The second period included the whole of the modern era of government, beginning with the seventeenth century, characterized by legislatures, lawmaking, and eventually by political parties and formally organized pressure groups. The third period has been emerging since the beginning of the industrial revolution and has not yet fully matured. The concern here is with some of the emerging characteristics of the third period.

The industrial revolution encompassed the same kind of three-stage evolution. At one time owners and managers had undisputed control over their own work organizations; then appeared the formal organization and special claims of trade unions and, later, of professional associations. Evidence exists that the militancy of trade unionism is declining and that the collective contract is less significant than it once was.[1] A new kind of *rapprochement* is developing.

A three-stage developmental process within whole professions and their whole context of work has been paralleled by comparable alterations in their relationships to public government. The development of major associations is part of this story.

INFORMAL RULE BY THE ELITE

Informal decision-making by an elite has frequently been the rule not only in such work organizations as hospitals and universities but also in professional associations and the circles out of which evolve proposals for public legislation.

Within Professional Associations

Historically, the professional association permitted the various types of specialists and leaders in all spheres of the profession's work to meet one another and come to informal agreement over problems of mutual concern—in clubrooms, over luncheon or dinner, in hotel rooms, and in lobbies. The issues did not necessarily become a matter of open debate; nor did persons of low rank or authority in the profession participate in decision-making. Academic associations still operate in this way. Almost no crucial issues are ever openly articulated and voted on by the profession. In other than academic associations this kind of informal decision-making is still important. Significantly, the persons who occupy positions of authority in the sphere of the work institution, in setting up scientific programs, or in leading the professional association have tended to be the same type of persons—often the same persons—as those who occupy powerful positions in the other spheres. Each profession or related group of professions has had its power elite.

Most professions today have one or more of the following divisions:[2] rural versus urban, young versus older, generalists versus specialists, administrators versus workers, prosperous versus nonprosperous, fee-basis versus salaried, and those with clients or students of high rank versus those with clients or students of low rank, whatever the criteria of rank may be. There are also divisions on the basis of sex, race, and religion, and divisions of thought, technique, or special function. Gradually special organizations have come to represent these divisions. In the meantime, the major professional associations have done what they could to curtail or control this more formal articulation of special interests: by making efforts to prevent specialization in the first place, as in the case of the bar; by merging special associations into one, as five separate specialist organizations merged to form the National Association of Social Workers in 1945; and/or by providing special sections within the main association for minority and specialist groups (in almost all the associations) and/or special provision for their representation in the association's government. This last might include a seat on the board for a representative of the student or young professional organizations; alternating presidencies for male and female educators; the election of one Negro as a delegate or officer or the selection of a woman as recording secretary for a professional association composed primarily of men. To offset the charge that it is dominated by urban specialists—a charge that is true—the American Medical Association gives an annual award to the General Practitioner of the Year.

Representation for weaker groups does not necessarily mean an equal voice in decision-making. Writing about Catholic sisters in nursing organizations, one sister commented that they were seldom adequately represented, but even if they were welcomed, the sisters' timidity, the dues, and night meetings were all deterrents. The sisters were often not useful on committees because their contacts were poor.[3] However, by making special provision for special groups or by making token gestures toward vocal minorities, the leading elite may actually enhance its own power as the spokesman for an only apparently unified profession.

Within Work Organizations

Within the organizations where professionals work, the decision-making process involves such issues as whether general practitioners shall be permitted to perform all types of surgery, whether, for example, more courses in political behavior and fewer in political theory shall be offered, or whether Research Project A instead of Research Project B shall be undertaken. Decisions have often been made informally, somewhat in the style of the king in consultation with his barons. Professional associations in the past have not necessarily played a formal role at all within the work organization, or they have not challenged the authority of those in charge.

Persons in positions of high authority within work systems formerly held unequivocal sway over most major professional associations. Often they were appointed or elected to associational office as representatives of institutions, rather than as individuals. They seemed to operate on the premise that what was good for the institutions within which professionals worked was good for the professionals who worked there. Rank-and-file members of the profession were not articulate. One of the aims and functions of professional associations in the past, therefore, was to keep unity within the profession and harmony within its work establishments.[4]

Library associations and teacher associations have traditionally been places where professional workers and their administrators have attempted to resolve their differences; some say at the expense of the workers. As conflicts of interest between teachers and administrators have become more articulate, to alleviate discontent from within and to counteract criticism from outsiders, the National Education Association has set up, and persuaded state associations to set up, a special classroom teachers' department, largely a paper organization, to provide a channel through which classroom teachers could be fed into the front-line leadership posts. Under constant accusations by teachers' unions of its being a company union, the NEA and its affiliates—having been for so long led by college presidents, superintendents of schools, professors, and administrators—have made increasing efforts to provide representation for classroom teachers. In 1957 the NEA's executive secretary claimed that 70 percent of the 6,000 delegates to the Representative Assembly were classroom teachers.[5] Critics responded by saying that administrators still ran the show and now more than ever claimed to speak for the whole profession.

Approaching Public Legislatures

In lobbying, too, there is usually a period in the development of intraprofessional associations when the main association is the dominant force, with elite members of the profession dominating the main association. For example, roughly between 1890 and 1910 in California, the main professional associations represented so small a segment of their respective professions and had so little power or influence that they were just one voice among many before the legislature in matters concerning the profession, and often that voice got lost in the crowd. Gradually they perfected techniques for mobilizing and keeping cohesive the members of their own profession—to make an impression on the legislature—until they came to dominate the process of lawmaking in their field. They relied on informal, behind-the-scenes prelegislative negotiations, with related and recognized groups, to keep overt conflict to a minimum. During this stage the associations came closest to writing the major laws affecting their profession, without much outside check or legislative hindrance. Dissident groups might take their case separately to the legislature, but this was sporadic, *ad hoc,* and often ineffective.

SPECIAL INTERESTS SPEAK AND ACT

In all three contexts, then—within work organizations, within the professional association, and between different elements inside and immediately relevant to the profession and legislation—the power elite, who occupy all the top posts, at one time speak for the profession or the work organization as if it were a united whole. However, despite efforts to the contrary, in all three contexts in the past several decades there has been a greater articulation of special vocational or authority-level interests. The issues between different special groups have become more clear-cut and verbalized, and more arm's-length methods have been used to resolve the issues.

One Professional Association to Another

Although attempts have been made to keep all or most segments of the profession within the main association, the centrifugal forces have been strong, resulting in the formation of independent associa-

archical work team. Professional associations have moved somewhat more in the direction of militantly representing the interests of the profession in the process of determining what the relationships shall be.[8]

Associations continue to attempt to mitigate differences between teachers and administrators within education associations, but as the teachers have gained more power in education associations, the associations have become more and more organizational weapons used to pressure administrators and work establishments from the outside. As hospitals have become larger and more complex and more sharp cleavages have occurred between medical staffs and hospital administrators, and as similar cleavages are occurring in other professions, many associations have been pressuring administrators, management, and perhaps third-party intermediaries.[9]

The most common form of pressure has been mild and indirect, through the publication and dissemination of information about salaries, fees, and work conditions. Even such weak intervention as this is fairly recent. In its early years the National Education Association looked askance at any concern with matters so mundane as salaries or pensions. After considerable pressure from classroom teachers the association appointed a committee to report on teachers' salaries and the cost of living. Since 1922 the Research Division has surveyed teaching salaries biennially and distributed the information to those who set salary rates.[10] National nurses' associations have disseminated comparative statistics as a way of raising nurses' salaries to a higher uniform standard.

When physicians' fees are set by third parties, the medical society may intervene more directly in the process of fee setting. As of 1962, the California Medical Association's Commission on Medical Services concerned itself not only with fees set by agencies of the profession itself but also with workmen's compensation fees, government program fees, and liaison with the insurance industry. The American Medical Association has exerted a powerful influence over hospital practices through its standards for hospital accreditation.

A more specific form of intervention has been used when the American Medical Association has been asked to mediate disputes between medical staffs and hospital administrators.[11] The National Education Association has also, on invitation, investigated local problems when there are major disputes between teachers and their administrators. This kind of mediation is one of the chief functions of state and local teacher associations.

There have been some moves in the direction of more militant collective bargaining. Although most nurses would bridle if their associations were called unions (for professional status is a precious thing to them), some state associations have an economic-security program, begun in California during World War II. Various categories of nurses wrote out what they considered to be minimum employment practices and attempted to persuade their employers to adopt them voluntarily. During World War II the California State Nurses Association considered collective bargaining. It signed its first major written contract with East Bay hospitals in 1946. By 1947 the association had helped to establish a forty-hour week for California nurses, and in 1952 the ANA House of Representatives resolved to try to establish a national forty-hour week standard.

Not all state nurses' associations have been willing to go as far as the CSNA. When the issue was being debated in the New York State Nurses Association in 1952, it was questioned whether the CSNA had managed to get a significant number of collective-bargaining contracts or that bargaining had raised nurses' salaries appreciably. Nonetheless, the CSNA had continued its efforts and by 1962 represented a high percentage of publicly employed nurses in California. It had collective contracts with individual hospitals and hospital associations, though some employers refused to recognize the association and some nurses were not in favor of the collective-contract program. In 1958 a budget statement indicated that $7.95 out of every member's $25 dues went to the CSNA's research and economic-security program.[12]

Observing the nurses' program, one California librarian asked of her state library association, "Why not a Salary Representative for CLA?" She said librarians should have a paid expert to represent members when salary adjustments were under consideration, "armed with formidable statistics, prepared to argue their cause with authority and skill."[13]

Although the professional associations as such have become more militant in relation to employers, they have been unwilling to go all the way. Despite the fact that administrators are forming associations of their own more and more, they often still belong to, and are powerful in, the main professional associations. The NEA and the American Library Association still maintain that professionals and administrators can work out their problems within one association. They say that a showing of unity is essential if the profession as a whole is to advance in competition with other professions and groups for public favor and public funds. Some teachers, unwilling to accept this point of view, have formed teacher unions.

The American Federation of Teachers claims that teachers can define and defend their rights only through an organization entirely their own, not in a "company union," and education associations and teacher unions actively dispute the issue of collective bargaining. The National Education Association holds that teaching is a profession, and therefore collective bargaining is inappropriate. The NEA and affiliated state associations prefer to gather statistics, publish guides for personnel policy, and lobby for minimum wages, tenure, and retirement benefits. The American Federation of Teachers regards these as merely pussyfooting forms of collective bargaining, and says it is better to call a spade a spade. The AFT contends that teaching is a craft, and that teachers should bargain collectively for their salaries and rights as other workers do. In 1961 the AFL-CIO United Federation of Teachers obtained bargaining rights for 40,000 teachers in New York City. In 1962 in California the teacher union was attempting to represent its members in negotiating collective group contracts with individual school districts. As a result of this kind of pressure, the NEA proclaimed in 1962 it would use nonstrike sanctions against school districts where teaching conditions were intolerable, but it continued to oppose teacher strikes. The AFT complained: "Collective negotiation with representatives of teachers' unions is still considered an act of grace rather than normal procedure."[14]

The same kinds of issues have occurred for engineers' and scientists' associations. Traditionally, the leaders of these associations have been management men. Management has encouraged its members to join the professional associations. A survey of seventy-three member companies of the National Conference Board indicated that fifty-six of them customarily paid the dues for membership in professional societies for their professional employees, and it was common practice for them to give time off for, and possibly pay the expenses of, attending professional-association meetings.[15]

When engineers' unions have attempted to engage in collective bargaining, they have often been as much opposed by professional engineers' societies as by business management. The most vehement opposition has been to heterogeneous unions, where professional engineers merge with other kinds of employees and cannot make decisions as a unified and separate group. In an attempt to prevent this, the National Society of Professional Engineers has set forth in its Statements of Principles what it considers are appropriate guides to engineers' behavior vis-à-vis unions and employer relations. It has held conferences with management and has helped individual engineers escape being unionized. In 1958, when five hundred to six hundred engineers and land surveyors were unionized in New York City, the society sent a notice to other professions to alert them to the danger. Kornhauser concludes, however, that neither professional associations nor professional unions have played a substantial role in influencing company policy toward professional employees.[16]

As the number of salaried professionals increases, unionism is beginning to appear among other salaried professions. Since many of the new salaried professionals work for government, new efforts are being made to legitimize collective bargaining for public employees. The stage of arm's-length negotiation between professionals and their employers may have only just begun. In the meantime the formal, mutually agreed-to statements of principles or collective contracts signed by professionals and their employers are comparable to the formal "treaties" between competing professional groups; they are halfway between private codes and public statutes in structural base, but like the written codes and public statutes in that they are written and in that they proscribe or prescribe rights and obligations in terms of general categories of people.

Why Not Tell the Legislature Our Own Story?

There has been a period of independent articulation of special interests within and among professional groups engaged in lobbying. While a major association is developing its legislative expertise and slowly accomplishing its purposes, through the aid of public government changes take place in the pattern of its relationships with the special groups inside and outside the profession that are combating one another over the many detailed and sometimes seemingly trivial issues centered around the basic question: "Who gets to do what work?" As different points of view become well articulated, the task of preparing legislative proposals may become too complex and vast for any one professional organization to handle. When the major associations attempt to embrace all the heterogenous elements of the profession in developing its legislative program, they have to search for common denominators and concentrate the program around them. There is a limit to the number of proposals any one organization, no matter how large, can handle effectively at any one legislative session. Legislators become impatient if the association appears to be asking too much. If an association has a very large legislative program, the legislative process becomes like the wars Tolstoy described: impossible to harness and control from on top. For both these reasons, the main association tends to neglect special interests within the profession, even when there might be no disagreement over those interests. People having those special interests learn to speak out for themselves. Their early lobbying is haphazard, disunited, unrealistic, *ad hoc*. Their lobbying activities follow some of the patterns of development manifested earlier by the main associations. Eventually they begin sending professional lobbyists to the legislature year after year. The conflict between them and the main association becomes militant and open, and although the main associations continue to dominate the public legislative process, legislators will not be entirely deaf to the new claims. Legislators normally react by refusing to pass the measure at all when there is open intraprofessional conflict on an issue primarily or only narrowly concerning that profession.[17]

SPECIAL INTERESTS INTEGRATE
WITHIN AND BETWEEN PROFESSIONS

To minimize open conflict, each profession has developed formal and informal channels of communication between professions and between the different groups within the profession. The formal ways of reaching agreement are still evolving and differ from profession to profession

1. *Leaders talk behind the scenes.* Some professions have only partially modified the old informal ways of making decisions. At both the national and state levels, taken all together, bar organizations resemble in form the old-time outdoor circus, with a number of shows going on simultaneously and independently within the main tent, and with a circle of minor shows going on in a semidetached manner on the grounds outside. Each of the ABA's sections has its own bylaws and officers; coordination is loose and sometimes nonexistent. Consensus for the whole profession is still reached, if it is reached, not so much through the private legislature of the main association as through behind-the-scenes communication among leaders of the various sections, special groups, and special associations.

2. *Coordinating councils.* Other professions are trying to perfect their coordinating mechanisms, but with only partial success. The engineering professions exhibit the most disjointed pattern of professional organizations. As of 1946, there were at least thirty-four national engineering societies. The number has been estimated as high as sixty.[18] The five so-called founder societies formed the United Engineering Society in 1904; the Federation of American Engineering Societies, renamed the American Engineering Council, which went out of existence in 1938; and with one other formed the Engineers

Joint Council in 1941. No agencies unified the many other independent engineers' organizations, although the National Society of Professional Engineers, organized in 1934, was discussing in the 1950's a functional plan for coordinating societies, with the Joint Council coordinating technical problems, the Council on Professional Development having primary responsibility for education problems, and the National Society of Professional Engineers being the voice of the whole profession on general professional matters. However, four out of five of the presidents of the five founder societies opposed this plan. The American Society for Mechanical Engineers proposed instead a federation of all existing units into an American Engineering Association.

Where several vocations have a continuing relationship with one another, sometimes standing joint committees are formed. The American Institute of Architects has had liaison committees with the Associated General Contractors, the Engineers Joint Council, the American Bar Association, and the Producers Council of building-materials manufacturers. An association may have unilateral standing committees on relationships with particular groups. The Northern California Pharmacists' Association has had a manufacturers' relations committee and the California CPA society has had a committee on cooperation wtih credit grantors.

A standing joint council may be set up under the auspices of the leading professions. A state-level example is the joint committee of architects, civil engineers and land surveyors, consulting engineers, structural engineers, and landscape architects brought together by the California Council of the American Institute of Architects or its joint committees with the California Association of School Administrators, the Associated General Contractors, and the School Library Associations.

3. *Federation or confederation.* Associations representing groups with a strong sense of separateness or organizations of different professions often join in federations. There are the Federation of American Societies for Experimental Biology, formed in 1913; the American Institute of Biological Sciences, 1948; and the American

Association for the Advancement of Science, which in 1960 had 286 affiliated organizations.

Then there are all-inclusive confederations, each called Organization of the Professions, being formed by the fee-basis professions in some states; some of these are attempting to form a national confederation of the professions.

4. *The holding company.* A variation of functional federalism is the National Education Association holding company. The NEA is holding company for thirty or more semi-independent national organizations, called departments, each with its own membership, dues, officers, staff, journals, programs. Members supposedly, but do not always, belong to the NEA. From 1907 to 1921 one of the departments was in turn a holding company for six lay women's organizations: the General Federation of Women's Clubs, the National Congress of Mothers, the Association of Collegiate Alumnae, the Women's Christian Temperance Union, the National Council of Jewish Women, and the Southern Association of College Women. The NEA, in turn, is a member of the American Council of Education. Consensus is reached through the NEA Representative Assembly and through interpersonal contacts among the leaders of the various organizations.

5. *Divided jurisdiction, functional federalism.* One approach to the problem of coordinating different elements of the profession is exemplified by the AMA and the medical-specialist associations that make clear-cut divisions of function, with the latter concentrating on authorizing specialists' credentials and the exchange of technical information, and with the former acting as the public policy-making forum for the whole profession. Members maintain dual membership. In 1962–3 the California Medical Association formed a thirty-six-member scientific board as a way to lessen fragmentization of the profession. The board was to have voting representation in the house and council, and its members were to be chosen by the CMA Council, and approved by the House of Delegates, from names submitted by CMA's eighteen scientific sections, by state or local divisions of independent national specialist organizations, by special colleges, and by the California Association of General Practitioners.[19]

6. *Special-purpose organizations.* There are presumably independent special-purpose organizations for, among other things, research, education, and accreditation whose directors are drawn from one or several professional organizations, sometimes within a single profession, sometimes cutting across professions.

7. *Interlocking directorates.* A glance at the biographies of the leaders of intraprofessional associations reveals another source of integration: the interlocking directorate. The leading officers of the ABA, for example, are ex officio directors of the American Bar Foundation, and some members of the ABA board of governors are also on the executive council of the National Conference of Bar Presidents.

As a result of these modes of integration that have been evolving over many decades, as have centrifugal forces, the national professional organizations are tied together in a complex web of formal affiliations and informal liaisons. Except in special circumstances, a main association's circle of formal intercommunication does not include representatives of independent special associations within the profession based on sex, religion, race, or ideology. Professional unions and some would-be competitor vocations are also outside the formal web.

The Bargaining Circle

With the advent of many related groups lobbying separately in public legislatures, prelegislative intergroup negotiation, as a way of minimizing public conflict, became an established part of the legislative process. At first the negotiation was informal and episodic, and came close to the time of the legislature's meeting. The more recent tendency has been for negotiation to begin earlier and earlier—in fact, to go on continually. Informal gatherings or temporary joint committees are being superseded or supplemented by permanent joint councils or even separate joint organizations to sift legislative proposals and negotiate and bargain before the proposals reach the legislature. The joint councils vary in scope and in the groups represented, so that the same professional association may participate in more than one prelegislative council, each council concerned with a different group of issues.

An example of limited coordination of groups within a single profession is provided by education associations in New York and California. During the 1920's, when many special education associations were being formed in California, they were not even loosely confederated. They were like a "basket of marbles of various sizes, thrown into contact, but without cement or mortar to bind them together."[20]

Since 1911 the California Teachers Association has had provisions for affiliating certain types of education associations. Most of them were content to let the CTA carry the main burden of legislative activity for the profession, interesting themselves only in those few problems most vital to their special interests. In this period they lobbied either through or for the State Department of Education or only sporadically on their own, on an amateur, *ad hoc* basis. Usually they were in communication with the CTA about their desires for legislation, taking independent action only when they were in conflict with the CTA or when they could not get the CTA to pay sufficient attention to their special problems. The CTA did not officially attempt to control their activities and policies, and sometimes the administrators' organizations were outspokenly dissatisfied with the CTA procedure. The California School Boards Association, strongly at odds with the CTA over tenure laws, first tried unilateral action before the legislature. Then when that failed it tried negotiation committees, in which the State Department of Education, the CTA, and administrator associations participated. When the committees failed to persuade the CTA representatives to back down sufficiently on tenure, the CSBA tried, with little success, unilateral action again, sometimes aligning with the supervisors' association, since school supervisors are often hired by school boards. Sometimes joint committees on nonlegislative issues helped to achieve consensus.

Occasionally, during the 1930's, one or another of the special education associations tried to form a more permanent council of associations, to which the CTA would be only one of the representatives, but because the organizations were apparently not willing to concede hegemony to any one of their number, the attempts failed. In 1943 the State Department of Education set up the State Education Council, with representatives from fifteen organizations. In the 1950's and after, the larger associations, beginning to hire lobbyists of their own, were depending less on the State Department to represent them before the legislature and were standing up for their special interests vis-à-vis the CTA.

During this period the California School Employees Association and the California Association of Public School Business Officials, among others, were created by nonprofessional vocational groups concerned with education to go before the legislature. The CTA faced the possibility of having its hard-won ascendancy in legislative matters cut away, this time by organized, skilled representation of interests close to the profession rather than by mere random and chaotic legislative activity. In 1947 the CTA reorganized the basis for affiliation of professional education associations; it created a special associate category for nonprofessional associations concerned with education, including the California Congress of Parents and Teachers. Since to be qualified for affiliation an association had to have five hundred or more members, 75 percent of whom were members of the CTA, dozens of smaller organizations claiming to be statewide were still operating autonomously, but the thirteen and then fifteen affiliates represented the major education associations that might have special interests to present to the legislature.

Each organization had a representative in the CTA's State Council. They were encouraged to take offices or to hold meetings in the CTA building, an offer to which many of them succumbed when the CTA put up its new state headquarters building in 1957. This did not prevent them from lobbying separately, but it enabled the CTA leaders to negotiate on many issues within the education family and hence to minimize the amount of conflict in the public arena. Negotiation with other education organizations on legislative matters was through personal contact of their leaders with the CTA leaders.

The education organizations divided primary responsibility for certain measures among themselves; gave mutual support where they agreed; amended controversial proposals to come as close to agreement as they could; and simply fought the remainder out before the legislature.[21]

New York City teacher organizations have been more successful in providing a formal setting for their negotiation. New York's bar associations have also been formally federated for public legislative purposes.[22]

Councils or organizations involving more than one profession range in degrees of formality and inclusiveness. Since 1956 representatives of various architects' and engineers' associations in California have met together regularly in a joint committee to exchange information and plan cooperative action on public legislation, subject to the approval of the constituent organizations.[23]

More formally organized and including a still larger number of different professions was the Public Health League, which the California Medical Association formed in 1934 as an organization separate though not altogether independent from the CMA. Members included licensed physicians, dentists, chiropodists, and nurses who were eligible for membership in their respective organizations, and administrators and superintendents of licensed hospitals eligible for registration by the American Medical Association or the American Hospital Association. Doctors of Veterinary Medicine could join as affiliates. The league maintained offices in the CMA's state headquarters building and in the state capital, published a legislative bulletin, and employed two highly experienced and able year-round lobbyists. (The senior of these in 1962 had been in that position for approximately 25 years.) The individual medical organizations also lobbied separately, but their lobbyists collaborated with those of the league.[24]

Permanent councils cutting across several professions are just beginning to make their appearance. In December 1958 representatives of the professions of architecture, dentistry, engineering, law, and medicine met to form the Michigan Association of the Professions.

Veterinary medicine, pharmacy, and education were later added. New York, North Carolina, Florida, and Texas soon followed the pattern. In the winter of 1962–3 representatives of nine professional organizations in California were exploring the possibility of a new liaison group "to set up a united line of resistance to any efforts by so-called 'non-professionals' to encroach on their fields of operation." In August 1960 the American Association of the Professions was incorporated in Michigan, growing primarily out of the Michigan association. If its publications and conferences were successful, the way might be paved for more systematically united action at the national and state level.

Individual associations also maintain special joint prelegislative committees with vocations, such as the architects with the contracting industry, that are not represented in the existing formal councils.[25]

Although such negotiation does not always prevent public conflict, it does eliminate or blunt some controversy. It operates somewhat as pretrial conferences are supposed to: it permits the groups to find their ground of common agreement prior to the public contest, to eliminate some issues, and to define others more clearly. Sometimes attempts to negotiate have broken down and one or both parties have taken their case independently to the legislature, but the associations prefer to avoid this kind of open conflict.

With this background of consultation and negotiation, the groups are also prepared to compromise and collaborate on legislation introduced by outsiders or on unexpected proposals at the time the legislature is in session.

The potency of intergroup councils in deciding on compromises enacted into law without much question depends not so much on the nature of the groups as it does on the nature of the issues. Technical modifications of existing law may be written entirely by the professional association, without any other group's taking an interest and with the legislature assuming a purely passive role. If the issue is superficially a technical one, appearing to touch no interests outside the groups concerned, then group negotiation might be the true legislative process and the legislature simply provides an official stamp of approval; or the legislature may referee residual issues upon which negotiations have broken down.

THE EVOLVING AMERICAN SYSTEM

A profession may be perfecting its integrating mechanisms at the same time that parts of the profession are pursuing a militant course on particular issues. Having arrived at a stabilized integration of its parts, a profession may then have to cope with new, militant demands from neglected segments of the profession or from outsiders.

Acknowledging partial deviations, it can be said with reasonable accuracy that the development of particular aspects of a profession often follows, in less time, the developmental patterns of the whole profession. The same can be said of the patterns of development of the whole profession in relation to the entire industrial revolution, which in turn has a similar relation to the whole Anglo-American political system. If we were dealing with static rather than mobile phenomena, we could say that each has fitted into the other as progressively smaller, but otherwise similar, wooden apples fit into a large wooden apple in a child's puzzle toy.

From an era of rule by custom and automatic deference to those in top socioeconomic positions, the English political system moved toward the concept of a state in which the people were citizens. Lawmaking and Parliament emerged. Can it not be said that, in some fashion, the trade union has been to the business corporation what Parliament was to the state? In each case the early intention was to define and protect rights, not to take over managerial decision-making. And are not these two phenomena similar to the stage in the maturing of professional associations when the associations moved to embrace all members of the profession in a single polity and set up representative legislative bodies, and when each professional association moved as a unit to make its claims for recognition and rights?

Note the collaborative relationships between management and trade unions; for example, the long honeymoon between Harry

Bridges' longshoremen's union and the employers' Pacific Maritime Association, or the relations of Dave Beck of the teamsters' union with many of the employers of teamsters. Are there not striking parallels between these relationships, the new modes of reaching agreement within and between professions, through formal councils and peaceable negotiations on details, and the new integrated relationship between public government and many segments of the economic structure?

The connections between the evolving political and economic systems go beyond a mere surface resemblance in growth patterns. The two systems are inevitably interdependent; changes in one sphere have produced or made possible subsequent changes in the other. The American industrial revolution probably could not have taken the forms that it did without the prior evolution of the political system. The industrial revolution in the United States began precisely in the decades when the American sociopolitical system was at its most atomistic. The work of dissolving the feudal order, necessary transformations in the old law of property and of human relationships— all these had to be done before the new industrial system could put down its roots and grow. The emergence of numerous private vocational associations, their increasing control over members, growing specialization and interdependence of the economic system, increasing regulation through public government—these have all occurred simultaneously and reciprocally *because they have been necessary to one another*.

As each new element of the total work system differentiates itself, it passes through a stage of self-conscious would-be autonomy, severing itself from its original matrix as children in late adolescence sever themselves from their parents. In each case some necessary conflict is produced, but the severance is never total. Once independent identity is achieved, there is a reintegration of the parts, this time with a more clear-cut recognition of their distinctive elements.

Public government is used to establish and reinforce the identity of the segments of the work system. It is also one arena in which the process of reintegration occurs. Professional associations seldom use public government to regulate intergroup relations directly. Public law may be used to define jurisdictional boundaries between professions and lines of autonomy and authority, when they are sure of what they want and that what they want will remain reasonably stable, when either there is consensus between the professions concerned or one is strong enough to impose its will on the others, inside and outside government. Otherwise each professional group seeks from public government the tools and recognition it needs to bargain more effectively in the private sphere. Although status-striving is often oblique in method, and the legislative aims of any particular group might appear to the uninitiated to be of interest only to that group, competing vocational groups know full well what advantages accrue from apparently technical or minor changes in public law or from slight changes in the structure of public government. Hence an individual group's apparently "personal" proposals become the subject for bargaining or of conflict between it and related groups. Slight readjustments in the total pattern of work relationships occur with each such change in public law.

When all of this is taken into account, the partial outline of the structure of government previously described needs revision and amplification.

Government takes place within professional associations, but more within the institutions where professionals work—universities, hospitals, research agencies, schools. Although outlines of the formal structure of such organizations are available, there are few thorough studies of the process of lawmaking and law enforcement within such organizations. Comparative studies, as well as studies tracing the transformation of the governmental process within different kinds of organizations over the years, are badly needed. Much groundwork must be done before valid generalizations can be made.

A good deal more needs to be known, too, about the structure and process of private governmental relations between professional associations and work organizations, professional associations and educational institutions, professional associations and intermediaries such as insurance companies, and between different professional associations. The strands in the web of relationships need to be traced; the patterns of change in these relationships must be explored in detail. These intergroup relations can be better understood as one intermediate phase of the total structure of public-private government.

THE ORDERING OF WORK THROUGH PRIVATE AND PUBLIC GOVERNMENT

Public and private law and government are linked in the task of regulating professional work, in systematizing professional work roles, work rights, and obligations. The linkage can be described in two ways: (1) both simultaneously perform different aspects of the same task in communication and collaboration; (2) the full articulation of a general principle governing a particular body of work relationships seems to take several decades—sometimes a century or more—to evolve from private *ad hoc* action and internal rules and codes to intergroup treaties and final crystallization in public law. Since problems are resolved at different rates, or the cycle of their resolution begins at different times, this means that at any given time different issues affecting the same profession will be at various points of resolution. The relationship between the professions and public government, between private rule and public law, varies from issue to issue, although the total, the sum, of the relationships is moving according to the general patterns already described.

Much of the systematization of work rights and relationships is still done obliquely. The existence of a professional association serves to define the work role more than it would be defined otherwise. The association indirectly affects managerial decisions about professional work—by defining professional function, setting boundaries of professional rights, motivating and helping professionals to identify closely with their vocational peers, making geographic mobility of employment easier, curtailing or advancing specialization and determining the channels in which specialization might move, and directing the advancement and spread of professional knowledge.

At certain stages in a profession's development much of the systematization develops through open, arm's-length, militant bargaining between whole vocational groups or with employers on behalf of those groups. The results of this intergroup bargaining may be a "statement of principles," a collective contract, or an agreement between the parties that would be enforceable in the public courts as a contract or is comparable in legal status to private accords in international law.

When jurisdictional issues at stake arise out of rapidly changing circumstances the dimensions of which have not been fully grasped, leaders of professional associations seem to prefer a private approach to intergroup problems. Private agreements are desired when the work situation is in flux, and alterations in the division of labor may be required. Sometimes statutory definitions of jurisdiction are too inflexible. The profession may fear that a statutory line may fence the profession in as well as others out. Sometimes licensing laws or related laws outline a core of work over which the profession has a monopoly, but leave the surrounding areas undefined. When this is the case, the profession may rely on its own resources and private agreements with its competitors to define and enforce jurisdictional boundaries. Some professions, such as psychologists in some states, have found it so difficult to arrive at an enforceable definition of their work that they have had to forgo licensing and rely on registration, certification, or the licensing of use of a title, with no clear-cut definition of the work it describes. They then try to erect jurisdictional fences by private agreement, trying to avoid a statutory line because it would be difficult to police; professions hesitate to place members in the position of being possible violators of public law for operating at the edges of jurisdictional boundaries.

Sooner or later there is resort to public law, particularly as the socioeconomic system becomes increasingly interdependent on bases transcending any particular organization's sphere of influence. Public government is the only agency with jurisdiction broad enough to back up a general principle affecting work relationships, so that those relationships will in turn have some kind of uniformity or predictability throughout large areas of the nation.

From the longer perspective, a "law" can be seen as evolving slowly through the private and private-intergroup stages before it becomes public law. In a more immediate sense, specific proposals for public law emanate from private groups and pass through a stage of intergroup negotiations before they enter the public arena, so that the structure of public government is integrated with, or embraces, the private and intergroup spheres.

CHAPTER **6**

Group-State Relations
and the Public Sector

Since there is a reciprocal relationship between the evolving economic system and changing governmental structure and process, it is difficult to generalize about public government for the United States as a whole. Both the overall structure and the process of government in the United States have differed historically and sectionally. They are not the same in all periods of economic development, and they vary from state to state, depending in part on the economic development of the particular state. Most of the debate over legislation affecting work roles and relationships goes on in state legislatures, but Congress is sometimes involved. The process in Congress differs from that in state legislatures, not only for constitutional reasons but also for reasons that are rooted in the socioeconomic-political structure of the entire nation. As the economy becomes increasingly integrated on a national basis—with nationalized business, possibly more nationwide collective contracts (for labor such as that pioneered by the teamsters' union), and more national uniformity of education and licensing requirements for the professions—it may be expected that the structure and process of federal government will alter accordingly.

It cannot be said that contemporary professional associations are *imperia in imperio*. Although at some points in the past professional associations have been relatively detached from public government, there is no group atomism today, as some guild socialists and other theorists would have it. Many contemporary professional associations have little or no direct relationship to public government, but these same associations do not attempt to govern their members directly, and many other professional associations are closely integrated with public government.

On the other hand, public government today is in no clear sense the detached instrument of natural law or of the abstract will of the people. It is not something clearly separate from the socioeconomic system. Organized groups do not merely pressure public government from the outside. And yet, as the major organized professions have evolved, they have passed through stages when they were pressure groups, and nothing more, in relation to public government. Less well-established modern professional associations are still in that category. However, one of their purposes is to establish a relationship that will link private association, group councils, and public government into an integrated structure in which the process of lawmaking operates.

By the time many bills reach the legislature numerous decisions about them have already been made: within the major associations, in bargaining between different elements of a profession and in bargaining between professions and/or other vocations, with public administrative officials and perhaps the chief executive involved in the process along the way. During prelegislative bargaining, licensing boards and certain narrowly based state agencies usually reinforce particular group claims; broader administrative agencies have their own cause to plead and also may serve as mediators among the elite groups of the profession with which they deal. Some issues may be resolved entirely by this kind of prelegislative bargaining, needing only the final touch of the legislative rubber stamp. When the issue touches interests of others outside the group council, then the group conference is a council of war among allies to develop strategy, or it is a temporary meeting of enemies to explore the possibilities of a negotiated peace if outside forces beyond the control of the negotiators might otherwise carry the day. In either case the public legislature is simply a new part of the process; new decision-makers enter the scene and help to shape the final result.

Today, at least in the large urban-industrial states, the professions approach both the legislative and administrative branches of government not individually but as members of one or more constellations of groups, with different but overlapping constellations for each type of issue. The consensus-reaching process on particular bills is almost entirely within that particular constellation. Some of the groups that meet at the public legislative level are the same ones that relate to one another in the private sphere, so that the public relationship is simply a continuation of the process of interaction and mutual adjustment beginning and ending in the private sphere. At the public level, however, the constellations usually expand greatly.

Since any major professional association does not speak for all the interests of the profession, the neglected interests may come to the legislature independently. Some of them are represented by formal organizations that are eventually represented at the legislature on a continuing basis. Others are temporary and make only *ad hoc* appeals to the legislature. Relations between groups will depend not only on the issue, and on the stage of development the major association representing the profession has reached, but also upon the current status of the division of labor within and around the profession and of organizations representing that division of labor. Is the profession still homogeneous, or is it now highly specialized? If specialized, are the groups on the same general plane of prestige and authority, or do divisions within the profession or outside the profession represent different levels of prestige and authority? Are certain forms of specialization in the process of disappearing or of gaining recognition? The answers differ not only from issue to issue—that is, from disagreement over one specific work task to disagreement over another specific work task—but also from profession to profession, and in different periods for the same profession.

Legislative constellations are very small (particularly around a new profession) or very large, and reach out into broad areas of the social system. In state legislatures relatively few of the bills in the legislatively fertile fields of education, law, and public health come from the main professional associations or the state government agencies. Out of a total of approximately 470 bills concerning education introduced in the California legislature in 1961, the state department of education sponsored only about eighteen.[1] The California Teachers Association, in the decade of the 1950's, sponsored about twenty-three or twenty-four bills each session. Most of the numerous other education organizations sponsored only a few bills apiece. Other bills came from major lay organized groups; for example, labor organizations and the American Legion. Others came from random individuals or less formally organized groups, a few from the independent thinking of the legislators themselves.

Bar associations are concerned with changes in procedural law that activate a wide number of organized economic interests—usually the same ones year after year. Medical associations interact with the many different categories of workers in the medical field, with drug manufacturers, insurance companies, and hospital representatives. Public accountants, on the other hand, may interact with only a few organized groups.

The total number of group constellations has greatly increased. At any given time, some are just beginning, others are well defined. Within a constellation, all groups may be in the formative stage, inchoate, random in their relations to one another and public government; one group may predominate, with some acquiescent and with others contending militantly for their own special viewpoint; or most of the groups may be organized into a formal prelegislative council with formal administrative advisory committees. Within each constellation are those who bargain on equal terms, those who are deliberately excluded from that bargaining, and those who are too dispersed and unorganized to be bargained with in this manner.

In the legislature different professions habitually meet certain representatives of outside groups with which the profession does not bargain but with which it must contend. These are part of the total constellation within which the professional association moves in its legislative activity. Conspicuously absent from each regular constellation are representatives of consumer and debtor interests; only on few bills do the few organizations representing those interests get involved in detailed "work" legislation relating to the professions.

The situation is never static. New groups are always rising, old ones changing. The changes emerge from the shifting division of labor in the entire economic system. All of this does not mean that public government is merely an arena where organized groups battle one another for hegemony. Although this is partially true, public government cannot be described totally in terms of social Darwinism.

First, the penetration of organized groups into public government is matched by the penetration of public government into the deliberations of organized groups. Individual groups temper their demands in anticipation of the probable counterclaims of related groups, the public mood, the political climate, the nature of governmental institutions, and the point of view of government officials. An important part of the public legislative process is the intangible yet very significant process of calculation that goes on in the minds of experienced professional-association leaders before they make a move. Great battles are forestalled because they have been discounted in advance. Representatives of public government participate in the councils and committees of private groups,[2] in intergroup prelegislative joint negotiating councils, and in intergroup *ad hoc* negotiating committees. These influences are reflected in group decisions and actions concerning both the content of proposals and strategy at each prelegislative stage.

At the public-lawmaking stage, public government plays two positive roles: (1) both the structure of public government and the orientation of its members not only affect the form and content of proposals brought to it but also stack the deck in favor of certain kinds of proposals and certain kinds of group interests; and (2) public officials as officials and public institutions as institutions have certain orientations necessary to their functioning and for maintaining their position. These orientations affect their decisions about particular proposals, no matter from which outside group the proposals may come.

THE ROLE OF PUBLIC GOVERNMENT

American public government in the twentieth century tends to reinforce the status quo, but at the same time it is receptive to pressures for change. A vehicle for change, at the same time it contains and channels that change. It forces any one imminent change to adjust to the existing system.

Formal Structure

The formal structure of public government at any given time will reflect and reinforce past changes in the socioeconomic sphere. As David Truman has said, "formal structure both reflects and sustains differences in power. It is never neutral. . . . Dispersed leadership and multiple points of control within one branch reflect and reinforce similar patterns in the other."[3]

For the professions, the formal structure of public government is a Maginot line composed of monuments to past group victories. A vocational group's past militancy may have eventually led to the establishment of a licensing board, perhaps even the creation of a broader administrative agency, and the forming of a legislative committee and/or grooves in legislative thinking that accommodate the group's special point of view. New groups do not have to fight the whole system, nor is their aim usually to overthrow. They are emulative: what they want first is a toehold; what they want ultimately is a place alongside the others. The others are not usually willing to move over, because a concession in the political sphere is tantamount to a concession in the work sphere.

The Executive Branch

Even within a single political jurisdiction, such as the federal government, the administrative activities concerning a single profession may be divided among a half dozen or more unconnected agencies. In the early 1960's the funds for the federal government's budget of over $4 billion for various medical and health activities were distributed among twenty departments and agencies. In many countries administration of public education is centralized under a Ministry of Education, but in the United States, as of 1949, the Veterans Administration, the Department of Agriculture, the Atomic Energy Commission, and the departments of army and navy all had more funds for education than the U.S. Office of Education had. The federal government's science and engineering activities are divided among numerous agencies, among which are the Atomic Energy Commission and the National Aeronautics and Space Administration.[4] Jurisdiction over public schools and, often, public health is widely dispersed at the state and local levels.[5]

The well-established professions campaign continually to try to effect consolidation of the administrative activities most vital to them under a single agency, preferably one whose jurisdictional boundaries are narrow enough to preclude effective access by other major groups. The National Education Association was displeased when the Federal Board for Vocational Education was established as an independent agency in 1917. In 1933 it finally managed to help transfer the board, as a major subdivision, to the Office of Education, which was then part of the Department of the Interior.[6] In the fields of science and medicine, too, there has been agitation for more centralized administration.[7]

Professions welcome the accrued status when a highly placed autonomous governmental agency is devoted solely to fields of their interest, just as they welcome the creation of a new department, school, or college for their field in a major university. The arrival of a profession at this exalted governmental state says a great deal about the whole socioeconomic system and its values.[8]

The organized professions also sturdily resist any reorganization of federal agencies that might result in downgrading the administrators who represent their profession. When the Department of Defense reorganized and abolished the office of assistant secretary for medical and health affairs, the California Medical Association published a protest because the man in charge of health and medical affairs would now be only a deputy assistant secretary.[9]

When a profession is highly specialized and each division has a professional organization, each group of specialists may seek to establish its own channels of access within the public administrative agencies affecting the profession. Administrative reorganization becomes difficult, and formidable obstacles to centralized coordination and direction of adminstrative activities may be created. Within the divisions of the Office of Education, the staffing pattern tends to correspond to important or articulate special interests within the education profession; staff members usually relate strongly to the specialist professional group with which their work is most directly concerned.[10]

The same problems occur on a smaller scale at the state level. Different, separate boards and agencies give points of access for different groups, which resist any efforts to change the status quo. All the while, rising groups are pressing for points of their own. As of 1952, the states licensed nearly seventy-five occupations. North Carolina had twenty-three independent licensing boards.[11]

Although authority relationships in professional work are not often spelled out as such in public statutes or administrative rules, they are affected by the composition of public regulatory boards and the relative position of those boards in the structure of state government.

Legally, the public boards are exercising the powers of the state. Actually, in many cases, as one political scientist has said: "Professional licensing boards are virtually the creatures of the professional societies . . ."[12]—although this is true only when the boards consist of representatives of the profession. Some boards are mixed; others are dominated by members of one or more other professions. A profession regulated by an independent board composed entirely of members of the profession is more clearly master of its own fate vis-à-vis its work than is one whose regulatory board is under the jurisdiction of the board of another profession or whose board includes members of other professions.

Once it has attained licensing, each profession strives for more complete self-regulation through piecemeal, minor changes in board composition, and these attempts are usually resisted by those higher in the professional pecking order. A profession highly placed may back the licensing of a subordinate group, even though this may mean more autonomy eventually for the latter, because control over licensing can give control over the supply of such subordinate workers and a measure of uniformity and predictability in their training and expected behavior on the job. However, the higher group endeavors to keep ultimate control over the licensing of the lower group; for example, by its presence on the latter's regulatory board.[13]

Issues pertaining to federal-government structure necessarily attract widespread attention, and are decided outside the closed circles of group bargaining. At the state level issues of government structure attract less lay attention, and it is here that the professions' joint prelegislative councils negotiate and bargain. Until a group has attained licensing and other forms of legitimization, it is usually not included in formal bargaining councils at all. Since established councils resist the claims of rising groups, pressure by new groups must be militant, and in the name of general principles. This tactic, once used by the older, now established groups, is a common one for a rising group that has a clear sense of itself but has not yet "arrived."

In medicine, for example, some clear-cut separations were established and recognized very early—for general medicine, veterinary medicine, dentistry, pharmacy, and optometry. In some states these groups eventually all became participants in the formal prelegislative councils, which are dominated by medical doctors. For years nurses battled for recognition and the degree of inclusion in group negotiating that they now have. They, in turn, have resisted similar efforts by psychiatric technicians to get independent licensing and recognition. The medical profession has taken two courses in response to various other claims: either it has agreed to a special licensing board or advisory committee under the jurisdiction of a board of medical examiners (as in California, for drugless practitioners, midwives, chiropodists, and eventually physical therapists and psychologists) or in some other way has forestalled complete self-regulation; or it has resisted licensing of the outsiders (*e.g.,* chiropractors). None of the latter groups participates in prelegislative group councils on equal terms with the more established participants, although there may be *ad hoc* prelegislative negotiation between representatives of medical associations and one or more of the weaker groups.

Architects have fought attempts of building designers to get licensing or other recognition. Of a somewhat different but related order have been the attitudes of professional teacher associations toward efforts on the part of teacher unions to get legislative recognition. However, architects' representatives have been willing to negotiate behind the scenes with the representatives of building designers.[14] Teacher associations generally have considered teacher unions beyond the pale of negotiation.[15]

Counterefforts have included such measures as grouping licensing boards together in one department or division under one director (as in Illinois in 1917, Washington in 1921, Pennsylvania in 1923, California in 1939, and New York); giving that director veto power over board actions; establishing budgetary controls and perhaps pooling licensing fees and placing them in the state's general fund rather than having them retained in separate accounts; creating independent hearing officers and pooling investigators rather than having these functions performed by each board's staff; adding one or more lay members to each board (which California did in 1961); and ensuring more rotation of board members.[16] Established professions have opposed all these moves as a curtailment of their influence over the licensing boards and therefore over their use of the boards to reinforce or advance the profession's position in the work sphere.

Whenever zealous administrators or students of public administration introduce proposals to reduce the number of independent boards and to alter relations between those in illogical conjunction with others, they encounter both resistance and cooperation. For example, to effect economies and greater efficiency, a governmental task force in California recommended in 1959 that the osteopathic and chiropractic boards, the landscape architect and architect boards, and the nurse and vocational-nurse boards be consolidated in each of the three cases, and that dispensing opticians be licensed by the optometry board rather than by the board of medical examiners. These seemed like sensible recommendations, but they immediately produced static from the professions, for they failed to take into account the status-strivings and power struggles underlying much of the external structure.[17] Public administrators generally fail to acknowledge *the extent to which the structure and composition of regulatory boards affect the division of labor and authority in the work world.*

Also of concern to the professions is the method of selecting relevant public administrators. Normally the professions prefer that these men be appointed rather than elected. Education associations deplore the fact that in many states superintendents of public instruction are elected.[18] Bar associations have campaigned for decades to have judges appointed rather than elected. The professions reason, and rightly so, that they can have more influence upon appointments.

Most of the well-established professions, as represented by the major associations, prefer that administrative appointments be as nonpartisan as possible. Sometimes this is because the professional association finds it easier to deal directly with a politically neutral man on a technical level. Sometimes it merely reflects the conservative orientation of the profession; the partisanship feared is primarily Democratic partisanship, which gives more voice to interests not represented by the professional elite. Often it means that the profession prefers to keep to a minimum the number of people influencing decisions directly affecting the profession, because the quality and nature of the decisions tend to vary according to the number of participants or interested observers. And, again, it probably means that the profession can have more influence over the choice of a man in the first place and more influence over him after he is in office or at least the reassurance that he shares the profession's values and outlooks.

The President of the United States normally consults with the

NEA and the AMA on policy-making administrative appointments
in their respective spheres. One of the problems is the unwillingness
of top men to serve. Through the attorney general, the ABA has in
recent years had a kind of veto power over federal judgeships,
although many members of the Senate Judiciary Committee, which
must confirm judicial appointments, strongly resent the ABA influence. Bar-association influence on judicial appointments at the state
level ranges from active official participation in selection to informal
veto power. Sometimes the chief executive will deliberately pass the
burden of selecting a department head on to representatives of the
profession concerned, because he wishes to sidetrack a controversial
problem.

One part of the associations' power over state licensing boards
derives from their power over appointments to the boards. There
were numerous examples in the nineteenth century of boards appointed directly by professional associations. Recently it has been
more common for the governor to make appointments from lists
initially presented by professional associations. The dental boards in
eighteen states are drawn from men nominated by dental associations;
in twenty-two states the same holds true for pharmacy, in sixteen
states for nurses, and in thirteen states for physicians.[19]

When the governor is not required to appoint from association
lists, he usually solicits or obtains unsolicited recommendations from
associations. How much weight he gives to these may depend on
how long he and his party have been in office. If he and his party
come in after a long time out of power, the need to satisfy patronage
pressures may outweigh other considerations. After his first year in
office, California's governor for the years 1958–66 made it a practice
to obtain information on the professional background of each pro-
spective appointee so that professional factions could be balanced,
and he (that is, his appointment secretary) tried to see that all
recognized elements of the profession were represented. This, of
course, is still another way by which new, rising, and not-yet-
legitimized elements of the profession are excluded from special access to government. Some persons recommended by the professional

association were chosen. Others came from different sources, but usually no one was appointed to whom the associations objected. Appointees had usually been members of the association and had perhaps held minor office, only rarely a major one.[20]

Legislative proposals frequently arise that would affect the selection process. In all of these and other matters the professions are ever watchful, pressing for advantage in a myriad small ways, vying with as well as occasionally assisting one another.

Legislative Committees

The same kinds of structural factors and issues arise with respect to legislative committees. Although bills affecting any one profession or related group of professions may be, and usually are, dispersed among a number of committees, the orientation and jurisdictional boundaries of the committees have some effect on the kinds of decisions eventually reached. The fact that committees are more autonomous in the Congress than in the average state legislature—in which members may serve on a number of committees during a session—makes congressional committee structure especially significant in influencing ultimate decisions.

When a profession clearly dominates its field, it prefers to have a committee the jurisdiction of which coincides with that field, just as it prefers to have jurisdiction over the field concentrated in a single administrative agency over which it has influence. One of the oldest of the standing committees affecting the professions has been the House Judiciary Committee, established in 1813. Before the Civil War pro-public-education forces were clamoring for congressional committees on education.

On the other hand, a group opposing the advancement of a particular field through public action may resist the establishment of a committee for that field and prefer to have decisions affecting the profession made in several decentralized places. Before the Civil War southerners, who feared a threat to their labor system, fought off efforts to set up committees on education and labor; such committees were not established in the House until 1867 and in the Senate until 1860. There has been no standing committee for medicine as such in Congress, although in the Eighty-sixth Congress the Senate had a subcommittee on problems of the aging, which became an independent select committee in the Eighty-seventh Congress. In the House, medical bills might be referred to the committees on education and labor, on veterans' affairs, or on Washington, D.C.; most have gone to the Interstate Commerce Committee, and for several years before the Medicare bill was passed such bills went to the Ways and Means Committee.[21]

Combining committees or renaming them may affect the fate of subsequent legislative proposals. The 1946 Reorganization Act combined the education and labor committees in the House, and the Senate Education and Labor Committee was renamed the Labor and Public Welfare Committee. This meant that one Senate committee handled many labor, welfare, veterans', medical, and education problems, and so committee members might be chosen to provide balance on one topic with only incidental attention to the others, or their attitudes on one set of problems might influence their attitudes on others. For example, if they were chosen on the basis of their stand on labor-management problems, this would affect their stands on education or medical care. Ordinarily bills must be drafted to correspond with existing committee jurisdictional lines.[22]

The structure of congressional committees is most relevant to the resolution of consumer issues affecting the professions. Attitudes on consumer issues do not necessarily carry over to issues more narrowly concerned with work relationships.

There have been no precise empirical studies of the effect of committee structure on decisions affecting the professions either in Congress or in state legislatures. However, close observation of the California legislature indicates that when there is a committee squarely related to a particular professional field—a public-health committee, a judiciary committee, an education committee, a social-welfare committee—each one has a unique personality and orientation persisting through changes of legislative personnel, and the organized professions in each field can predict and rely upon that orientation. Many of the social presumptions underlying the committee's orientations are the same as those operative in the private field of work over which the committee has jurisdiction; that is, a judiciary committee accepts the traditional methods of administering justice and then decides minor issues within that frame of reference—it does not begin with an assumption that perhaps an entirely different system might be desirable. Therefore the prevailing status relationships in the private work sphere tend to be reflected in the relative advantages of contending groups before the legislative committee. There is a particular constellation of groups appearing time and again before each particular committee. The elite groups tend to be the most effective in putting across their point of view, partially because they have the most authority in the private work sphere within the committee's purview.

In California, licensing proposals for many professions have gone before the Senate Business and Professions Committee and the Assembly Government Efficiency and Economy Committee. The title of the latter committee suggests what its predisposition has been toward the establishment of new licensing boards. Since rising professions are the ones that usually want licensing, this built-in orientation of resistance to establishing new boards automatically gives an advantage to already established professions, which want to preserve the status quo.[23]

Our Conservative Legislatures

Changes do occur, of course. New groups rise and win a place in the sun. But the changes do not come all at once; they come a bit at a time. The legislative process is slow. Legislatures are designed to be both conservative and yet permeable to change. Change is contained and channeled by the nature of the lawmaking institutions.

American public legislatures are like the Anglo-American common-law system generally in that they are reactive rather than active and disposed toward a piecemeal solution to individual problems, a predisposition hospitable to the point of view of many fee-basis professions. Commentators have spoken accurately of the "dead hand of seniority rule," the "paralyzing hand of the filibuster," "government by deadlock," of slowness, delay, and nay-saying in Congress.[24] When a major new law slips through this mesh of obstacles, it makes news by reason of its rarity. Nearly every aspect of the structure of state legislatures conspires to encourage single-shot, piecemeal, pragmatic action on a variety of issues treated separately, rather than large-scale, long-range, well-rounded, integrated programs of action, whether such programs come from groups, the executive branch, or the legislators.[25] The system favors the essentially conservative legislative proposals of those professions whose own work is often on a small person-to-person scale, with an a-bit-at-a-time approach to change. It favors the professions already established. And it forces those who would like to make drastic or large-scale alterations in the dispensing of professional services to do most of their initial experimenting, and to build up consensus, in the private sector.

Heritages from their prototype, the English Parliament; time pressures, turnover, and lack of staff; and the background and predispositions of the legislators are some of the reasons legislatures are this way.

The Passive Tradition

Repeatedly political scientists have concluded that "Very little legislation ever originates with the legislature itself. Few bills are conceived out of the independent thought and judgment of the individual legislator."[26] In a study of the 1929 Ohio Senate, Harvey Walker found that only 26 percent of the bills introduced were originated by senators and that more than half of these came from committees; 74 percent came from outside sources. In 1939, he found, the figures were 24 percent and 76 percent, and in the House about three-fourths of the bills came from the outside.[27] Legislatures are for the most part passive and receptive. They act on proposals coming from a variety of outside sources, and each new act must fit into a large body of existing law.

Part of the reason for this passive, receptive stance of the legislature is historical. A passive, piecemeal, resolution-of-specific-interpersonal-conflicts attitude toward lawmaking has been part of the essential and traditional nature of the Anglo-American legal system. It may even be fundamentally the nature of *all* legal systems, despite surface evidence to the contrary. Until the seventeenth century in England, the prevalent theory was that law was found rather than made. The law of custom, the feudal law, the common law, were altered by the slow rubbing of the centuries rather than by men's conscious will. The finding of law was required only when there were individual disputes to be settled. Decisions, made on the basis of precedent, were confined to the facts of the particular issue.

Parliament for a long time was not a lawmaking body. In its early stages it could be compared with the conferences called by modern American governors and Presidents to build up consent to executive actions; then, as now, consent was a useful prelude to the collection of taxes. It was also utilized by feudal subjects to assert to the crown their rights. When the lawmaking function did begin, it was exercised in the same spirit as the customary law and common law had been interpreted: pragmatically, in piecemeal fashion, governed by a keen sense of continuity with the past.[28]

English history was paralleled, in miniature, in the American colonies in the relations between colonial representative assemblies and the royal or proprietary governors. American legislatures, by the eighteenth century, thought of themselves as making law, but they did not break radically with the procedural heritage of the feudal and common-law traditions.

Renewed stress on natural law in the eighteenth century enabled legislators to appeal to a higher authority in case they disagreed with English laws, and Americans made this kind of legalistic appeal to justify their revolution. But they did not offer the idea of natural law as a rationale for wholesale remaking of existing laws. Only in a very limited way did they appeal to reason rather than to history. In the long run, they behaved more in accord with Edmund Burke's concepts of continuity with the past and change by accretion than with the a-historical radicalism of the Enlightenment.[29]

No Time and Not Much Staff for Large-Scale, Long-Range Study

In addition to the formative historical influences, some very practical contemporary expediencies help to make the state legislatures'
approach to legislation passively receptive and primarily piecemeal.
State legislators are very busy men, usually too busy to develop a
full-fledged, comprehensive program in more than one field or sometimes even in one field. While serving on perhaps several committees
when the legislature is in session, they must be concerned with internal legislative politics, must serve their constituents and carry on
correspondence, and must vote on bills that come to the floor of
the legislature. There is no time during a session to do the research
and thinking necessary to develop a radical, new, long-range program. Legislative sessions in most states are normally biennial and
run from sixty to ninety days, plus special sessions.[30]

Nor do legislators have much time to develop programs in interim
periods. They must campaign for office every two or four years, and
this may mean campaigning in both the primary and general elections. For years members of the lower house of the New Jersey
legislature had to campaign for re-election annually. Legislators must
make speeches and give reports to their constituents. Normally they
must attend a number of political events—meetings, fund-raising affairs, conferences. And since a legislator is generally not paid enough
to support himself and a family, the legislator without independent
means must also earn a living.

In 1949 about three-fourths of the states did not provide research
assistants for committees.[31] Some do not even provide office space for
legislators. A move in the direction of more related, comprehensive,
long-range programs in many states began with the hiring of legislative assistants, more secretarial help, the establishment of legislative
councils or expanded use of the legislative counsel and the legislative
analyst, the increased use of interim committees to hold hearings and
make studies while the legislature was not in session, and increased
use of law-revision commissions and other continuing commissions.
But none of these steps has been enough to surmount all the obstacles

in more than a few fields per session, and even then, as Bertram M. Gross has said, many bills are "minute insertions in a long-standing legislative framework."[32]

The situation is reinforced by rapid turnover among legislators. Partisanship is one cause: there is least turnover in one-party states.[33] Another reason may be relatively low compensation in relation to outside opportunities. In 1949 salaries ranged from $5,000 a year in New York and Illinois to $200 for two years in New Hampshire.[34] Most states compensate legislators on a per diem basis.[35] Legislators stay in office for relatively long periods in California, New York, New Jersey, Pennsylvania, Wisconsin, and Minnesota.[36] In the thirty years from 1929 to 1959 the membership of the California assembly changed almost once every five years. The median length of service for assemblymen in the 1959 session was four years. One study based on thorough interviewing of the legislators in New Jersey, Ohio, Tennessee, and California in 1957 led to the conclusion that "the legislative career appears to be only a temporary episode in their total life space."[37] Turnover is greatest in the rural states.[38]

A legislator who knows he will be in office only temporarily, not to mention the fact that he may be defeated in the next election, is not psychologically oriented to embark on long-range studies or to favor legislation that makes major changes that he has not had time to understand. Since elections every two or four years may also mean a turnover in administration, the minority party in the legislature is sometimes reluctant to commit itself to programs transcending changes in political fortunes.

Several factors make these generalizations about state legislatures less true of Congress. Congress is in session every year, rather than biennially, and for far longer periods each year than is the average state legislature. This, plus the great distance of the national capital from the homes of the midwestern and western congressmen, means that more of them work full time at the job of being a legislator. Higher salaries, too, reflect and reinforce this difference. Congress has more staff assistance and can draw on the resources of the Library of Congress. The administrative branch of government does much preparatory work on many major bills. Congressmen have fewer committee assignments than do state legislators—usually only one or two committees for most members of the House of Representatives and two or three for a senator—and they tend to stay with their committees year after year, building up expertise in the subject matter. A congressional committee may take several years to study all the ramifications of a particular legislative proposal.[39]

However, Congress, in that it must process many more bills, has a greater workload than do state legislatures. Often the California and New York legislatures have the highest number of bills—4,000 to 10,000 presented each session. Congress, in contrast, may have more than 30,000 for a two-year period.[40] Although congressional committees may do thoughtful, creative work on major bills, they may rubber-stamp narrow technical bills of a seemingly noncontroversial nature in much the same way that state legislatures treat such bills. In both cases, because of the sheer press of legislative business, small, piecemeal changes have more chance of slipping through because their lack of complexity apparently requires less consideration.

Middle-Class Legislators

These factors help to determine the kind of men who become legislators, and the prior occupational experiences of the legislators make them particularly comfortable with a pragmatic approach. A man with a demanding job, requiring constant attention, permitting no extended leaves of absence, cannot run for the legislature even if he should want to. Nor can the man on a salaried job, if his employers would not readily accept his frequent absences, take a legislative post without jeopardizing his career. Politics either has to be a career in itself, for those with some form of independent means, or it has to be an adjunct to the kind of vocation that lends itself to and may profit from the legislative experience.

Numerous studies have been made of the occupations of state legislators, and all of them point to the same conclusions. In 1949 an American Political Science Association committee tabulated the occupations of 7,475 state legislators and found that 23 percent of them fell into the business category—1,063 merchants, 311 in insurance, 212 in real estate, 142 bankers and investors, and 40 undertakers. The next-largest group were lawyers, 22.6 percent, with 1,078 in the lower house and 596 in the upper. Farmers averaged 19 percent. Teachers, with 198, constituted 2.5 percent. There were 80 doctors and dentists; 327 gave no occupations.[41] Since the businessmen were often in small, independent businesses, the occupations were almost entirely middle class.

Like the state legislatures, Congress is made up primarily of middle-class men, with an even higher percentage of lawyers. From the Seventy-first to the Seventy-fifth Congress the proportion of lawyers in the Senate ranged from 61 to 76 percent, with a tendency to fluctuate.[42] In the 1951 Congress approximately 64 percent of the members of both houses were in the professions, with 56 percent lawyers—by far the largest single occupational group. There were 297 lawyers, 28 in education, 3 engineers, 3 in social welfare, 3 dentists, 3 accountants, and 2 pharmacists. Business, industry, and finance, the second-largest group, constituted only about 16 percent, of which 17 were in real estate and/or insurance, 9 were bankers, and 3 were investors.[43] Of the remaining occupations, there were 26 in agriculture, 19 who had previously held public office or worked for government, 41 journalists, and only 3 laborers. In 1961, 62 out of 100 senators and 241 out of 437 representatives were lawyers.[44] The average lawyer-legislator bases his law practice in a small town.[45] Most congressmen are from small towns and used to working independently. America's legislators generally are drawn primarily from the ranks of self-employed, middle-class purveyors of services.

Almost all of the nation's legislators have been from occupations that customarily deal with issues, problems, and people on an *ad hoc,* pragmatic, person-to-person, piece-at-a-time basis. They have not drastically or creatively altered the status quo as large business enterprises may for a given area or even the whole country through, say, technological changes or the establishment of large plants in new areas. Accustomed to such methods in private life, legislators naturally approach the task of lawmaking in the same *ad hoc,* piece-meal fashion.

It is interesting to speculate on what legislatures would be like if they were dominated by educators instead of lawyers. Possibly the whole process of lawmaking would be different, less in the procedural traditions of the English common law. As it is, the influence of lawyers on procedural norms is one more factor making legislatures receptive to established groups who want to make minor adjust-ments in the status quo and resistant to groups pressuring for drastic, large-scale change. The lawyer's conception of procedure permeates the whole legislative process and undoubtedly affects the substance of the law.

The federal government was designed and has been manned to a considerable extent by lawyers, and state governments have imitated that model. Lawyers have for many decades constituted from one-fourth to one-third of state legislatures, having also had a dispro-portionate share of legislative leadership positions. In New Jersey, for example, in the late 1950's, two-thirds of the officer positions and more than one-half of the procedural committees of the legislature were manned by lawyers, although they had fewer committee chair-manships than nonlawyers. High proportions of lobbyists, too, are lawyers.[46]

Although nonlawyers in the legislature criticize lawyers for allegedly representing clients in the legislature, for making laws complicated in order to create more law business, or for being too interested in technicalities to see the practical problems with which a proposed law is trying to cope, lawyers in the legislature have quite a different picture of themselves. Speaking to the American Bar Association convention in 1958, the Solicitor General of Great Britain said that a lawyer made a good lawmaker because of his "lucidity of expression, a belief in courteous debate, refusal to reach a conclusion until the evidence and arguments of each side have been heard, and a conviction that his opponent must have his say, however much he disagrees with him."[47]

This, of course, does not prove how much they influence the workings of the legislature, but observation is corroborative. The lawyer-legislator who brings his bill before a legislative committee behaves as he does before a court; in fact, he often refers to elements of the legislative situation as if they were elements of courtroom procedure. This style is in turn often imitated by nonlawyers. The lawyer's conception of due process influences the whole legislative system.

It is for all these reasons and undoubtedly for other reasons as well that the legislature often functions like a court to which individuals or groups bring their disputes for settlement or adjustment, although without the court's elaborate procedural safeguards.

THE LEGISLATIVE PROCESS AND RELATIVE GROUP ADVANTAGES

Undoubtedly the public legislative process affords the greatest advantages to the elite groups in each constellation. These groups generally dominate the bargaining process in both the private and the public spheres. Group relations at the legislature correspond roughly to those outside the legislature. The more well established a profession is in the private sphere, the more it is apt to prevail on most issues within the legislature. Advantages, besides those previously discussed, accruing both from legislative structure and process and the group's knowledge of that structure and process, merit further elaboration.

Even if the various groups of a constellation were all equal at the time the legislature convenes, which they are not, they are not all equally advantaged in maneuvering their bills through the legislative obstacle course, and there is no well-established principle of handicapping in the legislature. Each stage of a bill's progress through the legislature not only reveals differences in advantage but also demonstrates how individual proposals affect, and are affected by, the total context.[48]

In the state legislatures in which the legislative sponsor of a bill assumes responsibility for piloting it through the legislature, the choice of that legislative sponsor can be crucial. The professions often choose a fellow member in the legislature to carry bills. It is normal practice to have an educator-legislator carry legal bills and a lawyer-legislator carry legal bills. Physicians may turn to one of their number in the legislature. Sometimes a legislator may be quite frankly the spokesman in the legislature for his profession. D. D. McKean wrote about a physician who was majority leader of the New Jersey Assembly in 1935 and speaker in 1936 and at the same time was also president of the New Jersey Medical Society and managed all public-health bills on its behalf.[49] This is an unusual case, however. Physicians rarely seek legislative office, because their patients may transfer permanently to others. As Max Weber pointed out long ago, the lawyer's work gives him not only the skills but also the time necessary to be politically active, whereas the physician's work leaves him little time to spare.[50] The one osteopath in the California legislature in 1961 had the advantage of having an osteopath wife who could sustain his practice, and the one veterinarian was one of three partners in a veterinary hospital.

For many professions, when there is no one exactly of their profession in the legislature, a member of a related profession might be useful; for example, a social worker–legislator may be asked to carry bills for psychologists. Except for attorneys, however, there are not enough members of the professions in legislatures so that their services as bill sponsors per se provide any more access for the professions than other vocational groups are afforded by legislators with different backgrounds.

The chairmen of appropriate committees are popular as bill carriers. The chairman of the Senate Judiciary Committee in California carries a large number of State Bar bills; the California Teachers Association seeks the aid of chairmen or members of the education committees in both houses. Sometimes legislators are chosen for reasons other than their vocation or committee position. If a bill has political overtones or has the backing of the administration, it may be carried by a member of the legislative faction with most power. Since some bills are used as dry runs, or propaganda vehicles, or are otherwise not seriously designed for passage, another type of legislative sponsor may be useful. If the bill will probably be so controversial that it will arouse the whole political community, the sponsor may be chosen for his symbolic value or his reputation as a fighter. The more experienced organized groups are almost always at an advantage because they choose their sponsors cannily, whereas individuals or groups without much legislative experience do not have the know-how needed for making shrewd choices.

The way a bill is drafted may affect the eventual fate of a bill. The legislator-sponsor of the bill, of course, may have very little to do with its drafting. The organized bar association may draft its own bills and the legislator-sponsor will accept them as is. Other groups with less internal drafting skill will rely on external services of the legislative counsel's office. In states without such services, groups without drafting skill or without the means to hire experts may find themselves at a considerable disadvantage at the outset.

Advantage comes not simply from knowledge of the law or technical skills of drafting, for these can be obtained from politically neutral craftsmen, but also from mastery of the strategic considerations that enter into determining the content of a bill: whether several bills or one omnibus bill is more appropriate, how much to ask for, how much bargaining leeway to allow, how to bury controversial items, how to highlight politically advantageous requests, when to be precise and when to be vague or ambiguous. The way a bill is couched may greatly influence the probable numbers and kinds of participants in the legislative process. On the other hand, in tempering bills to make them pass smoothly over the legislative terrain, the authors have permitted that terrain to influence their point of view and hence the form and substance of the law that eventually emerges. In this way special interests and public pressures interact and blend.

Timing and the choice of one or both houses are also used to best advantage by experts in the legislative process. If a bill comes as an official request of an administrative agency or as part of the chief executive's program, its fate may also be predetermined.

Since bills represent issues at different stages of consensus-reaching, some have been before the legislature many times, some may have been studied by interim committees or investigating committees, others are relatively new. Sometimes the last group of bills, when the extent and nature of probable opposition are not known, are introduced as feelers. The early stages of introduction—the first standing committee hearing—alert possible opponents, and they can then voice objections. Strategy may then be either a tactical withdrawal of the bill, once the terrain is seen, or behind-the-scenes negotiation. Much invisible negotiation takes place between the group sponsors and their opponents, with the legislator-sponsor awaiting the outcome and contributing to both sides his judgment as to what will probably be acceptable to the legislature and what will not. He may submit negotiated changes as author's amendments, which the hearing committee will accept as a matter of course before debate on the bill.

In California the sponsor of a bill carries it through to conclusion, working through a member of the other house when the bill reaches the floor of that house, so that in considerable measure a bill's fate depends on the attitude of the legislator-sponsor toward it. Some bills he may accept simply as a matter of courtesy or because he does not want to say no to constituents. These bills tend to lie inert or receive perfunctory treatment unless outside pressure is brought to bear on him. Some bills he is willing to trade for an affirmative vote on others that are more important to him. For some he feels personally responsible, but does not consider them crucial. Some are at the core of his interest and perhaps central in his own strategic political and legislative position. The politically naïve professional group, perhaps not cognizant of this, may fail to exert sufficient pressure to keep the bill in motion. The legislative sponsor is similar to an attorney in private life: theoretically all his clients get equal treatment, but actually some are more equal than others. The ones who have an advantage know what they are doing, have established access and influence far in advance, and are continuously alert and on the spot.

The same kinds of partially unconscious biases reflected in committee structure also seem to be inherent in the process of assigning bills to legislative committees, although there have been no precise empirical studies to document this. On rare occasions the power of assignment is used deliberately to affect the fate of bills relating to professional work. One incident has been reported for Idaho, when the state bar association was sponsoring a bill to incorporate the state bar. The Senate Judiciary Committee, composed principally of lawyers from smaller towns, was opposed to the bill and prepared to let it die, so representatives of the bar association got it re-referred to the Livestock Committee, of which a sympathetic senator was chairman, and so it passed.[51] More often this kind of power is employed for bills of a political nature. Dean Mann reports that presiding officers in Arizona utilize the power of referral to kill bills, when this is desired, by referring the bills to committees known to be unfavorable.[52] However, not many professional work bills receive this kind of attention. Since so many bills come before the legislature, prejudging obviously can take place for only a comparatively few bills. More often the way bills are drafted determines initial assignment: an omnibus bill may go to one committee; several narrow bills may be divided among several committees, depending on the primary emphasis of each bill. Only the knowledgeable professional association knows how to exploit the possibilities. Even more important are the unconscious presumptions underlying more routine assignments. Certainly if a bill calling for placing nonprofit hospital prepayment plans under the jurisdiction of the state insurance commissioner is referred to the Finance and Insurance Committee, its treatment will be different from what it would be if referred to the Public Health Committee. A bill on commitment procedures for mental reasons will be treated differently if sent to Criminal Procedure, or one on independent adoptions if sent to Social Welfare instead of to the lawyer-manned Judiciary Committee. Judiciary committees still seem to have an adversary-contract approach to legal problems, rather than an administrative, rehabilitative one. It is of great significance which set of orientations are brought to bear. Ordinarily, unless an issue has become a political one, unconscious presumptions tend to favor the status quo.

Established groups also have an advantage because a bill must run an obstacle course through the legislature. In state legislatures it usually passes through a standing committee, perhaps a ways and means or finance committee, a vote on the floor of the house of origin, a standing committee in the second house, a vote on the floor of the second house, perhaps a conference committee, and finally the governor's office. Up to this last point amendments may be made. As Samuel K. Gove and Gilbert Y. Steiner have said, legislative organization and procedure are designed to present a series of impediments to the easy enactment of laws, and each of the hurdles presents, differently on different issues, opportunities for bills to be killed by particular groups.[53] In Congress the obstacle course is equivalent to that of state legislatures. Although, of course, details vary, many a bill has been sidetracked in the House Rules Committee or by Senate filibuster.

Elite groups have an advantage not only because of their knowledge of the whole process, and because they can afford to keep lobbyists on the spot and so are constantly alert, but also because they often are on the defensive and want bills killed rather than passed.

The role of public legislatures and their degrees of accessibility and inaccessibility to elite and non-elite groups are vividly illustrated by the operation of state legislative committees, which are not usually creators of legislation. They act on bills brought before them and rarely on their own initiative make major amendments to bills, although they may suggest a minor technical change or perhaps a graceful (or ungraceful) compromise. Sometimes a committee may suggest an amendment, but not hold up the bill, and pass it with the understanding that it will be amended later. Gove and Steiner found that as many as one-fifth of all bills referred to committee in the Illinois legislature in the 1950's had been amended in committee, but most of the amendments were either technical or had been agreed upon between the legislator-sponsor and affected groups in advance of the hearing.[54]

If a committee does not pass a bill, its chances are slim indeed.

In California roughly half of the bills are killed in committee. Committees in Illinois tend to be unwilling to assume responsibility for formally killing a bill. If they do, usually participants knew in advance that this would happen. In the Illinois legislature in 1955, of a total of 1,666 referrals to standing committees in the House and 1,408 in the Senate, there were 103 "do not pass" recommendations, 3.3 percent of all referrals. Similar statistics prevailed in 1957.[55]

Legislative parties rather than committees make the crucial decisions in New Jersey. In many states the committee hearing is a stage in the consensus-reaching process for all parties involved. The role of the committee in the hearing and the function of the hearing itself vary for different bills, depending on the scope of a bill, on the number of proponents and opponents and the intensity of their interest, on the size of government expenditures that would result, and on the political implications of the bill. Treatment of bills varies according to who the legislator-sponsor is and whether a bill comes up early or late in a hearing and early or late in a session.

In California the legislator-sponsor may be an all-important factor in influencing committee reaction. If he is the chairman of another powerful committee or holds some other position of power in the legislature, and if he indicates to the committee that it is important to him that this particular bill be passed, the committee will be highly predisposed to act favorably. If he has a less powerful position, his degree of persuasiveness may depend on his total record of behavior toward his fellow legislators: whether he has accorded them a fair hearing when they have asked for his vote on bills in the past, whether the other bills he has carried or is carrying are regarded as good bills, whether he is known to be an honest and hard worker, what regard he has had for the feelings and problems of other legislators and particularly those of the committee members, who his friends are. In committee legislators handle bills with varying degrees of skill as well as different degrees of commitment.

Detailed procedure and the role of the committee vary. In the case of purely technical bills the committee may rely entirely on the word of the legislator-sponsor or an expert witness or two, ask a few questions, and then rubber-stamp the bill, without really having examined it in detail. On "agreed" bills, when the interests involved are relatively narrow and after conflicting parties have come to an understanding, the committee will make sure it understands what the situation is and then pass the bill. As Gove and Steiner have said, there is a general understanding that the committee process makes no preliminary demands on anyone, least of all the committee itself. "Logrolling explains most committee votes." The committees are able to move at a fast, amiable clip because they do not go seeking controversy when no controversy is brought to them. "In the absence of opposition, most members automatically and cheerfully support the colleague who is sponsoring a bill." However, the committee wants to make sure that it has not excluded from the preliminary bargaining any groups with a direct interest.[56]

When a bill is controversial but affects only a few individuals, the committee hearing may be like a pretrial conference or court hearing. The legislator-sponsor marshals his witnesses, including representatives of the people likely to be directly affected by the bill and possibly a distinguished expert. Having heard the proponents, the committee then hears the opposition. An attorney-lobbyist may represent opposition witnesses. If the differences between the two groups are reconcilable, the chairman of the committee commonly puts the bill aside for two or more weeks so that the parties can come to terms. Often the whole hearing procedure is a kind of discovery process for the bill's sponsors. They may not have known what the nature of the opposition would be; having learned, they then proceed to negotiate. If larger organized groups are involved in controversy over a bill, but the controversy is still not of major public interest, the advantage tends to be on the side of the group wanting to maintain the status quo.

When decisions are to be made at the hearing, a committee may function like a multi-member European court, but there is no swearing in of witnesses, there are no rules of evidence, and the rules of procedure are much more informal. The "judges" may be members of the group whose cause is being pleaded. They may have decided the case before it is heard, but they do not disqualify themselves. Sometimes the "judges" act as advocates and argue with or preach at the witnesses. They may give disproportionate time to one side and may decide to hear only a few of the witnesses who came to testify. Witnesses do not necessarily have to speak "of their own knowledge," although committees apparently prefer witnesses who either have some direct interest at stake and testify as to that or who are reliable, detached, expert witnesses. Committees exhibit a degree of discomfort when the witnesses are lobbyists who represent several different types of clients or new clients from session to session. They prefer to have lobbyists who identify closely, and can be identified closely, with the interests the lobbyist represents, so that the man has symbolic value. Very often this is carried to the point that if legislators dislike the lobbyist as a man, they are not favorable to the interests he represents or vice versa. In many states paid lobbyists must register, but committees sometimes do not make a systematic attempt to explore the qualifications and credentials of the witnesses who appear before them to find out, for example, for how many persons they speak. Committee decisions often appear to be made in response to the personalities and issues, with only an occasional tendency for members to think in quantitative terms about how many people will be affected or to consider the issues more objectively and in the abstract. Witnesses are not permitted to cross-examine witnesses for the other side.

California committees in the early 1960's appeared to be biased toward the familiar—to like precedents (although they were often uninformed about precedents), to like to know what other states were doing (yet they could sometimes be persuaded to take pride in having their state assume leadership). They were prejudiced against forming new licensing boards and exhibited a natural politician's wariness about controversy until its measure had been taken, it was under control, and there was some evidence of its being put to constructive use.

Despite all the factors tending to disperse committee members' loyalty in state legislatures, the more well-established professions often manage to gain special access to—some even say capture—the committees most central to their concerns. For example, for many years the California Senate and Assembly judiciary committees have held interim meetings at the time and place of the State Bar convention; the chairman of the Senate Judiciary Committee (the same man for many years) has had a close working relationship with the State Bar and the more well-established judges. Charges have often been made that the California Assembly Public Health Committee has been particularly accessible to organized medical interests.[57]

On bills without broad public impact that are introduced at the request of special groups, a congressional committee may act, as state legislative committees often do, like a "court, listening to the evidence of fact and law brought before it by interested parties"; Congress tends to accept the committee's conclusions on bills of this sort. The concept of the legislature as a referee between interest groups may apply in this case, or the legislature may even rubber-stamp a technical bill prepared by a single group when there is no opposition.[58]

On the surface the major professional associations do not appear to have as much access to congressional as to state legislative committees. Congressional committees have repeatedly failed to pass or have delayed for years the passage of proposals initiated by the American Bar Association. However, the ABA has also been frequently successful in passing its proposals on bankruptcy and commercial law. Congressional-committee chairmen have called on ABA and NEA talent and advice in the drafting of some bills.

The fact is that the established professions do have special access to congressional committees, but it is not so direct as their access to those in the state legislature. Many bills Congress considers originally come from administrative agencies, so that the American national legislative process more and more resembles the British system. Bills to the judiciary committees come from the Department of Justice, the administrative office of the United States courts, and the Conference of Judges. Medical, education, and welfare bills come out of the Department of Health, Education, and Welfare. Space and aeronautics committees pass on proposals originally drafted by the National Aeronautics and Space Administration. So, although it is true that congressional committees are much less passive than state legislative committees in the preparation and modification of legislative proposals, and therefore less apt to let high-prestige professional associations write their own technical law, the administrative agencies do work closely with such professional associations. It is through this back door that the more well-established interest groups get special access.[59]

In 1919 the ABA began the custom of holding an annual three-day meeting in New York City, permitting trade organizations, lawyers, railroads, women's clubs, and every business interest to appear and testify. The ABA adopted a resolution that in making recommendations for legislation affecting American social and economic affairs, it was a quasi-public association, and therefore its committees considering recommendations should hold full public hearings and make their proceedings open to the public.[60] The National Education Association, too, has held public hearings and acted as a liaison between groups, government agencies, and Congress in developing bills.[61]

In terms of group-state relationships, the committee system—in Congress and in some states—produces certain results, which can be summarized as follows: it favors already established groups; groups presenting problems in familiar and accepted ways, that is, groups whose liaisons and councils coincide with the frame of reference of the relevant committees. The system favors the position of elite groups within each field or area for which there is a committee—in other words, the most established ones in each field. However, established groups must not press too hard or display their power or influence too openly and arrogantly, for a reaction may set in. The operation of committees is such that they are conservative and permit a process of accommodation between groups sufficiently delineated and sufficiently strong to be recognized as interests. Groups not in this category can use committee hearings as a sounding board and may be able to force some small compromises in open hearings that they could not achieve behind the scenes. When it is up against the opposition of a more well-established group, very often the most a rising group with a new proposal can hope for is the referral of the bill to interim study.

Elite groups are also effective at all other stages of the legislative process because communication with their allies is easy and they have the skills of negotiation; because they have broad programs that enable them to bargain with a wide variety of groups for support; and because they have technical knowledge and many of their bills are beyond the comprehension of the average man. As one left-wing lawyer-legislator, who had attended night law school, said in 1961, "If the bar association's program is purely technical, I accept it because I don't want to show my ignorance."

Also, and here is a paradox, they may win because many of the legislators are middle-class upward-mobiles who, in the legislature, defer to the same kinds of persons as in the private sphere. In 1949 a bar-association committee commented on the "extreme courtesy shown us by members and committees of the Legislature. While our views were not always concurred in, we found sympathetic and respectful consideration." Or, as another California legislator, commented, "Most of the legislators are awed by doctors."

The elite groups do not always succeed. Power changes occur in the legislature, usually resulting in power-redistributing legislation. How and why do the elite groups sometimes fail? First, some bills fail, whether sponsored by elite groups or not, because they were never intended to pass. Some groups use bills as a gesture to the public to demonstrate their good will, to gain public sympathy, or to dramatize a situation. Some take a militant but losing position on certain issues and do not bargain quietly to win, because they are really talking over the heads of the legislature to certain people in the private sphere: members of their organization, persons they want to recruit into their organization, or employers. Introducing a bill may be a tactical maneuver in a process of conflict and adjustment taking place primarily in the private sphere. Such a group going to the legislature is analogous to a wife going to a divorce lawyer when she has no intention of getting a divorce but wants to win concessions from her husband.

Often the nature of legislative life is such that the most prestigious members of a profession cannot afford to run for office, and men of lesser note are found in the legislature; for example, professors from small rural or teachers colleges rather than from major universities. When these two types of educational institutions are at odds on issues, the legislators may side with the institutions from which they came. Many teacher-legislators have worked at other occupations and hence do not identify solely with the teaching profession. One former teacher in the 1961 California legislature was also listed as a businessman and former president of a junior-college school board. Another lived in farm country and had worked summers as a lumber-jack, construction worker, salesman, and machine operator.[62]

It should not be assumed that lawyer-legislators, as a bloc, act as agents for the legal profession. Lawyers in Congress display attitudes toward the American Bar Association's proposals that range from active sponsorship to active hostility.[63] Lawyers in the California legislature in 1961 did not necessarily carry bills for the organized bar; they also carried bills opposed by the bar, and some were alto-gether indifferent to the bar's program. The exigencies of political strife or broad constituency pressures may more strongly influence legislators than their special vocational ties.

Lawyer-legislators may not vote as a bloc on roll-call votes, even on issues affecting lawyer welfare. In his study of the lower houses of the Illinois, Indiana, and Missouri legislatures in 1955 and 1957 (with farmers and a random group as controls), David R. Derge found that lawyers had a less consolidated vote than the random group: ". . . as the degree of controversy on policy increases, high lawyer cohesion, which is infrequent at best, decreases until it dis-appears when the chamber is fairly evenly divided." In another study of the 1957 and 1959 sessions of the Indiana General Assembly, it was found that on all roll calls but one, lawyers divided in approxi-mately the same way as nonlawyers.[64] Of the lawyer-legislators who constituted 30 percent of the Illinois legislature in the 1950's, Gove

and Steiner have reported: "In matters of constitutional judicial review, compensation for court appointed counsel, grand jury terms,
amendments to the Civil Practice Act, and other issues of special
interest to lawyers, their voting behavior has been more in accord
with a political party interest or a regional interest than with an occupational interest."[65]

In state legislatures one reason for this lies in the age differences
between lawyer-legislators and the leaders of the state bar organizations. Lawyers often come to the state legislature while they are still
quite young, so that their average or median age is considerably
below the average or median for the legislature as a whole, and considerably below that of bar leaders. For many years the median age
for a California assemblyman has been fairly constant at forty-five
(forty-four in 1937). In 1961 the age range for nonlawyer assemblymen was thirty-one to seventy-four with the median somewhere near
fifty, whereas the average lawyer-assemblyman was between thirty-
nine and forty-one. In 1960 the ages of members of California's
State Bar board of governors ranged from forty-eight to sixty-eight,
with an average of fifty-three and a median between fifty-four and
fifty-six. Lawyer-assemblymen were, on the average, twelve to fifteen
years younger than the top leaders of the State Bar.[66]

Another factor is that lawyer-legislators have often had only nominal
connections with the organized bar prior to reaching office. Also, in
California very often leaders of the San Francisco and Los Angeles
bar associations and the State Bar are from large urban law offices,
which normally have corporate and other business clients. Lawyer-
legislators, on the other hand, often practice as individuals or with
associates who are not necessarily partners, and have a general practice with middle-class clients. Some are district attorneys in rural
areas.

On issues of special interest to lawyers as professionals, in committees and behind the scenes, lawyer-legislators have often been more
solicitous about the economic well-being of lawyers than have bar
associations in their official legislative programs. In California they
have complained that the State Bar is not interested enough in the

welfare of the average lawyer, that it has been unwilling to support measures to increase lawyers' fees and has not been vigorous enough in seeking statutory remedies against lay competition when that competition comes from the kinds of business corporations that are clients of some bar leaders.

They apparently are more sensitive to the economic and other problems of the average practicing attorney than many bar leaders. This fact has probably deterred them from pushing a plan for the substitution of a commission hearing for court trial in automobile-accident cases in California. When social workers advocate laws that would prohibit independent adoptions, lawyer-legislators often balk.

Organized bar leaders do not object to the lawyer-legislators' concern for the economic welfare of the lawyer: in California the State Bar's official reticence in this area is strategic. Like the professional teacher associations, the organized bar is most likely to get its official programs passed if it projects an image of objectivity and appears to be interested only in the public welfare. The California State Bar attempts to keep its legislative program as technical as possible.

On some kinds of issues lawyer-legislators tend to vote *against* the organized bar. When the bill to create a State Bar came before the California legislature in 1927, lawyer-legislators fought on both sides.

Bar-association efforts to raise educational standards for the bar often fail because many lawyer-legislators happen to have come up the hard way. California lawyer-legislators, in 1929, voted en masse to abrogate the delegation to the State Bar of power to set educational standards. They were on both sides in the subsequent debates over raising educational standards for the bar.[67]

In many states the organized bar has attempted repeatedly to make judgeships appointive rather than elective, and to have the organized bar given more voice in the selection of judges. Bar-association efforts to depoliticize the selection of judges fail because this runs counter to the interests of many legislators, many of whom want to be judges eventually, or have friends who do, or think of judicial patronage as a valuable element of the party machinery.[68]

There is some indication, at least for California, that Republican lawyer-legislators tend to vote more for the bar association's position on issues of bar organization, education for the bar, and judicial selection than Democratic lawyer-legislators. Republican lawyer-legislators usually have had more prior activity in organized bar associations.

All bills that come before the legislature, whatever their source or sponsorship, are affected by the legislature as a self-contained social institution. Friendships among legislators may affect voting patterns. Studies of the effect of legislative friendship patterns have been few, but interviews of lawyer-legislators in the California legislature in 1961 indicated that legislators of the same party and approximately same age, who were freshmen legislators in the same year, tend to become friendly. Sometimes proximity of offices or floor seats may produce friendships. Lobbyists who work in residence at the state capital on a year-in, year-out basis may become part of various friendship configurations, with different lobbyists in different configurations. There are correlations between friendship patterns and power. In 1961, when California lawyer-assemblymen were asked who were their best friends in the legislature, they most frequently named the man who subsequently became speaker. The ones who named this man also named one another, and the total number in this particular circle was greater than the number in other friendship circles. In other words, the subgroup within the legislature was both comparatively large and cohesive. It was not surprising that this group moved into power.

Holding the whole legislature together are rules that influence behavior and voting. As a result of their interviews with state legislators, John C. Wahlke and others identified over forty rules of the game and placed them in five functional categories: (1) rules affecting group cohesion and solidarity, (2) rules for predictability of behavior, (3) rules channeling and restraining conflict, (4) rules expediting legislative business, and (5) rules to give tactical advantages to individual members.[69] All but perhaps the last category are similar to professional-association codes of ethics, indicating that legislators, like other groups, are bound by certain principles that enable them to function as a group. Outside pressures that try to countervail or ignore these principles are not apt to meet with much acceptance and may activate legislative resistance or hostility.

Administrative agencies also have interests that they strive to protect, sometimes even in direct conflict with contrary interests on the part of the profession they otherwise serve. Friendship patterns and rules of the game also affect, for example, a governor's behavior toward legislation.

Sometimes pressure from one person, if that person is close enough to the governor or to a legislator, may make the difference between life and death for a bill. This can easily happen in Congress because of the power of committee chairmen. More than one ABA bill has been blocked for years by one man in the Judiciary Committee. One powerful man in the House Rules Committee or the House Ways and Means Committee may block—and has done so—passage of medical and education bills year after year.[70]

Professional associations may also fail to put their point of view across simply because of the accidents of vote trading, or they may fall victim once in a while to politicians' apparent desire to give everyone a little something.

If a non-elite group is vocal enough, and wins the support of powerful lay organizations (*e.g.,* the American Legion or trade unions), it may force some concessions. Another approach is to turn to politics, either directly, through an appeal to the governor or the President, or if he is unreceptive, through a longer drive using a political party. Resorting to politics and increasing the number of participants in deciding a policy issue are tactics used by those who cannot win their way through quiet negotiation in the legislature. Although public government per se is not an alternative power system for the weak, political partisanship is the channel through which the weak make themselves heard, a most effective channel when it involves the chief executive.

If an outside group fails in its legislative efforts, in eleven states it may attempt to place initiative propositions on the ballot. This costs large amounts of money and requires widespread organization to accumulate the necessary number of signatures, so it is a luxury for only the most desperate or well-financed groups. The California Teachers Association, however, has used the initiative successfully to have guarantees of state aid to education written into the state constitution. The direct legislation approach is most often the method of the very weak and the very strong. Direct appeal to the public is usually not an isolated strategy, but only one tactic in a campaign that continues in the legislature.

The public legislature, generally speaking, acts as an administrative rubber stamp, with perhaps a minimum of policy review, for non-controversial proposals emanating from high-prestige groups; referees and ratifies the bargains and compromises among relatively equal high-status groups; and acts as a sounding board or a propaganda vehicle for rising groups. The public legislative process is simply part of continuing negotiation and adjustment, which begins at the prelegislative level and continues after legislation has been passed.

Integration between the socioeconomic and political systems in individual states may once have been as Marx suggested. Public government may have been the agent of those who owned the means of production. There may even have been a centralized power elite. Certainly railroad interests had a substantial amount of control over public government in some states in the late nineteenth century. At least for the urbanized industrialized states, however, the Marxian analysis has not been valid for the twentieth century. Since different segments of the economic order have become differentiated in the present century, public legislatures and administrative branches—for all policy issues other than those affecting their own institutional self-interests or issues that have become broadly politicized—provide numerous channels for multiple elites in the private sphere. There is no one power elite; there are multiple elites, one for each constellation of groups, in labor, business, industry, the various professions. Public policy issues are often raised between older, established elites in each of the fields and the next-highest groups in that field. Sometimes the latter succeed, but when they do it is because they have succeeded first, or are about to succeed, in the private sphere.

GOVERNMENT AND THE ECONOMIC ORDER

This slow and difficult process forces innovation in the private sphere. Government in America is a conservative force. The real radicalism, the real instigation of radical change, occurs in the private social and economic spheres. Legislation comes after social change has substantially begun or even reached a plateau. It is the seal of approval on an accomplished fact. If proposals for legislation come before social developments are ripe for them, the proposals are not likely to be accepted, or if they are passed into law, they are not apt to be fully effective. At the point the time is ripe for legislation and the legislation is passed, social change is often already moving in new directions.

Even when the rising groups succeed in staking a claim or establishing a foothold, often campaigning for their rights in the name of broad, liberal principles, the net result is simply to legitimize one more element in the work system. The effect of their efforts is still conservative. The whole process centering around work issues is one of defining, ordering, rationalizing, and stabilizing professional work, helping to create a social order in which rights adhere to functional status. As each of the various work layers gains definition, recognition, and reinforcement through the use of public law, the final outcome may be a vast, complex, precisely differentiated network of work groups, each with its status, rights, and authority spelled out by public law.

The economic system and the public government and law are in this way intermeshed. The growth of private power and the growth of public regulation are inevitably concomitants of each other and of a developing complex industrial system. In the anonymity of an urban society, in an age of high social mobility, in a system at once pluralistic and interdependent, this public reinforcement of work roles and rights is probably essential to the economic system, but on the other hand, it does erect a formidable obstacle to the early adoption of technological improvements or to any major change in the form and substance of professional services to meet rapidly changing social needs.

≈

PART IV

Epilogue: The Dialectic Continued and Revised

CHAPTER 7

The Status Society

In the degree of organization, the hierarchical ordering of some relationships, the nature and aims of professional associations, the merger of public and private government, the drift away from contract and toward status as a way of defining individual rights—in all of these ways the American socioeconomic-political system is closer to its medieval ancestor than it is to the preindustrial system of the early nineteenth century.

The medieval guilds determined who should learn the craft skills by regulating apprenticeship or by operating schools such as those for legal training in the Inns of Court. They set and enforced standards for craft performance, regulated prices, protected their members against the competition of outsiders and of one another. They provided fellowship, brotherhood, and security for those within the fold. They gave to their members not only a sense of belonging but also a definition of the individual's rights, privileges, and duties. The guilds gave to the community direct service and the benefits of their self-regulation in terms of quality enforcement and the just price. In turn, their right to self-regulation was recognized and sanctioned by the community. The net effect of their activities was to help freeze the status quo.

And so it is again today.

227

Scholars disagree widely about the relationship of medieval guilds to medieval town governments. Brentano has taken the view that the guilds were entirely free and autonomous, Seligman that they were entirely subordinate. Others—Ashley, Lipson, Renard—have suggested that the relationship lay somewhere in between. It is probable that every gradation of relationship existed then, just as a gamut of relations between groups and government exists now. Although Church, lords, town, and guilds each had its customary sphere of power, the English kings did have a direct and immediate jurisdiction over certain matters and over the population on particular lands, just as public government today may operate in some spheres without benefit of group intermediaries.[1] In either era there has been far less separation of society and government than there was, for different aspects at times, in early-nineteenth-century America.

While the broader aspects of the historical dialectic have been presented here in terms of the professions, related manifestations have appeared throughout the American socioeconomic-legal system. Trade unions, particularly among skilled workers, and even trade associations exhibit many of the same characteristics also displayed by professional associations. In each case there is need for group cohesion; for control over group boundaries; for establishing, reinforcing, and advancing the position of the group in relation to others. In each case the techniques for accomplishing this are to a remarkable degree the same. Trade associations have their codes of ethics, which attempt to minimize intragroup competition. All kinds of vocational organizations utilize conferences, journals, workshops, group insurance, and so forth, for comparable functional purposes. Broad trends toward increases in association staff and toward bureaucratization or professionalization of staff are manifest in all three kinds of organizations. The multiplication of special organizations has been rampant within each broad grouping. Many of the problems of intra- and inter-group relationships are roughly the same. Relationships with public government are strikingly similar, too.[2]

The professions' efforts to exert some control over income floors and ceilings and to curtail competitive bidding have been matched by trade-union efforts to eliminate wage differentials for related categories of workers to discourage the setting of wage levels on the basis of individual merit.[3] Business has made similar efforts, too. Since the Second World War, fair-trade regulation has become so prevalent that to be unethical in the lexicon of some businessmen is to charge below the just price—now a floor rather than a ceiling—or to compete unduly. Administered prices are replacing the cash nexus.[4]

Vocations other than the professions have also been returning to a situation where rights adhere to status: the worker has certain rights because he holds a particular job, not because he is John Jones or because he has specifically entered into a contract for those rights; the president of the corporation gets the use of a private airplane and a beach place in Florida because he is the president, and when he leaves that position the perquisites pass on to his successor. What is true of rights is also true of obligations. Public law very often reinforces status relationships.[5]

Other changes have taken place beyond the individual group orbit, which bring the contemporary system closer to the medieval one—changes in property rights and relationships, in the law governing the individual's relationships to the community.

The economic system as a whole has moved far away from the cash nexus, which at one point governed so many relationships. Steeply progressive income taxes and inheritance taxes were intended to be contemporary equivalents of the medieval proscription against usury and have the same aim as the just price; that is, in each case one intent was to curb the rise of individuals too far in economic power above their fellows. During the two great world wars, government regulated prices. With the New Deal, wage regulation became an established practice. The concept of an interdependent economic commonweal is as entrenched today as it was before Adam Smith.[6]

All of these resemblances between modern institutions and the medieval or postmedieval order are not fortuitous. In each era similar traits appeared for the same functional reasons.

The medieval guild members—that is, the masters—worked as self-directing individuals. Their towns were enclaves within the feudal system. They formed guilds to protect and reinforce their individual autonomy the only way it could be protected and reinforced, through collective action. The modern professional association was designed, as medieval guilds and contemporary trade unions of skilled workmen were designed, to define the position of the worker in the hierarchies of authority in which he found himself, and to define, enforce, and defend his rights and obligations. Professional associations, like craft-union organizations, were responses by the middle strata in new hierarchical power structures to feelings of powerlessness and loss of prestige. Peer-group-enforced rationalized procedures and impersonal standards were created by these organizations to act as a buffer between the individual members and those with authority or power over them. For the same reasons impersonal standards were being developed in the fifty years between 1880 and 1930 to protect the civil servant in American government.

The guilds rationalized and justified their organization and activities in the name of the public interest through emphasis on, for example, service, craftsmanship, and the just price. Modern professional organizations have claimed to regulate themselves and to enforce professional standards for the public's welfare. American businessmen today talk not so much about rugged individualism as about teamwork for the corporation "family" and service to the community.

Much of the new emphasis on the confinement of individualism within certain peer-group or publicly defined bounds is so that the various functional groupings of an interdependent economic system are definable, predictable, and reasonably stable and balanced in relation to one another. Ordering the medieval system required equivalent actions. In each case all elements of the system—ethics, attitudes, institutional patterns—were in fact necessarily interrelated. Thus was spun the web of neo-medievalism.

There is some evidence to indicate that the American system may be moving beyond resemblance to late-medieval patterns—when guilds were, after all, the forerunners of the dissolution of the feudal system—and back to those of an even earlier time. Max Weber long ago predicted such a sequence.

For many decades the most conspicuous modern professional association was one whose members worked individually or in small groups and served the public on a fee basis, as did members of medieval guilds. The pattern of private organizations has been changing. Education for the most well-established professions has been given over to independent professional schools, and no longer rests entirely in the hands of the profession or of individual members, who formerly took apprentices. Although some professions that were formerly entirely salaried have begun, in a small way, to offer services on a fee basis (*e.g.,* economists, psychologists), for the most part the trend is the other way: toward higher and higher percentages of the professions working on salary.[7] In a general way, professional work has been moving away from the prototypes of the later Middle Ages— when free men worked individually, guided by self-governing guilds— and more toward something resembling the earlier medieval model, when most professional work was done through the Church. Today large secular organizations and public government itself have filled the place the Church once held, and there has been a trend toward wholesale bureaucratization of work, which Max Weber predicted. The professional association still functions as a buffer, perhaps more importantly than ever, but now it is a role in relation to and within other organizations as well as in relation to dispersed patients or clients.

It would be a gross oversimplification, however, to say that the term "neo-medievalism" fully describes the American situation today. A dialectic does not move full circle; it moves from thesis, to antithesis, to a new synthesis. Many of the traits evolving in the eighteenth and early nineteenth centuries are still manifest today. Bureaucratic rules, rational laws, and money or money symbols hold the contemporary system together; time-worn custom and personal loyalty are not the primary social bonds.

Many modern institutions that resemble earlier medieval institutions manifest, on closer examination, some crucial differences. Professional associations do not regulate all aspects of their members' lives, as guilds once did. In fact, professionals in the United States may belong to a variety of organizations other than vocational ones— each expressing a different facet of their interests.[8]

There are other vital differences, too. Socioeconomic organizations span larger geographic areas, even taking ecological distance into account, and although many activities of professional associations today and many processes of government have either the intent or the effect of preserving the status quo, they are at odds with the speed of adjustment that rapid technological change appears to require. The really important question is not, How does the contemporary child resemble his medieval ancestor? It is, rather, What is there in the contemporary American situation different in degree or kind from anything that has gone before?

If many of the socioeconomic patterns that once sustained free-enterprise capitalism and liberal democracy are gone, if the resemblance of the current order to medievalism is only partial and superficial, as indeed it is, then one of the most urgent tasks for American social scientists today is to analyze the present situation more comprehensively, with more accuracy and insight, because there are signs that a new order is already rapidly emerging—a new antithesis.

CHAPTER 8

Democracy and Dynamism

Despite all the pressures toward a stratified society, rigidification of the whole system, and resistance to change, contemporary America is characterized by a high degree of political and economic equality, and the political-legal-economic system is not static, but highly dynamic.

This is only a seeming paradox. As a continuum of private-public government orders and integrates the work system, egalitarianism in consumption and political institutions provides a bond that holds the whole sociopolitical order together. The adjustment of work relationships is not like the movement of a given number of blocks within a static framework. New elements are being added all the time at a remarkable speed, with rapid cumulative effects on the whole framework. (This dynamism is closely linked to the fact that in the present system law is still made, not found.) In the face of all the other developments, which separate men from one another and tend to make the system more rigid, it is these two features that give the whole American system its cohesion and its forward thrust.

DEMOCRACY RECONSIDERED

Every system has to have a bond that holds the whole together, whatever the mechanisms for integration of the parts.

In medieval times the binding force was an overarching body of ethical and religious dogma—and belief—that gave medieval life point and direction and helped to unite the whole of Christendom, at least for a while.

When the American industrial revolution was incipient, the socio-economic system was necessarily at its most atomistic: the parts broken into separate pieces so that they could be reassembled into a new industrial order. Each part of the system interacted with other parts through private contract and the cash nexus. But something more was necessary to keep them all within bounds and related. And the cohesive element was provided by nationalism, national patriotism, and even the imperialism of Manifest Destiny.

National patriotism still plays such a role, but new sources of cohesion have evolved, some of them reminiscent of the Middle Ages.

Christian churches—which have been splintered for so long—are moving more and more in the direction of a new unity, both in terms of organization and of dogma. Protestant churches are merging or confederating, and even the Roman Catholic and Protestant churches are coming closer together. There has been a steady rise in the percentage of Americans who are church members, whatever that may signify.[1]

In economic relationships there has been a marked shift away from the fee-for-service, money-for-object cash nexus, and away from the fee-simple basis of land ownership and the emphasis on tangibles as property (property wholly owned, severable, and interchangeable), which were essential elements of the atomistic order of the early nineteenth century, an atomism that was in turn an essential part of liberal democracy and evolving free-enterprise capitalism. The fact that workers have begun to think in terms of property rights to certain perquisites of their jobs is only one example of many changes in the American conception, and law, of property, which exhibits a marked tendency to return to a whole system of intangible rights rather than severable absorptive ownership: for example, in the long-term leasing rather than buying of land, in long-term financing arrangements for housing, in a multiplication of laws restricting individuals' right to use and alienate their land. As population mounts and the land-man ratio drastically changes, outright individual ownership of land may possibly disappear altogether. With the evolution of the modern corporation, even the ownership of stock is more ownership of a right than a thing.[2] Modern credit practices and the leasing of business machines illustrate the tendency to substitute a series of rights for absorptive ownership in movable property. More and more, important ownership rights adhere to intangibles rather than to tangibles.[3] The member of a "closed panel" plan for professional services owns a continuing right to those services. The new monetary and property relationships are symptomatic of an organic economic system—an integral whole with differentiated yet interdependent parts.

Growing adoption of the concept of social or civic rights to goods and services, based on membership in the human race rather than on any direct economic exchange, carries the evolutionary process one step further.

Other phases of the new emphasis stress the obligations of individuals to the general welfare and social responsibility for unfortunate individuals. Zoning laws, building codes, and governmental regulations of all sorts limit antisocial use of property. In the law, there has been the growth of the doctrine of liability without fault. *Caveat emptor* has given way to the principle of manufacturers' liability and *caveat vendor*. There are marked limits on freedom of contract in every sphere and especially in such fields as labor and insurance law. The insurance principle, the socialization of risk, has spread into more and more spheres of activity in America. The welfare state looks after its halt and its poor.[4]

Today's professionalism in many vocations, implying an ethic of service rather than the unrestrained pursuit of self-interest, is one facet of this larger picture (of course the ethic does not necessarily describe the fact—but then the medieval guildsman did not always live up to his code of ethics, either!). Even the pressures that some professionals resist—toward socialization of risk in the payment of professional services and toward the substitution of social-work philosophy and techniques for traditional law enforcement and trial by adversaries for the settlement of some kinds of social problems— are concomitants of these general social changes. All of these modern characteristics correspond to medieval traits that bound the community together.

However, two of the major suppliers of social cohesion in the present order—political democracy and egalitarianism of consumption— depart from the medieval prototype. There is a close correlation between these two traits. Each reinforces and enlarges the other.

Political Democracy and the Redistribution of Consumption

Increased stratification of work roles and of authority in the American industrial system has not been matched very clearly by stratification in consumption, though status symbols do exist. The maturing of the industrial revolution has brought with it certain changes in the direction of, not away from, egalitarianism: the spread and lengthened time span of public education for all citizens; a tendency toward equalization of the income of wage and salary workers; the rise of real per-capita income, giving most people the necessities for sustenance; the cultural assimilation of previously self-conscious ethnic groups; and the instant mass communication afforded by radio and television. Contemporary America has no sumptuary laws governing consumption. In income and consumption, the contemporary American middle class is so large that the social structure is more diamond-shaped than pyramidal, whatever the niceties of gradation of authority within that middle class.[5]

One of the manifestations of this egalitarianism, discussed earlier, is the rising expectations of American citizens with regard to the consumption of professional services. Whereas many of those rising expectations have been met, in the case of medicine, by the spread of private insurance and prepayment plans, constant pressure exists for more public governmental activity to make professional services more widely available—for more direct dispensation of services through public government, for public governmental subsidy of private enterprise, for public government to act as a third-party intermediary in the administration of prepaid funds, or for public government to effect redistribution of consumption through piecemeal regulation. As a consequence of such pressure, education, once nearly all private, by 1958–1959 had reached a point where only about 14 percent of the elementary- and secondary-school enrollment in the United States was in private nonprofit schools, over 95 percent of which were controlled by or affiliated with religious denominations.[6] Also by 1958, 2,200 of the 6,786 hospitals listed by the American Hospital Association were government-operated (439 federal and 1,191 state, county, and local).[7] Social work and legal assistance have increasingly been available to the indigent through the auspices of public government rather than through private charity.

In the governmental structure and process for issues pertaining to detailed work relationships, relations for intercommunication pre-exist in the private sphere, and the problems to be resolved are ones of consolidating or slightly readjusting relationships that already exist. The issues come up through individual organizations and intergroup negotiation to the legislature, where the group process continues, often with little outside intervention.

However, for the resolution of issues concerned with the redistribution of consumption of professional services, both the process and structure of government are different. There is, to be sure, a measure of private government here, too. When insurance companies decide to expand their medical insurance program, or various groups set up prepayment plans, or business corporations decide to allocate sizable percentages of their annual budgets to research and development, decisions vitally affecting the distribution of professional services are being made in the private sphere. In fact, their total effect is often far more radical than the effect of public decisions on the use of public funds to redistribute consumership. Some decisions are also made at the private intergroup level. But those consumer issues resolved through appeal to public government follow a pattern, both at the prelegislative and the legislative levels, different from the patterns previously described.

Whereas the resolution of a work issue may take anywhere from fifteen to seventy-five years, the complete resolution of a consumer issue may take a century or more. The steps leading to universal public education began almost simultaneously with the American colonies. Since these issues have developed so slowly, it is difficult, even impossible, to ascertain their original source. The first and leading proponents of change in distribution of consumption often appear to be special segments of the profession that would be dispensing the services (teachers in professional schools, people already working for government) and/or spokesmen from the organized groups representing the consumer point of view (labor, old-age associations). In the early stages the proponents usually do not include the main body of the profession involved, either because the profession itself has not yet been organized (as in the case of teachers when tax-supported education was first an issue) or because it is dominated by people who perceive themselves to have a vested interest in the status quo (as in the case of medical men in the past half century). As cumulative steps have been taken to establish medical and welfare programs that bring higher percentages of the relevant professions into public employ, the balance may turn for them as it long since has done for teachers. Those professions may then be in the forefront, pressing for an expansion of consumership of the profession's services with government as an intermediary.

When consumer issues reach the public arena, many groups enter the controversy. The contending forces—racial, regional, economic, religious—are giant in scale and deeply rooted in American culture.[8] Because not all of the contending groups are formally organized, only partial prelegislative bargaining can take place. Consumer issues do not evolve so narrowly out of going associations and intergroup councils of categories of people closely related to one another in their daily work. Developing consumer issues requires patterns of communication; organizations, often ephemeral, have to be created; relations between broadly dispersed categories of people must be articulated, reinforced, sustained. Mass propaganda becomes important, and the need for mass communication necessitates reliance on the instruments for mass communication, including political parties and the President (who not only has ready access to communication media but also has the added advantage of being the symbolic head of State).[9]

The chief executive is the transmitting agent through which issues reach the political stage in the legislature. His role is such that groups on the defensive or with a vested interest in the status quo prefer a weak executive; those wanting change prefer a strong one. Though administrators and the chief executive may bargain with various interested pressure groups to ensure maximum support and to minimize objections,[10] once the proposal reaches the legislature, pressure groups are more "front" than they are active decision-makers, and decisions by the legislature are determined by a combination of prior ideological commitments (that is, deep-seated ones), political forces, constituency pressures, and public opinion. In resolving these issues the legislator plays a much more active role than he does in resolving work issues. And legislative parties play a much more active role. Although Congress is bipartisan or nonpartisan on most issues, when an issue has been politicized, as issues of federal aid to education and the federal health program have been, then the operation of parties in Congress becomes important. In attempting to implement his legislative programs, the President must work closely with congressional party leaders, and governors work through legislative party caucuses or they foster partisanlike coalitions.

If broad consumption issues reach the stage of a floor vote, the vote is apt to divide along partisan lines. As David Truman has said, "Ample evidence already exists to support the proposition that, at least in the act of voting, the party label is constantly the most reliable predictor of a legislator's actions"—though individual legislators often dissent.[11] On consumer issues the legislature is no rubber stamp for group interests. The public has a say.

Many and effective are the tactics of delay, so that private adjustments vis-à-vis these issues may take place. But in the long run the proponents usually have managed to succeed. This remaining democratic element, this debate that embraces large sections of the body politic, is like the broadening of the suffrage base within professional organizations. It is the necessary "consent" upon which the rest of the superstructure depends. By having this political outlet, by having its fruits, the American people are given a stake in and identification with a system they are then willing to support. Thus the trends toward a more stratified work system and toward some forms of political egalitarianism and egalitarianism of consumption have all developed side by side.

PROGRESSIVE CONSENT

On work issues, although American democracy does not work the way American children are taught that it works, as if all citizens held up their hands to vote on each issue or did so by proxy through their representatives, yet there is still a form of democracy, through operation of what might be called progressive consent, that applies to lawmaking within and between organizations and to public lawmaking as well. Even on work issues, major policy decisions are not made in one fell swoop in a single setting or in a single year. It takes anywhere from fifteen to seventy-five or more years for a major policy to evolve. Sometimes a single major change is called for, and it will take years for a decision to be reached to make this change. Sometimes there is a series of small decisions, moving by degrees toward, and within, an overall policy goal. Sometimes there is a series of adjustments, adaptations to changing circumstances, even after a policy has been established. The "consent" in these cases develops from one generation to the next. It also may widen, as the policy evolves, from agreement within a small circle within a private association, through intergroup consensus, to discussion by and eventual assent of broad segments of the public. Each new generation and new group of participants must reaffirm or expand upon what has gone before. Law of all sorts—whether the law enacted within private associations, between them, or in the public legislature—evolves slowly, but it does evolve through the will and purpose of successive categories of men. It does not just happen; it is made.

Succeeding generations of professionals inherit their codes of ethics from foregoing generations. Associations imitate one another. Many codes have a core that originated long ago, having first been compiled out of pre-existing literature by local associations before there were national associations to incorporate and expand the older codes. It also takes much time for treaties between organizations to emerge, as successive generations have their say and the issues move from level to level.

Enacting a public law involving a major policy change frequently requires twenty years and often several decades from the time of the first sign of unrest and discussion of need for change to the final stages of legislative action. Often the formation of a professional organization is one step, and not the earliest, in this process. Intragroup rules or intergroup treaties may be another stage. Many years pass before the issue gets to the legislature, and usually it has to be tried out there two or three or more times before it is finally enacted into law.

Consumer issues evolve on even larger time scales. It took about half a century of agitation and conflict to produce in the United States the transition from partial to total tax support of public schools. Consent to universal public education emerged by degrees, beginning with small grants of public funds to charity schools and moving through a number of other stages before the principle of tax-supported education, available to all, was fully established. The process of consent is still going on over such issues as tax support to adult education. It took about 150 years for the issue to move from local to state to federal levels of debate. Federal support to public education derives from a series of limited appropriations and grants for special purposes. Full consent to federal aid for elementary and secondary education in general has not yet been achieved.

The sequence of public issues concerning the consumption of medical services at times has resembled the sequence for public education. The federal government provided for special medical care for merchant seamen from the earliest days of the Republic. As rapidly as scientists discovered the connections between sanitation and disease and as the facts of communicability of disease were learned, government at all levels began to act in the field of public health.[12] The federal government, in medicine as in education, has undertaken the task of providing special services for certain types of people under federal jurisdiction—for example, men in the armed services and veterans. Pressures for governmental intervention in the field of medicine came with increasing intensity in the first half of the twentieth century and, in 1964, scored a major success when Congress passed a Medicare bill. In medicine and education the principle has only gradually been evolving that medical care is a right to which every citizen is entitled.

To sum up: While only a few people may have a real voice in the settlement of an issue at any particular stage of its evolvement, much larger numbers participate in its resolution, if cumulative numbers are taken into account. There is progression of consent not only contemporaneously from private association, to intergroup bargain, to the public arena, but also from one generation to the next. Just how large the circle is will depend in part on the social function of the evolving law.

The Functions of the Lawmaking Process

American legal scholars and social scientists have done far too little research on the functions of both privately and publicly enacted law.

Not all the planks of a professional association's code of ethics are meant to be taken in the same spirit. Some are merely costumes the profession puts on to impress outsiders. Some are preachments to be honored but not necessarily obeyed. Some are guides, but permissive ones. Some are tactical moves in controversies with outside groups. Some are really seriously intended. There have been no studies of the function of these different types of rules in the social system. Nor have there been such studies of the planks of private intergroup treaties. The public law, too, deserves far more analysis along these lines. Statutes are not all the same in force and intent. Some set up a program for government action. Others are statements of rights and remedies, with varying provisions for enforcement or the lack of it. Some are merely declarations of opinion or perhaps statements of ideals or even smokescreens or propaganda.

More attention, too, should be given to the functions of lawmaking as a process. Even when legislative proposals are not enacted into law, they have a positive force. Through debate over issues, people explore and help to create both the boundaries and the possibilities of the social system in which they find themselves. The issues help to create a conceptual framework, on the basis of which private adjustments are made.

Policy issues are significant not only on their own merits but also because they play a functional role in the creation and maintenance of organizations and of a structured pattern of relations between different elements of the socioeconomic-political system. In other words, a professional association often has to have a purpose, a sense of direction, to hold itself together and to maintain the position of the profession or improve it in relation to other vocations. Different associations, whose respective members require some kind of relationship with one another in their everyday work, need to have something to communicate about, even when the most important by-product of their intercommunication is an intangible sense of connection. The same is true of political parties and of legislatures in their internal group life and in their relations with other significant groups. It is also true of the chief executive in relation to the public or some elements of it and to the various parts of government for which he must provide some kind of unity and direction. Verbal issues provide a bridge between groups that need to interact and have a common bond, but whose basis for interaction is otherwise tenuous.

Some verbalisms, some issues, are more useful than others. The kinds of issues raised at each level have a functional utility in sustaining organization or interrelationships at that particular level. Issues within political parties depend on the jurisdictional level at which the particular segment of the party is operating and on the dispersal, transiency, and degree of permanent commitment of party members. The more dispersed or transient the members, the greater the need for policy issues to hold the party together and give it a sense of purpose. Local party-organization members who have an ongoing party role as an end in itself, or at least as part of a permanent set of social relationships, may not need policy issues to provide internal cohesion. Issues may be raised only at campaign time to win the allegiance of voters. There are issues political parties adopt in a vital sense, other than resolutions the parties merely passively accept, when the organization's members are widely dispersed and have very tenuous and sporadic relationships with one another, or when the party is appealing to the whole public. These must be issues with a broad common denominator, that touch the minds and feelings and needs of large numbers of people, that can be stated simply, that appeal to self-interest and at the same time provide outlets for possibly unexpressed fears and desires.

Since the mid-twentieth century, and particularly after approximately 1957, consumer issues concerning education and medical care have served this kind of need. They touch everyone or nearly everyone. In the case of medicine they touch on the very mysteries and terrors of life itself. In the case of education they clearly bear upon national strength in a time of great fear about international affairs; they are loaded with power implications—for the hand that rocks the cradle rules the world—and bear upon the vital subject of social consensus in an age of pluralism. In general the subject is loaded with all the social potency that religious issues once had.

In an era when communication and transportation have become increasingly nationalized, and job markets and organizations are increasingly national, political issues, too, must serve a function of national integration. For the Democratic party in recent years, promises to have the federal government do something for the consumers of professional services provide some of that needed integration. The Republican party, or at least its leaders, resisting such nationalization in the name of those who already have power in the private sphere and preferring instead a doctrine of militant individualism, has offered national patriotism as a substitute bond—combining individualism and patriotism as frontiersmen did in the age of Jackson. A unifying principle of one sort or another there apparently has to be!

At the same time that lawmaking performs a differentiating and integrating function it also assists in the process of change. Resort to broadly and formally stated principles may be the weapon of a rising group. It is a stage in the evolution of a system and of its various parts.

Most of the professional organizations, even the conservative ones, are purposive, and this is what holds them together. Theirs is not a static, but rather a dynamic, cohesion. They are oriented toward future goals. Much of the interaction between organized groups, as well as most of the interaction between groups and public government, is of this purposive type. It gives political parties both their cohesion and their cutting edge. Debate over broad policy issues holds a whole community together and gives it its forward thrust.

To sum up: Debate over policy and potential law performs a motivating and integrating function for private associations, political parties, legislatures, communities, and nations. Certain kinds of policy issues, in the stages when they are being debated and before they become law, bind different elements of the social order together, whether the bond is one of unity or of conflict. The kinds of issues raised within groups and organizations, between different categories of people, and with varying degrees of openness are determined in part, both in form and in content, by the integrative needs of those elements of the social order in which the issues are viable. As changes in communication, transportation, and other technology have broadened the geographic spans over which men relate and need to relate, so policy issues have arisen, and have been needed, that weld large numbers of people together in debate and are therefore couched in terms of broad common denominators. At the same time, as technological changes have produced an increasingly refined division of labor, separating men into groups of vocational specialists, policy issues have arisen, and have been needed, to differentiate and bind together each specialist group. Whether an issue is visibly articulated or whether its verbalization is kept to a minimum, the nature and number of people who participate in its resolution and the course it runs before it is resolved are all determined in part by the subrational social function of the issue. Laws, after they are enacted, also perform these same kinds of subrational functions, although it is clear that a formal law performs a cohesive function different from that of a policy issue before it becomes a law. The process of fully developing a law takes many decades, so that one of the functions of that development is to provide paths of continuity between past, present, and future.

Obviously much more research is needed before the full scope and nature of the dynamics of law development can be understood, or before we have a clear idea of the function of those dynamics in the processes of stabilization and change in the sociopolitical system. In modern American industrial and urban society, debate over policy issues has provided both stabilization—welding groups and organizations together—and thrust toward change. Taken all together, these debates provide a dynamic cohesiveness for each of the parts and for the system as a whole.

THE DAY THE WORLD STANDS STILL

Everything that has been said throughout this book has referred to phenomena within the bounds of the evolving American nation-state. There are, however, some indications that a broader frame of reference is required.

As business is conducted increasingly on an international scale, and as powerful private international organizations create a body of law or agreement transcending national boundaries, nineteenth-century conceptions of the nation-state begin to seem anachronistic. If we assume a perspective that looks beyond today's awesome and terrible dance of power of the Communist bloc and the "free" world, and beyond the thrusting nationalism of contemporary Africa and Asia; if we look at regional "common markets" and other evidence of economic integration—perhaps we may see emerging a new, secular equivalent of the medieval concept of united Christendom, bonded together by quasi-public or quasi-private organizations.

All the processes of development, the changes in law and government and society, that have been described appear to be taking place, over centuries and now decades, on a worldwide scale. Since socioeconomic-governmental integration on a universal basis is far from completion, it can be expected that in the world as a whole and in its parts the phenomena that are both the causes and symptoms of dynamism will persist for a long time to come.

And after that? It would be presumptuous to say, but a thought Max Weber published in 1906 may be applicable: "Everywhere the house is ready-made for a new servitude. It only waits for the tempo of technical economic 'progress' to slow down and for rent to triumph over profit. The latter victory, joined with the exhaustion of the remaining free soil and free market, will make the masses 'docile.' " Then would come, he said, a move in the direction of *caste*.[13] Neo-medievalism may have its antidotes today, but how long will these antidotes last?

Appendix

Professional Associations in the Eighteenth and Nineteenth Centuries in the United States (*a partial list*)

EDUCATION

Local

New York City; Utica, N.Y.; Essex County, Mass.	1794–1800[a]
New England, New York, Pennsylvania	1820[b]

Regional

New York, Ohio, Illinois	late 1820's
Indiana, Kentucky	early 1830's

State

Rhode Island, New York, Massachusetts	1845	Wisconsin, Illinois, New Jersey	1853
Ohio	1847		
Connecticut	1848	Iowa, New Hampshire, Indiana	1854[c]
Vermont	1850		
Michigan, Pennsylvania	1852	Missouri	1856

[a] Usually the date refers to the time of the association's crystallization, rather than to the time when it was first conceived in some organizer's mind. For a more complete list, see *Encyclopedia of Associations,* Vol. I (Detroit: Gale Research Co., 1961); U.S. Department of Commerce, *National Associations of the United States* (Washington, D.C.: U.S. Govt. Ptg. Off., 1949); Albert Byron Crawford, *A Critical Analysis of the Present Status and Significant Trends of State Education Associations of the United States,* Vol. IV, No. 4 (Bulletin of the Bureau of School Service, College of Education, Univ. of Kentucky [June 1932]), p. 12.

[b] At least 30 in this region by this date.

[c] By 1855, 23 states out of 31 had associations.

National

American Institute of Instruction[d]	1830
National Teachers Association[e]	1847
National Association of Friends of Education[f]	1849
National Association of School Superintendents[g]	1865
National Education Association[h]	1870

MEDICINE

Local Medical

Boston	1735	Philadelphia	1765
New York	1749	New York	1766
	Wabash Valley	1846	

State Medical[l]

Massachusetts	1781	Maryland	1798
New Hampshire	1791	New York	1806[j]
Connecticut	1792		

National

American Psychiatric Association	1844
American Medical Association[k]	1846–7
American Society of Dental Surgeons	19th cent.
American Dental Association	1859

LAW

Local

New York	1748	Other New England states by 1790's
Rhode Island	1755	Philadelphia, Boston, New Orleans,
Massachusetts	1761	by 1799

Association of Bar of City of New York   1870
159 city or county organizations by   1890

[d] Begun in Boston; most members from New England.

[e] Sponsored by 10 state associations.

[f] Merged with NTA.

[g] Merged with NTA when NEA created.

[h] Formed from merger of, among others, American Normal School Association and NTA.

[l] Numerous associations in early 19th cent. of the various schools: regular, homeopath, eclectic, physio-medic, botanico-medic.

[j] New legal status. Earlier antecedents.

[k] Delegates from 40 medical societies.

State

Short-lived state associations, late eighteenth and early nineteenth centuries; unsuccessful attempt to organize in Massachusetts, 1849; New Hampshire, Connecticut, Iowa, New York, Illinois, Alabama, Vermont, Wisconsin, New Jersey, Nebraska, Washington, D.C., by 1870's; twenty-eight state associations by 1890

National

American Bar Association   1878

ARCHITECTURE AND ENGINEERING

Local

Chemical Society of Philadelphia (students)	1792
Columbian Chemical Society (Philadelphia)	1811

National

American Society of Civil Engineers[1]	1852
American Institute of Architects[m]	1857
American Institute of Mining Engineers	1871
American Chemical Society	1876
American Society of Mechanical Engineers	1880
American Electro-Chemical Society	19th cent.
American Society of Irrigation Engineers	19th cent.
Society of Naval Architects and Marine Engineers	19th cent.
Society of the Chemical Industry	19th cent.

COLLEGE PROFESSORS AND SCIENTISTS

Attempts to found Association of American Geologists	1838–9
American Association for Advancement of Science[n]	1848
American Social Science Association	1865
American Philological Association	1869
Archaeological Institute of America	1879
American Association of Naturalists	1881
American Economic Association	1883
Modern Language Association	1883
American Historical Association	1884
Geological Society of America	1888
American Psychological Association	1892

[1] Originally included architects.

[m] Merged with Western Association of Architects in 1889.

[n] Grew out of Association of Geologists and Naturalists. By 1950 AAAS had more than 200 affiliated scientific societies.

OTHERS

American Philosophic Society°	1769
American Library Association	1876
American Association of Public Accountants	1887
American Nurses Association^ᴾ	1896

° Grew out of Junto Club in 1727.
ᴾ American Society of Superintendents of Training Schools for Nurses organized in 1893. With delegates from local alumnae societies, organized the Nurses' Associated Alumnae of the United States and Canada in 1896, which became the American Nurses Association.

Notes and Bibliography

INTRODUCTION: *Historical Trends and Political Theories*

1. Joseph A. Kahl, *The American Class Structure* (New York: Holt, Rinehart & Winston, 1960), p. 67. Alba M. Edwards, *Comparative Occupation Statistics for the United States, 1870 to 1940* (Washington, D.C.: U.S. Govt. Ptg. Off., 1943), p. 102, states that professionals were 2.6 percent of gainful workers in 1870. See U.S. Department of Commerce, *Historical Statistics of the United States, Colonial Times to 1957* (Washington, D.C.: U.S. Govt. Ptg. Off., 1960). As of March 1961, there were 7,998,000 professional and technical workers, 4,977,000 agricultural, and 60,539,000 nonagricultural; see *Statistical Abstract of the United States,* 82nd ed. (Washington, D.C.: U.S. Govt. Ptg. Off., 1961), p. 215.

2. Bonnar Brown and Janet H. Tate, *Income Trends in the United States* (Menlo Park, Calif.: Stanford Research Inst., 1957).

3. For a general picture of medieval life and government see G. G. Coulton, *Medieval Panorama* (New York: Macmillan, 1946); George L. Haskins, *The Growth of English Representative Government* (Philadelphia: Univ. of Pennsylvania Press, 1948); Edward Jenks, *Law and Politics in the Middle Ages* (London: J. Murray, 1919); Ernst H. Kantorowicz, *The King's Two Bodies* (Princeton: Princeton U.P., 1957); John L. La Monte, *The World of the Middle Ages* (New York: Appleton-Century-Crofts, 1949); A. F. Pollard, *The Evolution of Parliament* (London: Macmillan, 1920); Brian Tierney, *Medieval Poor Law* (Berkeley and Los Angeles: Univ. of California Press, 1959); Paul Venogradoff, *Roman Law in Medieval Europe* (London: Oxford U.P., 1929); A. B. White, *Self-Government at the King's Command* (Minneapolis: Univ. of Minnesota Press, 1933).

4. For discussions of the medieval guilds see W. J. Ashley, *An Introduction to English Economic History and Theory,* I (London: Longmans, Green, 1913); Lujo Brentano, *On the History and Development of Guilds and the Origins of Trade-Unions* (London: Trubner, 1870); G. N. Clark, *The Seventeenth Century* (Oxford: Clarendon Press, 1929); Rev. George Clune, *The Medieval Gild System* (Dublin: Browne and Nolan, 1943); Austin P. Evans, "Problem of Control in Medieval Industry," *Political Science Quarterly,* XXXVI (December 1921), 603; Stella Kramer, *The English Craft Gilds: Study in Their Progress and Decline* (New York: Columbia U.P., 1927); Joseph M. Lambert, *Two Thousand Years of Gild Life* (Hull A. Brown, 1891); Ephraim Lipson, *The Economic History of England,* Vol. I: *The Middle Ages,* 7th ed. (London: A. and C. Black, 1937); Arthur J. Penty, *A Guildsman's Interpretation of History* (London: Allen & Unwin, 1920); Georges Renard, *Guilds in the Middle Ages* (London: G. Bell, 1918); E. R. A. Seligman, *Two Chapters on the Medieval Guild of England* (Baltimore: American Economic Assoc., 1887).

On the subject of universities see Hastings Rashdall, *The Universities of Europe in the Middle Ages,* ed. F. M. Powicke and A. B. Emden, 3 vols. (Oxford: Clarendon Press, 1936).

Studies of the early history of the bar and the Inns of Court include: Michael Birks, *Gentlemen of the Law* (London: Stevens and Sons, 1960); Edmund B. V. Christian, *A Short History of Solicitors* (London: Reeves and Turner, 1896); *Halsbury's Laws of England,* Vol. II: *Barristers,* and Vol. XXI: *Solicitors,* 2nd ed. (London: Butterworth, 1938); W. S. Holdsworth, *A History of English Law,* II and VI (Boston: Little, Brown, 1922–51).

5. LaMonte, *op. cit.,* p. 568; A. Z. Reed, *Training for the Public Profession of the Law* (New York: Carnegie Foundation for Advancement of Teaching, 1921), p. 18.

6. R. M. MacIver, "The Social Significance of Professional Ethics," in *Annals of the American Academy of Political and Social Science,* CI (Philadelphia: May 1922), 5.

7. See Summerfield Baldwin, *The Organization of Medieval Christianity* (New York: Henry Holt, 1929); Alexander C. Flick, *The Rise of the Medieval Church* (New York: Putnam's, 1909); ———, *The Decline of the Medieval Church* (New York: Knopf, 1930); John R. H. Moorman, *Church Life in the Thirteenth Century* (Cambridge, Eng.: Cambridge U.P., 1945).

8. Carl Stephenson, *Medieval Feudalism* (Ithaca, N.Y.: Cornell U.P., 1942).

9. Holdsworth, *op. cit.,* I and III; Ewart Lewis, *Medieval Political Ideas,* 2 vols. (New York: Knopf, 1954); Max Radin, *Handbook of Anglo-American Legal History* (St. Paul, Minn.: West Publishing, 1936).

10. Ashley, *op. cit.,* I, 126.

11. Lipson, *op. cit.,* p. 313; Kramer, *op. cit.,* p. 162.

12. Kramer, *op. cit.,* p. 194.

13. Clune, *op. cit.,* pp. 35, 36, 49.

14. *Ibid.,* pp. 47, 99, 101–4.

15. Radin, *op. cit.;* Holdsworth, *op. cit.,* I and III; Lewis, *op. cit.,* Vol. II: *Regnum and Sacerdotium,* 506–51.

16. William R. Scott, *The Constitution and Finance of English, Scottish and Irish Joint-Stock Companies to 1720,* 3 vols. (Cambridge, Eng.: Cambridge U.P., 1910–12); Clark, *op. cit.,* pp. 32–9.

17. John D. Eusden, *Puritans, Lawyers, and Politics in Early Seventeenth Century England* (New Haven: Yale U.P., 1958).

18. Perry Miller, *The New England Mind—The Seventeenth Century* (Cambridge, Mass.: Harvard U.P., 1954); Emil Oberholzer, Jr., "The Church in New England Society," *Seventeenth-Century America,* ed. James M. Smith (Chapel Hill: Univ. of North Carolina Press, 1959), pp. 142–65.

19. In 1790 corporate organizations included only three bridge companies, a few insurance associations, a dozen canal companies, three

banks, and only one successful factory. See Joseph S. Davis, "Eighteenth Century Business Corporations in the United States," *Essays in the Earlier History of American Corporations*, Vol. II, No. 4 (Cambridge, Mass.: Harvard U.P., 1917).

20. Ashley, *op. cit.*, I, 131.

21. James Hall, *Sketches of History, Life, and Manners in the West* (Cincinnati: Hubbard & Edmonds, 1834); Joseph Schafer, *The Social History of American Agriculture* (New York: Macmillan, 1936), p. 52; Charles M. Wilson, *Backwoods America* (Chapel Hill: Univ. of North Carolina Press, 1934).

22. Henry B. Shafer, *The American Medical Profession, 1783–1850* (New York: Columbia Univ. Press, 1936).

23. Reed, *op. cit.*, p. 37.

24. Clarence H. Danhof, "Agricultural Technology to 1880," *The Growth of the American Economy*, ed. Harold F. Williamson (Englewood Cliffs, N.J.: Prentice-Hall, 1946), p. 113; Schafer, *op. cit.*, pp. 65–6.

25. Richard B. Morris, *Government and Labor in Early America* (New York: Columbia U.P., 1946).

26. John A. Krout and Dixon Ryan Fox, *The Completion of Independence* (New York: Macmillan, 1949), p. 296; see also Harold J. Laski, "The Decline of the Professions," *Harper's Magazine* (November 1935), pp. 676–85.

27. Arthur Schlesinger, *Paths to the Present* (New York: Macmillan, 1949), p. 2.

28. *Democracy in America*, 2 vols., ed. Philips Bradley (New York: Knopf, 1945).

29. See G. D. H. Cole's Introduction to the English edition of Renard, *op. cit.*, p. xxiv; see also R. H. Tawney, *The Acquisitive Society* (New York: Harcourt, Brace, 1920); ———, *Religion and the Rise of Capitalism* (New York: Harcourt, Brace, 1926).

30. In England the shift away from regulation of prices, wages, and craft standards had clearly made itself felt by the eighteenth century: William E. H. Lecky, *A History of England in the Eighteenth Century* (New York: D. Appleton, 1887), VI, 236–7. Of course some American states persisted in regulation long after the ideology of laissez faire had been widely expressed: Louis Hartz, *Economic Policy and Democratic Thought* (Cambridge, Mass.: Harvard U.P., 1948).

31. The American character in this period is vividly described by Tocqueville; see also Carl Russell Fish, *The Rise of the Common Man, 1830–1850* (New York: Macmillan, 1927).

32. See *Thomas Jefferson on Democracy*, ed. Saul K. Padover (New York: New American Lib., 1952); Louis Hartz, *The Liberal Tradition in America* (New York: Harcourt, Brace, 1955).

33. Noble E. Cunningham, Jr., *The Jeffersonian Republicans: The*

Formation of Party Organization, 1789–1801 (Chapel Hill: Univ. of North Carolina Press, 1957); Moisei A. Ostrogorski, *Democracy and the Organization of Political Parties* (New York: Macmillan, 1902); Robert V. Remini, *Martin Van Buren and the Making of the Democratic Party* (New York: Columbia U.P., 1959).

34. See comments of Marvin Meyers, *The Jacksonian Persuasion* (Stanford: Stanford U.P., 1957), pp. 199–202.

35. Chicago B & Q Railroad Co. *v.* Iowa, 94 U.S. 155 (1877), Richmond, F & P Railroad Co. *v.* Richmond, 96 U.S. 521 (1878).

36. Joseph L. Blau, *Social Theories of Jacksonian Democracy* (New York: Hafner, 1947); Adrienne Koch, *The Philosophy of Thomas Jefferson* (New York: Columbia U.P., 1943); Meyers, *op. cit.;* Charles M. Wiltse, *The Jeffersonian Tradition in American Democracy* (Chapel Hill: Univ. of North Carolina Press, 1935); Benjamin F. Wright, Jr., *American Interpretations of Natural Law* (Cambridge, Mass.: Harvard U.P., 1931); see also Robert Dahl, *A Preface to Democratic Theory* (Chicago: Univ. of Chicago Press, 1956).

37. Charles B. Kuhlmann, "The Processing of Agricultural Products in the Pre-Railway Age," p. 189, and Constance M. Green, "Light Manufactures and the Beginnings of Precision Manufacture Before 1861," p. 229, in Williamson, *op. cit.* Beginning in the 1790's, new corporations were being formed so rapidly that approximately 310 had been created by the end of the century. See Edwin Merrick Dodd, *American Business Corporations Until 1860* (Cambridge, Mass.: Harvard U.P., 1954), p. 11.

38. Schlesinger, *op. cit.;* Kenneth E. Boulding, *The Organizational Revolution* (New York: Harper & Brothers, 1953).

39. See Thomas C. Cochran and William Miller, *The Age of Enterprise* (New York: Macmillan, 1942).

40. W. W. Manross, *The Episcopal Church in the United States, 1800–1840* (Milwaukee: Morehouse Publishing, 1935); Leo Rosten, ed., *Religions of America* (New York: Simon and Schuster, 1955); Henry K. Rowe, *History of Religion in the United States* (New York: Macmillan, 1924); H. W. Schneider, *Religion in the Twentieth Century* (Cambridge, Mass.: Harvard U.P., 1952); W. W. Sweet, *The Story of Religion in America* (New York: Harper & Brothers, 1939); Leonard Trinterud, *The Forming of an American Tradition* (Philadelphia: Westminster Press, 1947).

41. C. F. Fuess, *Carl Schurz* (New York: Dodd, Mead, 1932).

42. *The Theory of the Leisure Class* (New York: Random House, 1934).

43. *Our Benevolent Feudalism* (New York: Macmillan, 1902).

44. *The Ethics of Redistribution* (Cambridge, Eng.: Cambridge U.P., 1951).

45. General Motors in 1960 had assets of $8,553,085,000 and 595,151 employees, and Standard Oil of New Jersey had assets of $10,090,437,000,

according to *Fortune* (July 1961), p. 168. According to Herrymon
Maurer, *Great Enterprise* (New York: Macmillan, 1955), p. 7, the Bell
System had more than 1,300,000 stockholders and nearly 700,000 em-
ployees.

46. William H. Whyte, Jr., *The Organization Man* (Garden City, N.Y.:
Doubleday, 1957); see also Thomas C. Cochran, *The American Business
System* (Cambridge, Mass.: Harvard U.P., 1957), pp. 75–6, and Arthur
M. Ross, "Do We Have a New Industrial Feudalism?" *The American
Economic Review,* XLVIII (December 1958), 903–20.

47. Roger Blough, *The Free Man and the Corporation* (New York:
McGraw-Hill, 1959), pp. 114–21.

48. Max Weber, *The Theory of Social and Economic Organization,*
Introduction by Talcott Parsons (Glencoe, Ill.: Free Press, 1947), p. 58.

49. The literature on groups and government tends to be either on
pressure groups or on groups and regulatory agencies. The literature on
private government tends to be either on the purely internal affairs of
organizations or on government regulation of organizations. There have
been few, if any, studies dealing with all these aspects of the problem
in relation to one another. Below are some of the books on pressure
groups, and a few more general works. Arthur F. Bentley, *The Process
of Government: A Study of Social Pressures* (Evanston, Ill.: Principia
Press, 1949); Donald C. Blaisdell and Jane Greverus, *Economic Power
and Political Pressures,* Temporary National Economic Committee Mono-
graph 26 (Washington, D.C.: U.S. Govt. Ptg. Off., 1941); Donald C.
Blaisdell, *American Democracy Under Pressure* (New York: Ronald
Press, 1957); Kenneth Crawford, *The Pressure Boys* (New York: Van-
guard Press, 1939); Henry W. Ehrmann, ed., *Interest Groups on Four
Continents* (Pittsburgh: Univ. of Pittsburgh Press, 1958); George B.
Galloway, *The Legislative Process in Congress* (New York: Thomas Y.
Crowell, 1953); V. O. Key, *Politics, Parties and Pressure Groups* (New
York: Thomas Y. Crowell, 1946); Bertram M. Gross, *The Legislative
Struggle* (New York: McGraw-Hill, 1953); E. P. Herring, *Group Rep-
resentation Before Congress* (Baltimore: Johns Hopkins Press, 1929);
Dayton D. McKean, *Party and Pressure Politics* (Boston: Houghton
Mifflin, 1949); Fred W. Riggs, *Pressures on Congress* (New York:
Columbia U.P., 1950); Karl Schriftgiesser, *The Lobbyists* (Boston: Little,
Brown, 1951); David B. Truman, *The Governmental Process* (New York:
Knopf, 1951). See also U.S., Congress, House Select Committee on
Lobbying Activities, Interim Report, Eighty-first Congress, second session,
1951, pp. 3–4, 62–5. More general works include: William Y. Elliott,
The Pragmatic Revolt in Politics (New York: Macmillan, 1928); R. M.
MacIver, *The Web of Government* (New York: Macmillan, 1947);
W. J. M. Mackenzie, "Pressure Groups: The Conceptual Framework,"
Political Studies, III (October 1955), 247–55; Frederick Watkins, *The
Political Tradition in the West* (Cambridge, Mass.: Harvard U.P., 1948).

50. This appears to be the view of John K. Galbraith, *American Capitalism* (Boston: Houghton Mifflin, 1952), Ch. 2.

51. Clark Kerr, *Unions and Union Leaders of Their Own Choosing* (Berkeley: Univ. of California Inst. of Industrial Relations Reprint No. 109, 1958); Henry S. Kariel, *The Decline of American Pluralism* (Stanford: Stanford U.P., 1961).

52. Earl Latham, *The Group Basis of Politics* (Ithaca: Cornell U.P., 1952), p. 35.

53. For a summary of theories on the public interest, see Glendon Schubert, *The Public Interest* (Glencoe: Free Press, 1960), and Joel Tussman, *Obligation of the Body Politic* (New York: Oxford U.P., 1960).

54. G. D. H. Cole, *Guild Socialism Restated* (London: L. Parsons, 1920); Kung Chuan Hsiao, *Political Pluralism* (London: Kegan Paul, Trench Trubner & Co., 1927); H. M. Magid, *English Political Pluralism* (New York: Columbia U.P., 1941); A. R. Orage, ed., *National Guilds* (London: G. Bell, 1914); Maurice Reckitt and C. E. Bechhofer, *The Meaning of National Guilds*, 2nd ed. (London: C. Palmer, 1920); see also Henry Creange, *The Guilds of America* (New York: The Guilds of America Foundation, 1934).

55. Reckitt, *op. cit.*, p. 199.

56. *Authority in the Modern State* (New Haven: Yale Univ. Press, 1919), p. 385; see also Harold J. Laski, *The Foundations of Sovereignty and Other Essays* (New York: Harcourt, Brace, 1921).

57. E. E. Schattschneider, *The Semi-Sovereign People* (New York: Holt, Rinehart & Winston, 1960), pp. 121, 123.

58. Maurer, *op. cit.*, p. 4: "For that matter, is big business private? It could as accurately be called public." Mathew O. Tobriner, "The Labor Union: Public Utility of Labor Relations," *American Bar Association Journal* (hereafter cited as *ABA Journal*), XLIII (September 1957), 805–8.

59. Lane W. Lancaster, "Private Associations and Public Administration," *Social Forces*, XIII (December 1934), 234.

Writers on public administration tend to stress the collaboration between groups and government in social control. See Avery Leiserson, *Administrative Regulation, A Study in Representation of Interests* (Chicago: Univ. of Chicago Press, 1942); J. M. Gaus and L. O. Wolcott, *Public Administration and the United States Department of Agriculture* (Chicago: Public Administration Service, 1920); E. P. Herring, *Public Administration and the Public Interest* (New York: McGraw-Hill, 1936); Fritz Morstein-Marx, ed., *Elements of Public Administration* (Englewood Cliffs: Prentice-Hall, 1959); Emmette S. Redford, *Administration of National Economic Control* (New York: Macmillan, 1952); ———, *Public Administration and Policy Formation* (Austin: Univ. of Texas Press, 1956).

60. David Spitz, *Patterns of Anti-Democratic Thought* (New York: Macmillan, 1949).

61. There are, of course, many economists who maintain that antitrust policies could be effectively enforced, *e.g.*, Walter Adams and Horace M. Gray, *Monopoly in America* (New York: Macmillan, 1955), and Walter Adams, "Public Policy in a Free Enterprise Economy," in *The Structure of American Industry*, 3rd ed. (New York: Macmillan, 1961), pp. 15, 533–63.

62. Bernard Bosanquet, *The Philosophical Theory of the State* (London: Macmillan, 1899); Mary Follett, *The New State* (New York: Longmans, Green, 1923).

CHAPTER 1. *Bread-and-Butter Professionalism*

1. Useful background histories of the professions, in addition to those cited in the Appendix and the Introduction, include:

ENGLISH BACKGROUND: Peter Allsop, *The Legal Profession* (London: Sweet & Maxwell, 1960); Alexander M. Carr-Saunders and P. A. Wilson, *The Professions* (Oxford: Clarendon Press, 1933); Roy Lewis and Angus Maude, *Professional People* (London: Phoenix House, 1952); Robert Robson, *The Attorney in Eighteenth Century England* (Cambridge, Eng.: Cambridge U.P., 1959); Beatrice and Sidney Webb, "Professional Associations," *The New Statesmen*, Special Supplements, IX (April 21–8, 1917).

ACCOUNTING: James D. Edwards, *History of Public Accounting in the United States* (East Lansing: Michigan State U.P., 1960).

CHEMISTRY: Charles A. Browne and Mary E. Weeks, *A History of the American Chemical Society* (Washington, D.C.: American Chemical Society, 1952).

DENTISTRY: Byron S. Hollinshead, *The Survey of Dentistry: The Final Report* (Washington, D.C.: American Council on Education, 1961); Robert W. McCluggage, *A History of the American Dental Association* (Chicago: ADA, 1959); Loren B. Taber, "A Period in California's Dental Education and 'Politicking,' from Ante 1885 to Circa 1906," *The Journal of the California State Dental Association* (hereafter cited as *Journal of the CSDA*), XXXVI (April 1960), 106.

EDUCATION: Commission on Educational Reconstruction, *Organizing the Teaching Profession: The Story of the American Federation of Teachers* (Glencoe: Free Press, 1955); Albert B. Crawford, *op. cit.*; Walter G. Daniel, "Negro Educational Organizations and Publications," *Journal of Negro Education*, VI (October 1937), 225–30; Paul Delanoue, *Teachers and the International Working-Class Movement* (London: World Federation of Trade Unions Publications, 1954); Mildred S. Fenner, *NEA History—Its Development and Program* (Washington, D.C.: NEA, 1945); F. W. Hubbard, "Professional Organizations in Education," *Annals of the*

American Academy of Political and Social Science, CCXXV (September 1944), 113–21; Theodore D. Martin, *Building a Teaching Profession, 1857–1957* (Middletown, N.Y.: The Whitlock Press, 1957); National Educational Association, *Handbook* (Washington, D.C.: NEA, 1960–1), p. 3; Timothy M. Stinnett, *The Teacher and Professional Organizations* (Washington, D.C.: NEA, 1956); J. C. Umstattd, "Teachers' Associations, Organizations and Unions," *Review of Educational Research,* VII (June 1937), 314–15; Edgar B. Wesley, *NEA: the First Hundred Years* (New York: Harper & Brothers, 1957).

ENGINEERING: Esther L. Brown, *The Professional Engineer* (New York: Russell Sage Foundation, 1936); Daniel H. Calhoun, *The American Civil Engineer: Origins and Conflict* (Cambridge, Mass.: Technology Press, 1960); John W. Lieb, Jr., "The Organization and Administration of National Engineering Societies," *Science,* new series, XXII (July 21, 1905). Blaustein and Porter, *op. cit.*

LAW: Other references not cited here are contained in Norbert C. Brockman, "The History of the American Bar Association: A Bibliographic Essay," *The American Journal of Legal History,* VI, No. 3 (July 1962); see Reed, *op. cit.,* p. 206; Esther L. Brown, *Lawyers and the Promotion of Justice* (New York: Russell Sage Foundation, 1938); James Bryce, *The American Commonwealth,* II (New York: Commonwealth Publishing, 1908); William W. Cook, *Power and Responsibility of the American Bar* (New York: Tudor Press, 1922); J. W. Hurst, *The Growth of American Law* (Boston: Little, Brown, 1950); Harold J. Laski, *The American Democracy* (New York: Viking Press, 1948), pp. 564–615; Roscoe Pound, *The Lawyer from Antiquity to Modern Times* (St. Paul: West Publishing, 1953); Max Radin, "The Achievements of the American Bar Association," *ABA Journal,* XXV (1939), 903, 1007, and XXVI (1940), 19, 135, 227, 318; James Rogers, *Law, A Century of Progress, 1835–1935* (New York: New York U.P., 1937); M. L. Rutherford, *The Influence of the American Bar Association on Public Opinion and Legislation* (Philadelphia, 1937); Edson R. Sunderland, *History of the American Bar Association and Its Work* (Boston, 1953); Charles Warren, *A History of the American Bar* (Boston: Little, Brown, 1911).

LIBRARIANSHIP: George B. Utley, *Fifty Years of the American Library Association* (Chicago: ALA, 1926).

MEDICINE: Louis G. Caldwell, "Early Legislation Regulating the Practice of Medicine," *Illinois Law Review,* XVIII (1923), 225; Morris Fishbein, *A History of the American Medical Association, 1857–1947* (Philadelphia: W. B. Saunders, 1947); Oliver Garceau, *The Political Life of the American Medical Association* (Cambridge, Mass.: Harvard U.P., 1941); David R. Hyde and Payson Wolff, "The American Medical Association: Power, Purpose, and Politics in Organized Medicine," *Yale Law Journal,* LXIII (May 1954), 938–1022; Lester S. King, *The Medical World of the Eighteenth Century* (Chicago: Univ. of Chicago Press,

1958); Louis S. Reed, *The Healing Cults* (Chicago: Univ. of Chicago Press, 1932); Richard Carter, *The Doctor Business* (Garden City, N.Y.: Doubleday, 1958); Richard H. Shryock, *The Development of Modern Medicine* (New York: Knopf, 1947).

NURSING: A. M. Brainard, *The Evolution of Public Health Nursing* (Philadelphia: W. B. Saunders, 1922); Esther L. Brown, *Nursing as a Profession* (New York: Russell Sage Foundation, 1936); Katherine Holmes, *History of Industrial Nursing Up to Date* (Detroit, 1931); Elizabeth M. Jamieson and Mary Sewall, *Trends in Nursing History* (Philadelphia: W. B. Saunders, 1940); Milton J. Lesnik and Bernice E. Anderson, *Nursing Practice and the Law* (Philadelphia: Lippincott, 1955); Leonard Reissman and John H. Roher, eds., *Change and Dilemma in the Nursing Profession* (New York: Putnam's, 1957); Mary M. Roberts, *American Nursing History and Interpretation* (New York: Macmillan, 1961); Lucy Ridgely Seymer, *A General History of Nursing* (New York: Macmillan, 1932); Mabel K. Staupers, "Story of the National Association of Colored Graduate Nurses," *American Journal of Nursing,* LI (1951), 222; A. B. Thomas, *Pathfinders, a History of the Progress of Colored Graduate Nurses* (New York: Kay Printing House, 1929).

PSYCHOLOGY: Samuel W. Fernberger, "The American Psychological Association: A Historical Summary, 1892–1930," *Psychological Bulletin,* XXIX (January 1932), 52–3; Abraham A. Roback, *History of American Psychology* (New York: Library Publishers, 1952).

SOCIAL WORK: Frank J. Breno, *Trends in Social Work, 1874–1956* (New York: Columbia U.P., 1957); Esther L. Brown, *Social Work as a Profession* (New York: Russell Sage Foundation, 1942); Abraham Flexner, *Is Social Work a Profession?,* Proceedings of the National Conference of Charities and Correction (New York: New York School of Philanthropy, 1915); Kathleen Woodroofe, *From Charity to Social Work in England and the United States* (London: Routledge & Kegan Paul, 1962).

See also Ralph S. Bates, *Scientific Societies in the United States* (New York: John Wiley, 1945); Eric F. Goldman, *Two-Way Street, the Emergence of the Public Relations Counsel* (Boston: Bellman Publishing, 1948); H. F. Gosnell and M. J. Schmidt, "Professional Associations," *Annals of the American Academy of Political and Social Science,* CLXXIX (1935), 25–33; Everett C. Hughes, *Men and Their Work* (Glencoe: Free Press, 1958); John A. Krout and Dixon Ryan Fox, *The Completion of Independence* (New York: Macmillan, 1944), pp. 292–6; T. H. Marshall, "The Recent History of Professionalism in Relation to Social Structure and Social Policy," *Canadian Journal of Economic and Political Science,* V (August 1939), 325; Talcott Parsons, "The Professions and Social Structure," *Social Forces* (May 1940); Jack Stednitz, "A Comparison of the Profession of Accounting with Architecture, Engineering, Law, and Medicine" (unpubl. diss., Univ. of California at Berkeley, 1956); and the fall 1963 issue of *Daedalus,* journal of the American

Academy of Arts and Sciences, "The Professions"; Sherwood Dean Fox, "Voluntary Associations and Social Structure" (unpubl. diss., Harvard, December 1952); U.S. Department of Commerce, *National Associations of the United States, op. cit.*; Daniel H. Calhoun, *Professional Lives in America, Structure and Aspiration, 1750–1850* (Cambridge, Mass.: Harvard U.P., 1965).

Historical information was also obtained from national, state, and local professional journals; for state and local associations: dissertations on state education and nurses' associations; a wide range of books, articles, proceedings, court cases, newspaper accounts, manuscript collections, and ephemeral literature; numerous personal interviews of representatives of professional associations; and visits to the national association headquarters of the ABA, AMA, NEA, and ACS and to numerous state and local association headquarters in Washington, Hawaii, California, Illinois, Missouri, Pennsylvania, and New York, during the years 1951–65.

2. Fenner, *op. cit.*, p. 26.

3. George W. Bristol, "The Passing of the Legal Profession," *Yale Law Journal*, XXII (1913), 590; Herbert U. Feibelman, "The Passing Independence of the Bar," *Commercial Law Journal*, XXVI (1951), 227; J. Ragner Johnson, "Economic Changes and the Practice of the Law," *Canadian Bar Review*, IX (1931), 239.

4. Council of State Governments, *Occupational Licensing Legislation in the States* (Chicago: Council of State Governments, 1952).

5. However, John Granrud stated in 1926: "Most [state education] associations can present few evidences of a continuous, constant effort to promote a well-rounded education program." *The Organization and Objectives of State Teachers' Associations* (New York: Columbia U.P.), p. 44.

6. Richard G. Boone, *A History of Educational Organization in California, 1849–1923* (San Francisco: Bancroft, 1926), p. 18.

7. *Ibid.*, p. 39; see also, Fenner, *op. cit.*, p. 17.

8. Granrud, *op. cit.*, p. 12, says most state teacher associations except New Jersey had either reorganized on delegate bases or planned to. See Blaustein and Porter on bar reorganization, *op. cit.*, p. 290.

9. Boone, *op. cit.*, p. 21. A later survey showed that in a great majority of state associations, the superintendent held no ex officio office but often was elected to an important office in the state association. His influence was often as much due to his personality as to his official position (Granrud, *op. cit.*, p. 9).

10. Council of State Governments, *op. cit.*, p. 22.

11. California Bar Association *Proceedings*, VI (1915), p. 8; Blaustein and Porter, *op. cit.*

12. See California Bar Association *Proceedings*, IX (1918); *The Recorder*, editorial, September 21, 1917, p. 12; S. B. Warner, "Procedural Delay in California," *California Law Review*, XVIII (September 1920),

369; "Courts *versus* Commission," *Transactions of the Commonwealth Club of California*, XXVI (January 1932).

13. California Bar Association *Proceedings*, XI (1920), p. 213; California *Statutes* (1921), ch. 700, p. 1189.

14. *Halsbury's Laws of England*, II, *op. cit.*, sec. 692, p. 510.

15. *Journal of the American Judicature Society*, II (December 1918), 111. See Quebec *Statutes* (revised), II (1909), law entitled Bar of the Province of Quebec, sec. 1, paras. 1-c, 4, 4483.

16. *Journal of the American Judicature Society*, IV (December 1920), p. 111.

17. See William A. Glaser, "Bibliography on the Integrated Bar," "The Debate over the Integrated Bar," and "The Organization of the Integrated Bar" (New York: Bureau of Applied Social Research, Columbia U.P., August 1960); D. D. McKean, *The Integrated Bar* (Boston: Houghton Mifflin, 1963). The story of the California bar is told in detail in Corinne L. Gilb, "Self-Governing Professions and the Public Welfare" (unpubl. diss., Radcliffe, May 1956).

18. NEA Research Division, *Local Associations . . . , 1958–9* (Washington, D.C.: NEA, 1960), p. 5.

19. Richard Hofstadter, *The Age of Reform* (New York: Knopf, 1955).

20. NEA *Handbook, op. cit.*, 1960–1; Roberts, *op. cit.;* Hyde and Wolff, *op. cit.*, pp. 938, 941; Fox, *op. cit.*, p. 154, dates the founding of the NMA from 1895, the NDA from 1913, and (p. 173) the NBA from 1949. The number of Negro professionals has been relatively small. The 1950 Census reported 4,026 Negro physicians and 1,450 lawyers. See Ira deA. Reid, in "Fifty Years of Progress in the Professions," *The Pittsburgh Courier*, July 1, 1950, p. 9. See G. Franklin Edwards, *The Negro Professional Class* (Glencoe: Free Press, 1959). See references under NURSING in Note 1 to this chapter. See W. Montague Cobb, *The First Negro Medical Society* (Washington, D.C.: Associated Publishers, 1939); J. H. Watkins, "History and Development of the Colored National Teachers Associations of Texas" (unpubl. thesis, Univ. of South Carolina, 1941); Walter G. Daniel, "Negro Educational Organizations and Publications," *Journal of Negro Education*, VI (October 1937), 225–30.

21. W. W. Robinson, *Lawyers of Los Angeles* (Los Angeles Bar Association, 1959), pp. 168, 169, 235. Also usually outside the pale were other special associations based on ethnic background. As of 1963, 61 percent of New York City lawyers were Jewish, with close to 70 percent of these Eastern European in origin. New York, of course, has a variety of other special ethnic groups. Two percent of New York City's lawyers in 1963 belonged to special ethnic bar associations, according to Jerome E. Carlin, *Lawyers' Ethics* (New York; Russell Sage Foundation, 1966). For somewhat different figures see Erwin O. Smigel, *The Wall Street Lawyer* (New York: Free Press, 1964). The Chicago bar also

had a mixture of ethnic groups, with a high preponderance of Jews of Eastern European background. See Carlin's *Lawyers on Their Own* (New Brunswick, N.J.: Rutgers U.P., 1962). This ethnic mix produced a variety of special bar associations: the Bohemian Lawyers Association of Chicago (1911), the Lithuanian American Lawyers Association (1927), the Justinian Society of Advocates, for lawyers of Italian birth, the Nordic Law Club of Chicago (1932), and the Jewish Decalogue Society of Lawyers (1934).

22. See Sister Mary Victory Lewis, "A Critical Survey of the Professional Relationship of Catholic Sisters Conducting Schools of Nursing" (unpubl. thesis, Catholic Univ. of America, August 1935). Some of my information derives from telephone conversations with Father Felix Flynn, San Francisco spiritual director of the Council of Catholic Nurses, and with staff members for the Archdiocese of San Francisco (April, 1962). Most special Catholic associations are of recent origin: The American Catholic Philosophical Association, 1926; the Guild of Catholic Lawyers (mostly in New York City), 1928; the National Federation of Catholic Physicians Guilds, 1932; the American Catholic Sociological Society, 1939; the National Council of Catholic Nurses, 1940; the Catholic Economic Association, 1941; the American Catholic Psychological Association, 1948; the Guild of Catholic Psychiatrists, 1950.

23. See Fox, *op. cit.*, p. 180; Carter, *op. cit.*

24. *The Journal of the American Medical Association* (hereafter cited as *Journal of the AMA*), CLXVI (April 5, 1958).

25. NEA Research Division, *Local Associations . . . , op. cit.*, p. 5.

26. American Medical Education Foundation (1951) and American Medical Research Foundation (1957) merged in 1962. National League of Nursing Education (1893), National Organization for Public Health Nursing (1912), Association of Collegiate Schools of Nursing (1933), and four national committees formed in the 1940's all joined to form the National League for Nursing in 1962. Note also the United Engineering Trustees (1904), the American Institute of Architects Foundation (1942), the American Bar Foundation (1955), the National Council for Accreditation of Teacher Education (1952), and the Joint Committee on Continuing Legal Education (1948).

CHAPTER 2. *Freedom Through Conformity*

1. E. L. Woodward, *The Age of Reform, 1815–70* (Oxford: Clarendon Press, 1938), p. 16; Holdsworth, *op. cit.*, VI, 436–7.

2. On the subject of professional education, see Reed, *op. cit;* Hurst, *op. cit.*, p. 256 *et. seq.;* Blaustein and Porter, *op. cit.*, p. 165; William K. Selden, "The History and Role of Accrediting in Higher Education," *Journal of the AMA*, LXXXI (August 8, 1962), 613; Ellwood P. Cubberly, *Public Education in the United States* (Boston: Houghton Mifflin,

1934), p. 379; Lloyd E. Blauch, *Education for the Professions* (Washington, D.C.: U.S. Govt. Ptg. Off., 1955); Lesnik and Anderson, *op. cit.,* p. 71; *Nursing and Nursing Education in the United States* (New York: Macmillan, 1923); Ernest V. Hollis and Alice L. Taylor, *Social Work Education in the United States* (New York: Columbia U.P., 1951); Mildred L. Montag, *The Education of Nursing Technicians* (New York: Putnam's, 1951).

3. Loren B. Taber, "A Period in California's Dental Education and 'Politicking' . . . ," *op. cit.,* p. 103; quotation from *The Daily Californian,* Univ. of California at Berkeley, October 26, 1956, p. 16.

4. Carter, *The Doctor Business, op. cit.,* p. 95; *Journal of the AMA,* CLXXXI (July 21, 1962), 30.

5. Selden, *op. cit.;* Victor Johnson, "The Historical Development of Accreditation in Medical Education," *Journal of the AMA,* CLXXXI (August 18, 1962), 616. See also William K. Selden, "What Is an Accredited College?" *Journal of the National Education Association* (hereafter cited as *Journal of NEA*), XLVII (January 1958), 43–4; Arthur F. Corey, "National Accreditation Is a Reality," *California Teachers Association* (hereafter cited as *CTA Journal*), XXXI (September 1955), p. 3.

6. Hyde and Wolff, *op. cit.,* p. 970; Selden, *op. cit.*

7. Blaustein and Porter, p. 184.

8. Council of State Governments, *Occupational Licensing . . . , op. cit.,* pp. 26, 52; Hyde and Wolff, *op. cit.,* pp. 969–70. See Senate Interim Committee on Licensing Business and Professions, *1957 Report to the Legislature* (Sacramento, Calif.), pp. 93–102; Hurst, *The Growth of American Law, op. cit.,* p. 277; Alfred McCawley, *Professional Engineering Registration Laws* (privately printed, backed by NSPE); Justin Miller, *The Philosophy of Professional Licensure,* Proceedings of the Annual Congress on Medical Education, Licensure and Hospitals, Chicago, February 12–14, 1954; Francis P. DeLancey, *The Licensing of the Professions in West Virginia* (Chicago: Foundation Press, 1938); Frank Bain, "Licensing of Businesses and Occupations in the South, 1900–1925" (unpubl. diss., Univ. of California at Berkeley, 1934); Francis R. Aumann, "The Growth and Regularization of the Licensing Process in Ohio," *University of Cincinnati Law Review* (March 1952), pp. 97–124; Fred C. Irion, *A Survey of Licensing in New Mexico* (Albuquerque: Univ. of New Mexico, 1949); Oklahoma Legislative Council, *The Licensing of Professions in Oklahoma* (1950).

9. Gilb, *Self-Governing Professions . . . , op. cit.,* p. 92; California *Statutes* (1937), ch. 503, sec. 1–3, p. 1492.

10. Dayton D. McKean, "Who's in Charge Here?" *The Colorado Quarterly,* VI (spring 1958), 395.

11. Hurst, *op. cit.,* p. 277; Council of State Governments, *op. cit.,* pp. 2, 16, 18, 21; Caldwell, *op. cit;* Lesnik and Anderson, *op. cit.,* p. 78.

12. Council of State Governments, *op. cit.,* pp. 28–9.

13. E. C. Hughes, *Men and Their Work, op. cit.*, pp. 141–2.

14. See James E. Brenner, Consultant, *Bar Examination and Requirements for Admission to the Bar* (Survey of the Legal Profession, Shepard's Citations, 1952); Edwards, *History of Public Accounting . . . , op. cit.*, p. 131; Council of State Governments, *op. cit.*, p. 51.

15. Carter, *op. cit.*, p. 90; Hyde and Wolff, *op. cit.*, pp. 972–4. However, the latter (p. 971) reported that the American doctor-patient ratio was 136 to 100,000, second only to the ratio in Israel.

16. Hyde and Wolff, *op. cit.*, p. 975. At the AMA's clinical meeting in December 1960, attempts to relax the AMA's policy on foreign graduates failed. See Note, "Refugees and the Professions," *Harvard Law Review*, LIII (1939), 112, 114. Despite the resistance of organized medicine to foreign doctors, shortages of physicians made mandatory their acceptance and even recruitment. See Herman M. and Anne R. Somers, *Doctors, Patients, and Health Insurance* (Washington, D.C.: Brookings Institution, 1961), p. 124.

17. Some state boards, notably those for accounting, have followed the equivalent standard doctrine, sometimes with additional requirements, including a special examination. Other state boards, including all of them for accounting and more than half of the medical boards as of 1952, have issued certificates to professionals from states that were willing to reciprocate. Sometimes reciprocity has been limited to states requiring equivalent standards. Other states have required out-of-state professionals to take examinations and be admitted *de novo* (Council of State Governments, *op. cit.*, p. 54).

Practices vary from state to state for any given profession. See Blaustein and Porter, *op. cit.*, p. 231 *et. seq.*; William D. Stratford, *Some Restrictions and Limitations to the Free Interstate Movement of Teachers*, Contributions to Education, No. 851 (New York: Columbia U.P., 1942); Bernice Anderson, *The Facilitation of Interstate Movement of Registered Nurses* (Philadelphia: Lippincott, 1950). Within a state, state laws and the practices of state boards have also varied from profession to profession in their treatment of out-of-state professionals.

Interviews with representatives of most of the California state licensing boards, Sacramento, 1962–3. See Frank Hanft and J. N. Hamrick, "Haphazard Regimentation Under Licensing Statutes," *North Carolina Law Review*, (XVII (December 1938), 1.

18. See Oswald Hall, "The Stages of the Medical Career," *American Journal of Sociology*, LIII (March 1948), 243–53; Howard S. Becker and James W. Carper, "The Development of Identification with an Occupation," *American Journal of Sociology*, LXI (January 1956), 289–98.

19. Fenner, *op. cit.*, pp. 23, 28, 36. The possibility of having one's expenses paid as a delegate or of deducting expenses from one's income tax has encouraged attendance. See "Tax Ruling on Deductions by Delegates," *Journal of the CSDA*, XXXV (December 1959), 415.

20. *Journal of the AMA,* CLXXXI (July 21, 1962), 32; Roberts, *op. cit.,* pp. 120, 401 *et seq.* Wesley, *op. cit.,* p. 313, says the NEA has had a commission researching supply and demand for teachers since 1946.

21. Comments on codes of ethics are based on an examination of the codes for educators of various sorts, architects, dentists, physicians, lawyers, engineers, and podiatrists. Works consulted on professional ethics include: Kenneth G. Young, "The Ethics of Accountancy" (unpubl. diss., Univ. of California at Berkeley, 1951); Annals of the American Academy of Political and Social Science, *Ethical Standards and Professional Conduct,* CCXCVII (Philadelphia, 1955); Arthur B. Willis, "Ethics," *The California Certified Public Accountant,* XXIV (November 1956), 18–26; J. E. Blumberg, "An Investigation into Some Perceptions of the Ethics of Nursing as Expressed by a Selected Group of Nurses" (unpubl. thesis, Univ. of California at Berkeley, 1958); Annals of the American Academy of Political and Social Science, *The Ethics of the Professions and of Business,* CI (May 1922); N. W. Dougherty, "Ethics and the Professional," *American Engineer* (April 1954), pp. 13–14, 35–7; American Bar Association, *Opinions of the Committee on Legal Ethics* (1947); American Law Student Association, *Lawyers' Problems of Conscience* (Chicago, 1953); H. S. Drinker, *Legal Ethics* (New York: Columbia U.P., 1953); Orie Phillips and Philbrick McCoy, *Conduct of Judges and Lawyers* (Los Angeles: Parker, for Survey of the Legal Profession, 1952); Maynard E. Pirsig, *Cases and Materials on Legal Ethics* (St. Paul: West Publishing, 1949); George Sharswood, "Essay on Professional Ethics," first published Philadelphia: T. & T. W. Johnson, reprinted in American Bar Association *Reports,* XXXII (1907); Symposium, *Rocky Mountain Law Review,* XXV (June 1953), 405.

22. "John E. Gurley . . . Dentists of the Century," *Journal of the CSDA,* XXV (April 1959), 80.

23. Edith Wensley, *Building Sound Public Relations* (New York: National Organization for Public Health Nursing, 1949). See Carter on public relations for the medical profession, *op. cit.,* ch. 11. See also Stanley Kelley, Jr., *Professional Public Relations and Political Power* (Baltimore: Johns Hopkins Press, 1956).

24. R. C. Gillingham, "The California Teachers Association" (unpubl. diss., Univ. of Southern California, 1949), pp. 177, 210.

25. Kenneth R. Brown, "The Tutor Who Tooted the Flute," *CTA Journal,* XLIX (September 1953), 12–13; "Joint Statement Hits Kickbacks," *ibid.,* LIII (October 1957), 42; Alfred E. Lentz, "Restrictions on Teachers," *Sierra Educational News,* XXXII (April 1936), 15.

26. As early as 1874 the California State Medical Association threatened to expel members who accepted rebates from druggists; in 1891 the society complained about the problem again. News stories on the ownership problem appeared in the Oakland *Tribune,* November 27, 1962, and in the San Francisco *Chronicle,* August 8, 1958, p. 1. See also Kern

County Medical Society *Bulletin,* Vol. IX, No. 8 (August 1962), 293–4, and Vol. IX, No. 1 (January 1962), 15.

27. *Halsbury's Laws of England,* XXXI, *op. cit.,* pp. 140–1.

28. F. B. MacKinnon, *Contingent Fees for Legal Services* (Chicago: Aldine Publishing, 1964).

29. Oakland *Tribune,* September 25, 1959; Berkeley *Gazette,* January 4, 1962.

30. President's *Report,* September 27, 1961, p. 21.

31. *California Business and Professions Code,* I, sec. 6068, p. 427; *ABA Journal,* XXII (1936), 339; First National Bank *v.* Superior Court, 12 Cal. App. 335, 107 Pac. 322 (1909).

32. See 12 Cal. 2d 93, 82 Pac. 442 (1938).

33. Comments on liberal censorship reported in Oakland *Tribune,* July 13, 1958; comments on ALA campaign in *Wilson Library Bulletin,* Vol. XXVIII, No. 1 (September 1953).

34. San Francisco *Examiner* report on AMA convention, June 22, 1958, p. 1; Hyde and Wolff, *op. cit.,* p. 959.

35. Fox, *op. cit.,* pp. 164, 167.

36. Blaustein and Porter, *op. cit.,* p. 207; Harrison Tweed, "Continuing Legal Education," National University Extension Association *Proceedings* (1949), pp. 40–4; American Bar Association Committee on Continuing Legal Education, *Handbook, op. cit.* (1949); Edwards, *op. cit.,* p. 229.

37. Somers and Somers, *op. cit.,* p. 114.

CHAPTER 3. *The Work Revolution and the Consumer Revolution*

1. George Rosen, *The Specialization of Medicine* (New York: Froben Press, 1944).

2. The American Patent Law Association appeared early in the century; Association of the Customs Bar, 1917; Federal Bar Association, 1920; Federal Communications Bar Association, 1935; Association of Insurance Attorneys, 1937; Consular Law Society, 1943; National Association of Claimants' Compensation Attorneys, 1946; American College of Trial Lawyers, 1950.

3. Robert E. Moore, "An Appraisal of Southern State Professional Associations of School Administrators" (unpubl. diss., George Peabody College for Teachers, Nashville, 1953).

4. Herman M. and Anne R. Somers, "Private Health Insurance," *California Law Review,* Part I, Vol. XLVI (August 1958), 396.

5. Herman M. and Anne R. Somers, *Doctors, Patients, and Health Insurance, op. cit.,* p. 33.

6. Cubberly, *op. cit.,*

7. Somers and Somers, "Private Health Insurance," *op. cit.,* pp. 384–5.

8. Figures presented by Charles Silberman, board of editors of *Fortune*

magazine, and James E. Bryan, speaking on Blue Shield, at the Conference of County Society Officers of CMA, February 17–18, 1962.

9. Emery A. Brownell, *Legal Aid in the United States* (Rochester, N.Y.: Lawyers Cooperative Publishing, 1951); news release of National Legal Aid and Defenders Association, July 31, 1962; John S. Bradway, *Legal Aid Bureaus* (Chicago: Public Administration Service, 1935); ———, ed., *Frontiers of Legal Aid Work* (Philadelphia: American Academy of Political and Social Science, 1939); conversations from time to time during the 1950's with Junius L. Allison, field director of the National Legal Aid Association.

10. Generally available sources include the committee report on "The Availability of Legal Services and Judicial Processes to the Low and Moderate Income Groups . . . ," *Lawyers Guild Review*, X (spring 1950), 8; Jerome E. Carlin and Jan Howard, "Legal Representation and Class Justice," *UCLA Law Review*, XII (January 1965), 381, 437; Mayer C. Goldman, *The Public Defender* (New York: Putnam's, 1917).

11. Washington *Statutes* (revised, annotated), sec. 10001–207 (Remington, 1940); see also R. H. Smith, "The English Legal Assistance Plan: Its Significance for American Legal Institutions," *ABA Journal*, XXXV (June 1949), 453; Note, *Yale Law Journal*, IX (January 1950), 320; Roy Lewis and Angus Maude, *Professional People* (London: Phoenix House, 1952), p. 206.

12. Somers and Somers, "Private Health Insurance," *op. cit.*, pp. 385–6. See also F. Sognnaes Reidar, "Dentistry at Its Centennial Crossroads," *Journal of the CSDA*, XXXVII (February 1961), pp. 28–33.

13. Somers and Somers, *Doctors, Patients* . . . , *op. cit.*, p. 230; Joseph Garbarino, "The Development of Health Insurance Plans," *Monthly Labor Review*, LXXXII (May 1959), pp. 572–8; see also report of the Conference of County Society Officers of California Medical Associations, held February 17 and 18, 1962; see Fox, *op. cit.*, p. 147, on the non-cooperation of the AMA with voluntary health insurance; see also Richard Shryock, *The Development of Modern Medicine* (New York: Knopf, 1947), p. 403, on the development of medical insurance and group practice.

14. California Medical Association *Newsletter*, Vol. VI, No. 6 (June 1961); *California Medicine*, XCI (August 1959), 103; Herbert Malley, *The Social Role of the California Medical Association* (unpubl. thesis, Univ. of California at Berkeley, June 1949); "Twenty Years After," *California Medicine*, XC (March 1959), 236; "C.P.S. Medical Care Plan for 'Over 65,' " *ibid.*, XC (April 1959), 291.

15. "C.P.S.—Its Strengths and Weaknesses," *California Medicine*, XCV (August 1961), 132–5.

16. Interview with Norman Brown, executive secretary of the Sonoma Medical Society, San Francisco, April 17, 1962; "San Joaquin's Medical Foundation," *California GP* (March 1959), p. 11.

17. Somers and Somers, *Doctors, Patients . . . , op. cit.,* p. 239.

18. C. Edward Rutledge, "Dentistry's Greatest Challenge," *Journal of the CSDA,* XXIV (November–December, 1958), 457–60; Lyall O. Bishop, "An Inside Look into California Dental Association Service," *ibid.,* XXXVIII (April 1962), 103, 151, 170.

19. Somers and Somers, "Private Health Insurance," *op. cit.,* p. 376.

20. Reported in Oakland *Tribune,* January 6, 1963, p. 29.

21. Los Angeles Bar Association *Bulletin,* XXVI (December 1959), 121; "The Availability of Legal Services . . . ," *op. cit.*

22. Don Cook, "Socialized Medicine, Ten Years Old," *Harper's Magazine* (May 1959), pp. 32–7; "State Health Aid Hailed in Britain," *New York Times,* July 6, 1958, p. 9; "Government Health Insurance Losing Favor in England," *California Medicine,* XC (February 1959), 42; see also "Should We Have a National Health Plan?" reprinted from *The Dispatcher* of the International Longshoremen's and Warehousemen's Union in the *Journal of the CSDA,* XXXV (June 1959), 163–7; "This British GP Likes the National Health Service," *California GP* (February–March, 1961), p. 12.

23. "100 Largest Architectural Firms in the U.S.," *Architectural Forum* (April 1963), p. 110.

24. See Corinne Lathrop Gilb, *Conformity of State Personal Income Tax Laws to Federal Personal Income Tax Laws* (California: Legislature, Assembly Interim Committee on Revenue and Taxation, 1964), pp. 53–61.

25. Kornhauser, *op. cit.,* pp. 3–5, 10.

26. Charles W. Letourneau, *Hospital Trusteeship* (Chicago: Starling Publications, 1959), pp. 30–1.

27. Hyde and Wolff, *op. cit.;* Kornhauser, *op. cit.,* p. 4.

28. Letourneau, *op. cit.,* pp. 69–76.

29. W. G. Fordyce, "Teachers' Unions and Labor's Weapons," *American School Board Journal,* CXII (May 1946), 43–4; Arthur B. Wagner, "A Study of Recent Organized Attempts to Promote Professional Independence for Teachers" (unpubl. thesis, Stanford Univ., 1937). Interview with Don Henry, executive secretary of the California Federation of Teachers, Berkeley, California, 1957.

30. "NSPE Compiles Figures on Engineers in Unions," *American Engineer* (July 1958), pp. 22–5; Peter W. L. Buck, "The Unionization of Engineers" (unpubl. diss., Univ. of California at Berkeley, 1948); Paul Richard Dolan, "Industrial Personnel Practice and the Professional Employee" (unpubl. diss., Univ. of California at Berkeley, 1955); Kornhauser, *op. cit.;* New York Engineering Societies Library, *Bibliography on Unionization of Professional Engineers* (New York, 1954); Herbert R. Northrup, *Unionization of Professional Engineers and Chemists* (New York: Industrial Relations Counselors, 1946).

31. Leslie R. Burnett, "The Unionization of Professionals" (unpubl. diss., Univ. of California at Berkeley, 1948), pp. 125–33; *California*

Librarian, XIV (March 1953), 185; interview in Sacramento, California, September 19, 1962, with the business agent for Hospital and Institutional Workers Union, Local 250, of San Francisco.

32. Somers and Somers, *Doctors, Patients . . . , op. cit.*, p. 106.

33. *Ibid.*

CHAPTER 4. *Professional Associations as Governments*

1. For works on organizations and the history of organizational structure in the United States see Henri Pirenne, "Stages in the Social History of Capitalism," in Bendix and Lipset, eds., *Class, Status, and Power, op. cit.*, pp. 501–17; William R. Scott, *The Constitution and Finance of English, Scottish and Irish Joint-Stock Companies to 1720*, 3 vols. (Cambridge, Eng.: Cambridge U.P., 1910–12); Davis, *Essays in the Earlier History of American Corporations, op. cit.;* E. M. Dodd, *American Business Corporations Until 1860* (Cambridge, Mass.: Harvard U.P., 1954); D. Lloyd, *The Law of Unincorporated Associations* (London: Oxford U.P., 1938); Berle and Means, *op. cit.;* Edward S. Mason, ed., *The Corporation in Modern Society* (Cambridge, Mass.: Harvard U.P., 1959); A. W. Gouldner, *Patterns of Industrial Bureaucracy* (Glencoe: Free Press, 1954); A. W. Gouldner, *Studies in Leadership* (New York: Harper & Brothers, 1950); Robert A. Gordon, *Business Leadership in the Large Corporation* (Washington, D.C.: Brookings Institution, 1945); K. E. Boulding, *The Organizational Revolution* (New York: Harper & Brothers, 1953); Clarence E. Bonnett, "Evolution of Business Groupings," *Annals of the American Academy of Political and Social Science*, CLXXIX (May 1935), 1; John Hutchinson, "The Constitution and Government of the AFL–CIO," *California Law Review*, XLVI (December 1958); Will Herberg, "Bureaucracy and Democracy in Labor Unions," *Antioch Review*, III (fall, 1943), 405–24; Richard A. Lester, *As Unions Mature* (Princeton: Princeton U.P., 1958); S. M. Lipset, "The Political Process in Trade Unions: A Theoretical Statement," in Morroe Berger *et al., Freedom and Control in Modern Society* (New York: Van Nostrand, 1954), pp. 2–124; William M. Leiserson, *American Trade Union Democracy* (New York: Columbia U.P., 1959); S. M. Lipset *et al., Trade Union Democracy* (Glencoe: Free Press, 1956); Robert K. Merton *et al.*, eds., *Reader in Bureaucracy* (Glencoe: Free Press, 1952); Max Weber, *The Theory of Social and Economic Organization* (New York: Oxford U.P., 1947); H. H. Gerth and C. Wright Mills, eds., *From Max Weber* (New York: Oxford, U.P. Galaxy, 1958); Philip Selznick, *Administrative Leadership* (Evanston: Row, Peterson, 1957); James G. March and Herbert A. Simon, *Organizations* (New York: John Wiley, 1958); see extensive bibliography in Mason Haire, ed., *Modern Organization Theory* (New York: John Wiley, 1959); G. E. Milward, *Large Scale Organization* (London: Institute of Public Administration, 1950); Perry Miller, *The*

New England Mind: the Seventeenth Century (Cambridge, Mass.: Harvard U.P., 1954), chaps. 13–15, bibliography, Appendix B, "The Federal School of Theology"; H. Richard Niebuhr, *The Social Sources of Denominationalism* (New York: Henry Holt, 1929); Hubert P. Beck, *Men Who Control Our Universities* (New York: King's Crown Press, 1947); F. Steward Chapin and John E. Tseuderos, "Formalization Observed in Ten Voluntary Associations," *Social Forces,* XXXIII (May 1955), 306; Sherwood D. Fox, *op. cit.* (A complete bibliography on this subject would run to several volumes.)

2. Sources for this section are the general books on the national professional organizations cited for Chapter 2. Also John M. Hancock, "Report on the Organization of the American Chemical Society," *Chemical and Engineering News,* XXV (February 17, 1947), 442; American Library Association, *ALA Bulletin,* LV (December 1961); constitutions and by-laws of the AMA, ABA, AIA, ADA, NSPE, NASW, and ALA (the ALA constitution is in the above-cited bulletin, p. 989 *et seq.*). Also state and local constitutions and by-laws for teachers, accountants, physicians, dentists, chemists, engineers, social workers, librarians, nurses, and lawyers. The author has attended national conventions of the ABA, ACA, ALA, and the National Society of Professional Engineers (NSPE), as well as numerous academic associations, and state and local meetings in California of judges, lawyers, physicians, dentists, social workers, teachers, and nurses.

3. Garceau, *op. cit.,* pp. 16, 17.

4. Board members, other than those who are seated ex officio, are either selected by the policy-making assembly or elected by members of the association on a decentralized, geographic basis (by regions, states, or —in the case of the ABA—federal judicial circuits). National boards vary in size, the largest being approximately 75 (NEA board).

Garceau, *op. cit.,* pp. 15, 17; Hyde and Wolff, *op. cit.,* p. 943; NEA *Handbook, op. cit.,* pp. 33–5; Rutherford, *op. cit.,* pp. 1–18 (on the ABA). Up to 1936 the ABA was governed largely by executive committee. See Granrud, *op. cit.,* pp. 13–14, on methods of selecting the boards of state teacher associations.

5. The NEA in 1961 had a representative assembly of 6,000. The ABA's house consisted of 254 delegates in 1962. A very large association legislature functions more like a convention than a legislature. Even a much smaller body, such as that of the AMA (192 members in 1957), can be cumbersome. This is a problem for state as well as for national associations. As of 1926, the average size of the delegate assemblies of state teacher associations was over 300 delegates (Granrud, *op. cit.,* p. 12).

Sometimes growth in the size of houses has been a response to pressures for more democracy, but proponents of limitation claim that a large house is undemocratic, that decisions are more likely to be influenced by a few active members, and that the small body is more democratic and less rigid, whereas the larger group takes on a machinelike character.

6. The unitary association is the form of organization for architects, social workers, the NSPE, various academic disciplines, and often for the independent associations based on race, sex, specialized functions, as well as the form associations often take in their early stages of development. For unitary associations there may be regional subdivisions, but an intermediate state organization to coordinate local chapters may be nonexistent or weak. If there is an intermediate state council, individual professionals usually do not belong to the council as such but rather to the local chapters. Representatives of the local chapters meet at the state level to confer on matters of common interest. Normally decisions by the state council are referred back to the chapters for approval. Sometimes the state council, such as the council for social workers in California in the 1950's, may be designed to facilitate communication between chapters and may not be a formal part of the national structure at all.

7. For teachers', lawyers', librarians', and certified public accountants' organizations, the links between the national association and state associations are weak. The individual professional may belong to the state association but not to the national or vice versa. Sometimes, in addition, there are also virtually autonomous local chapters. State associations may be affiliates of the national association, and the policy-making body of the national organization will include delegates from state and possibly also local associations, as well as delegates at large, but the state association has its own constitution and operates in a highly independent fashion.

8. Hyde and Wolff, *op. cit.*, p. 938.

9. Normally the national association requires that affiliate and state and local associations have constitutions that do not conflict with its own, and state associations require the same of their local chapters. Some associations require that changes in chapter constitutions or by-laws be ratified at the national level, or that changes in the constitution or by-laws of intermediate state associations be ratified by the member chapters and possibly by the national association.

Rutherford, *op. cit.*, p. 20, describes the connection between the ABA and state associations as rather tenuous and on p. 22 says the delegates had no power to commit their associations. The ABA's Conference of Bar Delegates has been mainly a forum for individual expression.

10. Garceau, *op. cit.*, pp. 116–17.

11. American Bar Association House of Delegates, Midyear *Proceedings* (1961), p. 184.

National associations may claim to speak for numbers far beyond their immediate direct membership. For example, in 1960 the NEA claimed to speak for 1,317,696 professionals; in 1962 the ABA reported that combined bar associations in the United States represented more than 250,000 lawyers (press release, "Fact sheet," 1962). For ABA membership requirements, see *ABA Journal*, XLVIII (February 1962), 101.

State-association membership has been growing steadily and is becoming less exclusive. As of 1926, 8 out of 42 state education associations in the United States were open to anyone who wanted to join (Granrud, *op. cit.*, p. 11). Gillingham, *op. cit.*, p. 72, says that from 1911 to 1924, 60 percent of all those eligible to belong did belong to the CTA. After 1924 over 70 percent belonged. Membership declined during the Depression, but was 74.8 percent again by 1948. By 1962 the CTA estimated that 80 to 85 percent of all those eligible to belong did belong. By 1962 dentists' and CPA's associations in California claimed over 90 percent membership. The nurses in California were an exception to the general rule, for the percentage of their membership climbed steadily during the years of World War II to a high of 55 percent in 1955 and declined steadily thereafter. In 1950 and 1951 the percentage was approximately 42, and by 1955 it had fallen to 33⅓ (interview with Robert McKay, February 8, 1962, Burlingame, Calif.; "Facts about Medical Practice in California for 1962," CMA leaflet).

12. Sunderland, *op. cit.*, p. 96. See also Martin, *Building a Teaching Profession, op. cit.* Membership may still be denied in ABA on the basis of four negative votes on the board of governors (*ABA Journal*, XLVIII [February 1962], p. 101).

13. Garceau, *op. cit.*, p. 132.

14. Hyde and Wolff, *op. cit.*, p. 941; Garceau, *op. cit.*, p. 105; Fox, *op. cit.*, pp. 155–73. See AB 1475, introduced in the California legislature in 1953.

15. *The Washington Teamster* (October 24, 1941), p. 6, col. 5; Fox, *op. cit.*, p. 203.

16. Complete Service Bureau *v.* San Diego Medical Society, 272 P2d 497 (1954); Group Health Cooperative *v.* King County Medical Society, 237 P2d 737 (1951); AMA *v.* U.S., 317 U.S. 519 (1943); U.S. *v.* Oregon State Medical Society, 343 U.S. 326 (1952). However, see Medical Society of Mobile County *v.* Walker (Alabama, 1949) 16 S2d 321, 324. Of interest is Lane Lancaster, "The Legal Status of 'Private' Organizations Exercising Governmental Powers," *Southwestern Social Science Quarterly*, XV (1935), 325–36.

17. Sunderland, *op. cit.*, pp. 97–8.

18. See Wesley, *op. cit.*, p. 326, on the election of the NEA's first woman president. Bowman, *op. cit.*, p. 82; Gillingham thesis, *op. cit.*, pp. 82, 101, 238. In 1947, 67% of the CTA's State Council were administrators; 33% were teachers. In 1958 the CTA elected its first woman president, but her husband was a county superintendent (*CTA Journal*, LIV [May 1958], 7).

19. Wesley, *op. cit.*, Ch. 23; see also Roy W. Cloud, "The History of CTA," *Sierra Educational News*, XXIX (October 1943), 9.

20. The charge that the leaders are a self-perpetuating clique has been

made against the NEA leaders prior to 1916 (Wesley, *op. cit.*, p. 329) and perpetually against the leaders of the AMA. There is often a manifest lack of democracy in the nominating process. The AMA, for example, allows the officers in power to have a dominant influence in deciding who their successors will be. At the state level the president often appoints the committee that nominates national delegates. At the county level the president often appoints the nominating committee (Hyde and Wolff, *op. cit.*, p. 944). See Garceau, *op. cit.*, and Hyde and Wolff, *op. cit.*, for a detailed discussion of tenure and turnover in medical societies. Some affiliates send the same delegates, with expenses partly paid, to the NEA year after year (Wesley, *op. cit.*, p. 333).

There is no proof, of course, that either short or long tenure affects voting characteristics. Garceau found that the Massachusetts society, with its low turnover, was often restive over AMA policies. Also, as Garceau points out, from 1899 to 1923, turnover in Congress averaged only 25.4 percent, markedly below the AMA house and many state medical societies (pp. 43–4).

21. Wesley, *op. cit.*, p. 397.

22. Seidman *et al., The Worker Views His Union, op. cit.*, p. 209.

23. Wesley, *op. cit.*, pp. 324–7.

24. Hyde and Wolff, *op. cit.*, p. 945. See Garceau, *op. cit.*, p. 80, on solicitation of votes. On p. 82 he states that there are often four names for president, but other offices may go uncontested.

25. Hyde and Wolff, *op. cit.*, p. 946.

26. *Encyclopedia of Associations, op. cit.*, Vol. I.

27. *Ibid.*, p. 945; Truman, *op. cit.*, p. 208.

28. Committee on Physicians, Garceau, *op. cit.*, pp. 147–51. On going along with the AMA, see Hyde and Wolff, *op. cit.*, p. 947, and Garceau, *op. cit.*, pp. 133–7. See also Oliver Garceau, "Organized Medicine Enforces Its 'Party Line,'" *The Public Opinion Quarterly*, IV (September 1940), 408–28.

In the 1930's there were bitter contests for office on the California State Bar board of governors, but when the economic tension that underlay these differences died down, apathy set in so that it was sometimes difficult to find men to run from the less urban districts. Some association officials make a deliberate effort to represent all interests in making appointments.

29. Hyde and Wolff, *op. cit.*, p. 944. On attendance at conventions, see Rutherford, *op. cit.*, pp. 14, 16.

As of 1950, only about 3 percent of California lawyers were members of State Bar committees. Until the principle of rotation in office was introduced in the early 1950's, it was not unusual for committeemen to serve for many years. The chairman of the most powerful committee screening legislative proposals was in office for approximately twenty years. (In a letter to the author, dated July 28, 1954, he objected to the principle of turnover.)

One student of the California Teachers Association reported that fewer than 10 percent of all members of the CTA had ever held office in a section of the CTA, attended section or state council meetings, or visited section or state headquarters. He added that the CTA literature often went unread (Gillingham, *op. cit.,* p. 239).

30. *California State Nurses Association Bulletin* hereafter cited as *CSNA Bulletin,* LII (January 1956), 8. In 1956 the CSNA reported that 70 percent of its members seldom had voted in an annual election, despite elaborate procedures for nomination from the grass roots, the use of questionnaires to inform voters on candidates' views, and the mail ballot. Many organizations have provisions for initiative and referendum, but have seldom used them and have found them to be more a technique for demonstrating solidarity among those who vote than a symptom of membership activity. The referendum has been referred to as "window dressing," and sometimes is not even taken as binding (Garceau, *op. cit.,* p. 22).

31. Wayne T. Toivanen, "The Occupational Composition of the Officers of Teachers Organizations in the Inland-Empire-States Region" (unpubl. thesis, Stanford Univ., 1942), pp. 112, 113, 169, 181–5; John Mongan, "The Professional Composition of the Controlling Bodies of Teachers Organizations" (unpubl. thesis, Stanford Univ., 1941), pp. 10, 68, 86, 93–4. For the combined associations in the United States as a whole, Mongan found that membership consisted of 20.6 percent men and 79.4 percent women, but office holders consisted of 80.9 percent men and only 19.1 percent women, with men 292.7 above a ratio proportionate to their numbers and women 75.9 below. Among the officers, board of directors, board of trustees, and executive committee of the NEA, 32.6 percent of the posts were held by superintendents and by the executive secretaries of state educational associations.

32. Garceau, *op. cit.,* pp. 54–5.

33. Hyde and Wolff, *op. cit.,* p. 947.

34. Garceau, *op. cit.,* pp. 52, 56–7.

35. *Ibid.,* p. 86. However, the Institute of Architects reported in 1957 that the role of executive secretary varied enormously from chapter to chapter, and Wesley, *op. cit.,* p. 380, states that though the NEA staff is very influential, staff members "prudently refuse to become involved in making decisions that might affect their status."

By 1961 the NEA had a staff of approximately 850 people; the AMA, 700; the ADA, 189; the ABA, 120; the ANA, 111. They were operating within annual budgets ranging from $4 to $12 million. As staffs grew in size and permanency, they were given pensions and other benefits, which resulted in low turnover in the higher offices. If they moved, it was apt to be from the professional association in one state to the association in another state. Staff men might belong to the National Association of Association Executives. Association staff work was becoming more and more bureaucratized and professionalized.

36. Donald R. Matthews, *Social Background of Political Decision-Makers* (Garden City, N.Y.: Doubleday, 1954), p. 23, states that the fathers of all categories of American public officials have been primarily from professional and proprietary vocations, and that among the officials there has been a higher percentage of college graduates than there was among the population at large over age 25 for the year 1940 (p. 29). He found that the higher the office, the higher the status of the prior occupation and the higher the education.

37. Fenner, *op. cit.*, p. 112; see *CTA Journal*, LI (January 1955), 13.

38. *Western Journal of Education*, XIV (March 1905), 9.

39. Fenner, *op. cit.*, pp. 24, 48–9; Wesley, *op. cit.*, p. 336.

40. Hyde and Wolff, *op. cit.*, p. 962.

41. See Granrud, *op. cit.*, p. 40, on state education association journals generally. *CSNA Bulletin*, XL (January, 1944), 7; (February 1944), 38.

42. Fenner, *op. cit.*, pp. 46–7.

43. Galloway, *op. cit.*, p. 481; Kern County Medical Society *Bulletin*, IX (November 1962), pp. 418–19.

44. Martin, *op. cit.*, p. 98.

45. In 1929 Herring, in *Group Representation Before Congress, op. cit.*, described the AMA as relatively inactive.

46. Speech of member of AMPAC board to Political Education and Action Seminar in Chicago, June 1962; reprinted in Kern County Medical Society *Bulletin*. Leaflet on AMPAC.

47. *Journal of the NEA*, XLVI (December 1957), 564. The NEA sends letters of praise to legislators who have been helpful. See Hyde and Wolff, *op. cit.*, p. 957; Ben Read, "How Legislation Affects Dentistry," *Journal of the SDA*, LXVI (April 1960), 98; Belle Zeller, *Pressure Politics in New York* (New York: Prentice-Hall, 1937), 169.

48. NEA *Handbook*, 1960–61, *op. cit.*, p. 6; Fenner, *op. cit.*, p. 17.

49. Hyde and Wolff, *op. cit.*, pp. 954–6.

50. Louise Overacker, articles in *American Political Science Review*, XXVII (1933), 776; XXXI (1937), 485; XXV (1941), 723.

51. Garceau, *op. cit.*, p. 122.

52. Norbert C. Brockman, *op. cit.*, p. 277.

53. ABA House of Delegates Midyear *Proceedings* (1961), p. 402, conclusion result of a recent questionnaire.

54. AMA Committee to Study the Relationships of Medicine with Allied Health Professions and Services, *Proceedings* (mimeographed). See Hyde and Wolff, *op. cit.*, p. 969.

55. Martin, *op. cit.*, p. 99.

56. ABA House of Delegates Midyear *Proceedings* (1961), p. 173. Smaller associations have to rely more on exhortation.

57. For years the executive secretary of the California Teachers Association identified himself and was identified with his organization, and the association's influence on school legislation derived largely from his reputation among legislators. Gillingham, *op. cit.*, p. 161; Bowman, *op. cit.*, pp. 31, 394, 396; Hyde and Wolff, *op. cit.*, p. 957; Zeller, *op. cit.*, p. 248. In New York the state bar association's legislative work was done by a committee until 1936, when a legislative reporter was hired to inform the association about legislation, but not to speak for the association unless expressly authorized to do so (Zeller, *op. cit.*, p. 193).

58. The national associations' legislative committees perform a mixture of tasks: policy-making, liaison, and direct lobbying. They are gradually assuming more importance. For many years the real work in all three areas was done by staff persons in central headquarters (Zeller, *op. cit.*, pp. 169, 175, 179, 183, 184, 249; Gillingham thesis, *op. cit.*, pp. 152–3).

The CTA's weekly newsletter goes to each school building, to presidents of all local CTA-affiliated associations, and to members of the state council. On CTA lobbying, see CTA *Journal*, LI (September 1955), 5.

59. See Zeller, *op. cit.*, p. 240.

60. Public Administration Service, "A Report on an Administrative Survey of the U.S. Office of Education of the Federal Security Agency" (Chicago: U.S. Office of Ed., 1960), pp. 4–5.

61. Hyde and Wolff, *op. cit.*, p. 960. Numerous other examples of complementary or collaborative activity could be given. Medical representatives have repeatedly asked the California legislature not to take a certain action (*e.g.*, not to make tissue reports subject to subpoena) on the grounds that the professions could police themselves and that state policing was unnecessary.

62. There were approximately 1,100 active disciplinary committees in county medical societies in the U.S. in the 1950's. California's State Bar conducted nearly 2,000 formal disciplinary proceedings in the first 20 years of its existence. On the other hand, in 1955–6, in the California Society of CPA's, the Los Angeles chapter reported only 14 complaints and 2 hearings, and the San Francisco chapter reported 5 complaints and 9 formal inquiries.

See Philip Taft, "Judicial Procedure in Labor Unions," *Quarterly Journal of Economics*, LIX (May 1945), pp. 370–85; ———, "Equitable Jurisdiction to Protect Membership in a Voluntary Association," *Yale Law Journal*, LVIII (May 1949), pp. 999–1006; Bernstein v. Alameda etc. Med. Assn. (1956), 139 Cal. App. 2d 241, 253: court held society could not impose its discipilne on this member because it had not arrived at its decision in accordance with the procedure prescribed by its own rules. On the responsibility of trade unions to follow due process in imposing discipline, see Matthew O. Tobriner, "Labor Under Attack," *Frontier* (Los Angeles, August 1958), pp. 17–18, 26. Also of interest is the description of the medieval jury system in Barnaby C. Kenny, *Judgment by Peers* (Cambridge, Mass.: Harvard U.P., 1949).

CHAPTER 5. *Differentiating and Reintegrating Special Interests*

1. Harvey Walker, *The Legislative Process* (New York: Ronald Press, 1948), p. 13, says Greek law in the Heroic Age was exclusively customary. The transition to statutory law was the result of political struggles of oppressed classes against the ruling classes, who controlled the courts. The statutes were supposed to be of divine origin; the law giver was considered to be inspired by the gods.

2. Browne and Weeks, *op. cit.,* for chemists. As early as 1888, the AMA began to worry about the divisive effects of specialist societies (Fishbein, *op. cit.,* p. 136). In 1960 the ADA approved revision of the section of its code of ethics on specialization and limitation of practice to make it more restrictive and to put specialization more rigorously under its control (California State Dental Association *Newsletter,* Vol. I, No. 3 [May 1961]. This was an attempt to prevent splintering of the profession. ABA Press Releases, July 19 and 31, 1962, indicated that changes were being considered in the ABA toward more formal recognition of specialization.

3. See Sister Mary Victor Lewis, *op. cit.,* pp. xi, 2, 34.

4. See *Journal of the American Association of University Professors* hereafter cited as *Journal of the AAUP,* XLI (summer 1955), 211.

5. See NEA, Department of Classroom Teachers, "The Organization and Programs of the State Departments of Classroom Teachers," November 1958. By 1958 there were 55 classroom-teacher departments in 44 states; Washington, D.C.; and Hawaii. However, the NEA department serves primarily to provide a channel for some teachers to be leaders. See Fenner, *op. cit.,* p. 35; see also Sarah Carter, "Who Runs the CTA?" *CTA Journal,* LVIII (February 1962), 2.

Work organizations have their own associations: the American Hospital Association (1898), the Catholic Hospital Association (1915), the American Protestant Hospital Association (1921), and the associations of colleges and universities. Administrators in work organizations have formed their own associations.

6. Kenneth D. Benne and Warren Bennis, "Role Confusion and Conflict in Nursing," *American Journal of Nursing* (March 1959), p. 381.

7. See "Those Worrisome Package Builders," *Architectural Forum,* CVIII (April 1958), 121. At the national level the AMA has played an increasingly active role as mediator in jurisdictional disputes affecting its members.

AMA Committee to Study the Relationships of Medicine with Allied Health Professions and Services, *Proceedings,* 1960 (mimeographed); "Interprofessional Principles of Practice for Architects and Engineers,"

American Engineer, XXVIII (May 1958), 23; for an account of bar treaties in California, see Gilb, *Self-Governing Professions . . . , op. cit.,* Ch. 6, and the bibliography on lay competition with lawyers. See also *Unauthorized Practice News; CTA Journal,* LIII (September 1957), 43.

As in the case of enforcement of professional ethics, usually both private and public government are involved. In the twilight zones where different professions and vocational groups function at the same time, where the statutory guidelines for jurisdiction may not be clear, the public licensing boards generally do not presume to tread or at the most tread gingerly. However, the public courts have played a more active role in defining jurisdictional boundaries. (See Council of State Governments, *Occupational Licensing . . . , op. cit.,* p. 6.)

8. General practitioners in medicine have used their association to try to protect or restore their privileges of practice within hospitals and of participation in hospital government.

9. See Edward H. L. Corwin, *The American Hospital* (New York: Commonwealth Club, 1946); Letourneau, *op. cit.;* Kornhauser, *op. cit.;* Emanuel Hayt, Lillian R. Hayt, August H. Groeschel, *Law of Hospital, Physician, and Patient,* 2nd ed. (New York: Hospital Textbook Co., 1952), p. 130.

10. Fenner, *op. cit.,* Ch. 7; Wesley, *op. cit.,* pp. 334–7.

11. For example, the Santa Clara County Hospital (California) incident reported in the Oakland *Tribune,* October 20, 23, 24, 27, 1961, and November 1, 4, 10 1961.

12. *CSNA Bulletin* LIV (June 1958), 141, on the budget. The story of the California association's economic security program can be found in numerous issues of its bulletin, from 1950 to date. The author interviewed the organization's bargaining representative and also a representative of a trade union that included nurses, in Sacramento, Calif., November 1962. See also the typewritten and edited transcript of a tape-recorded interview by Corinne L. Gilb with J. Paul St. Sure, "Some Comments on Employer Organizations and Collective Bargaining in Northern California Since 1934," conducted in San Francisco, March–June 1957, on file in the libraries of the Univ. of California at Berkeley and Los Angeles. Mr. St. Sure was at one time counsel for the nurses. On the ANA conference, see *CSNA Bulletin,* XLVII (July 1951), 281–2. The New York association's objections are stated in the *CSNA Bulletin,* XLVIII (November 1952), 319. ANA statements are reprinted in "Collective Bargaining," *CSNA Bulletin,* LVII (October 1951), 387.

13. Pauline Coleman, "Why Not a Salary Representative for CLA?", *California Librarian,* XIV (December 1953), 131.

14. Ben Rust speech at Univ. of California workshop, August 7, 1958; accounts in the CTA *Journal,* LVIII (January 1962), 2, and *California Teacher* (for the unions), XIII (November–December 1960), 1. Com-

mission on Education Reconstruction of the American Federation of Teachers, *Organizing the Teaching Profession* (Glencoe: Free Press, 1955), p. 99.

15. The attitudes of engineer societies toward management problems are obviously affected by the fact that high percentages of the members are administrators. The Engineers' Joint Council Survey in 1947 noted that 34 percent of those questioned (38,000 members of 6 major national engineering societies) were doing primarily administrative work. The National Society of Professional Engineers' Income and Salary Survey (Washington, 1952–3), p. 8, found that over one-third of the respondents held executive-administrative posts. (Buck, *Unionization of Engineers, op. cit.*, p. 2). See Kornhauser, *op. cit.*, pp. 52, 88.

16. The author attended the national convention of the National Society for Professional Engineers in October 1958. See the NSPE's "Statement of Principles, Collective Bargaining by Professional Employees." See also *American Engineer* (July 1958), pp. 22–5.

17. The ABA has difficulty coordinating even the lobbying of its own sections, which proceed independently, often without clearing or working through the ABA's Washington office. (See ABA House of Delegates Midyear *Proceedings,* 1961, p. 173.) However, that office reported to the author in an interview in December 1963 that coordination had become much more effective in recent years.

18. See William F. Ryan, "Professional Organization of Engineers," *American Engineer* (April 1946).

19. CMA *Newsletter,* Vol. VII, No. 3 (March 1963).

20. Bowman, *op. cit.,* p. 76.

21. Gillingham thesis; Bowman; other California sources previously cited. Interview with George E. Hogan, California State Department of Education, April 5, 1962, Sacramento. In 1962 the American Institute of Architects was debating the possibility of admitting members of certain related professions and vocations to affiliate membership in the AIA.

22. Zeller, *op. cit.,* p. 192.

23. Interview with staff members of California Council of the AIA, San Francisco, July 14, 1958.

24. Ben Read, *op. cit.*

25. The Buchanan congressional committee investigation showed an emerging pattern of group alliances, mutual financial support, sale or exchange of publications, and interlocking directorates among all kinds of organizations that lobby Congress (Galloway, *op. cit.,* p. 482).

CHAPTER 6. *Group-State Relations and the Public Sector*

1. Interview with George E. Hogan, California State Department of Education, April 5, 1962, Sacramento.

2. The journals of state associations are replete with accounts of cooperation and collaboration between the associations and government agencies.

Fenner, *op. cit.*, pp. 63, 94, 122, 131, states that the NEA is in constant contact with federal agencies, though Public Administration Service, *A Report on an Administrative Survey of the U.S. Office of Education of the Federal Security Agency* (Chicago, 1960), p. 27, says the office is not always effective in its relations with Congress. Zeller, *op. cit.*, p. 240, describes the frequent contact between New York associations and state administrative agencies.

The 1962 ABA convention was attended by justices of the U.S. Supreme Court, the U.S. Attorney General, members of the Federal Trade Commission and the Interstate Commerce Commission, the chairman of the National Labor Relations Board, the Postmaster General, the former director of the Central Intelligence Agency, governors, mayors, senators, the former supreme allied commander in Europe, the president of the Canadian Bar Association, and the Lord Chief Justice of England (to name only a few). U.S. Commissioners of Education speak at NEA conventions. Superintendents of education have often been officers of state education associations, either ex officio or elected.

3. *The Governmental Process, op. cit.*, pp. 332, 437–8, 441, 449.

4. U.S. Department of Health, Education and Welfare, *Education in the United States of America* (Washington, D.C.: U.S. Govt. Ptg. Off., 1960), p. 7; Hollis P. Allen, *The Federal Government and Education* (New York: McGraw-Hill, 1950), pp. 5, 210; A. Hunter Dupree, *Science in the Federal Government* (Cambridge, Mass.: Belknap Press, 1957); CMA *Newsletter*, Vol, No. 3 (March 1961); David Truman, *Administrative Decentralization* (Chicago: Univ. of Chicago Press, 1940).

5. See Clyde F. Snider, *American State and Local Government* (New York: Appleton-Century-Crofts, 1950), p. 438, on public-health administration. See also Frederic N. Cleaveland, *Science and State Government* (Chapel Hill: Univ. of North Carolina Press, 1959).

6. Fenner, *op. cit.*, pp. 128–30.

7. Dupree, *op. cit.*, pp. 215–30, 258–9, 260, 269–70.

8. Milton F. Lunch (NSPE legislative counsel), "Engineering and Science Involved in Defense Reorganization Controversy," *American Engineer* (May 1958), pp. 21–2. Dupree, *op. cit.*, pp. 35, 216, 258–60, 269–70, 365, 370; Wesley, *op. cit.*, pp. 243–4; Allen, *op. cit.*, pp. 305–8.

9. *California Medicine*, XCV (July 1961).

10. Public Administration Service Report, *op. cit.*, pp. 5, 17, 32. U.S. Department of Health, Education and Welfare, "A Federal Agency for the Future" (April 1961), pp. 6, 35–7, criticizes the Office of Education as being too oriented to the profession, which results in fragmenting policy and inflexibility. See also Walter Gellhorn, *Federal Administrative Proceedings* (Baltimore: Johns Hopkins Press, 1941).

11. Council of State Governments, *Occupational Licensing . . . , op. cit.,* pp. 21, 29.

12. James W. Fesler, "Independence of State Regulatory Agencies," *The American Political Science Review,* XL (1940), p. 943; ———, *The Independence of State Regulatory Agencies* (Chicago: Public Administration Service, 1942), pp. 60–1.

After boards are appointed their ties with the professional association are cemented by constant formal and informal communication. Many boards appoint advisory councils, often consisting of representatives of the various associations representing or affecting the profession the board regulates. One dentist (program director of the Illinois State Dental Society) wrote glowingly in a professional journal: "Our Board of Examiners in Illinois is tops! . . . We discuss mutual problems and cooperate on almost a daily basis" (Edgar T. Stephens, "Law Enforcement Is Dentistry's Responsibility," *News and Views of the Dental Laboratory Craft,* Vol. III, No. 2, pp. 3–4). See also Note, "Delegation of Governmental Power to Private Groups," *Columbia Law Review,* XXXII (1932), p. 80.

13. Interviews in Sacramento with staff and/or board members of California boards for veterinary medicine, medicine, nursing, social work, accounting, vocational nursing, landscape architecture, engineering, 1962–3. Interviews with professional-association representatives in Chicago Philadelphia, and New York, 1963–4.

14. The author attended the hearings of the California Senate Interim Committee on Business and Professions, November 13 and 14, 1958, relevant to building designers. See Report of California Assembly Interim Committee on Governmental Efficiency and Economy, 1955–7; CCIA *Counciletter,* Vol. IX, Nos. 1 (January 1959) and 9 (September 1959); Vol. XII, No. 5 (May 1962).

15. "We do not reply in kind," said the CTA's executive secretary about teacher union charges and statements. (Quoted in William M. Harriman, unpubl. paper, "A Case Study in Associational Law-Making," May 1963, Univ. of California at Berkeley, Law School, p. 10.)

16. Council of State Governments, *Occupational Licensing . . . , op. cit.,* p. 16; Fesler, *op. cit.,* pp. 55, 63.

17. See Frank Hanft and J. N. Hamrick, "Haphazard Regimentation Under Licensing Statutes," *North Carolina Law Review,* XVII (December 1938). An interesting account of an attempt by a governor and state board of control to exercise budgetary control over the state board of accountancy is in William Dolge, "Highlight of State Board History," *The California Certified Public Accountant,* XX (May 1953), 25. See Fesler, *op. cit.,* pp. 55, 63.

State professional journals are replete with accounts of resistance to efforts to alter the composition of boards. For California, in addition to the interviews previously cited, the author interviewed John G. Clarkson, chief of the Division of Administrative Procedure, Department of Professional and Vocational Standards, fall 1962. See "Tentative Proposal for Reorganization of California State Government" (Sacramento, September 10, 1959); "Report to the Governor on Reorganization of State Government by the Task Forces" (November 1959); "The Agency Plan for California" (December 1959); statement to the legislature by Governor Edmund G. Brown, "Reorganization of State Government" (February 13, 1961).

18. Snider, *op. cit.*, p. 468. See CTA *Legislative Letter*, Vol. XI, No. 8 (March 31, 1958).

19. Council of State Governments, *Occupational Licensing . . . , op. cit.;* on the ABA's role in the selection of judges, see Joel B. Grossman, *Lawyers and Judges* (New York: John Wiley, 1965).

20. Interviews with board staff and members in Sacramento, 1962–3; interview with May Bonnell, governor's office, Sacramento, March 27, 1962.

21. Gross, *op. cit.*, pp. 267–8.

Interviews with staff of House and Senate judiciary committees, House Interstate Commerce Committee, House Education and Labor Committee, Senate Labor and Welfare Committee, and House and Senate space and aeronautics committees, September 12 and 13, 1963, in Washington, D.C. George Goodwin, Jr., "The Seniority System in Congress," *The American Political Science Review*, LIII (June 1959), 412–33; ————, "Subcommittees: The Miniature Legislatures of Congress," *The American Political Science Review*, LVI (September 1962), 596–600.

22. There is more than usual turnover in the House Committee on Education and Labor, and members are generally appointed to this committee on the basis of strong ideological and partisan commitments that intensify divisions within the committee. Richard F. Fenno, Jr., "The House of Representatives and Federal Aid to Education," in Robert L. Peabody and Nelson W. Polsby, eds., *New Perspectives on the House of Representatives* (Chicago: Rand McNally, 1963), pp. 195–235. Floyd M. Reddick, *The United States Congress Organization and Procedure* (Manassas, Va.: National Capital Publishers, 1949), p. 159.

23. The author has attended and observed numerous committee hearings from 1957 to 1963 in California.

24. Abbot Low Moffat, "The Legislative Process," *Cornell Law Quarterly*, XXIV (1939), 223.

25. See Gross, *op. cit.*, p. 186.

26. Galloway, *op. cit.*, p. 38.

27. Harvey Walker, "Where Does Legislation Originate?" *National Municipal Review*, XVIII (September 1929), 565–7; ————, "Who Writes Our Laws?" *State Government*, XII (1939), 199–200.

28. G. M. Trevelyan, *History of England* (London: Longmans, Green, 1937).

29. See Louis Hartz, "American Political Thought and the American Revolution," *The American Political Science Review*, XLVI (June 1952), 321.

30. Walker, *The Legislative Process, op. cit.*, p. 156.

31. Belle Zeller, *American State Legislatures* (New York: Thomas Y. Crowell, 1954), p. 156. About one-fourth provided special assistance during the session. On legislative councils, see Harold W. Davey, "The Legislative Council Movement in the United States, 1933–53," *The American Political Science Review*, XLVII (September 1953), 786.

32. Gross, *op. cit.*, p. 186.

33. Zeller, *American State Legislatures, op. cit.*, p. 69.

34. *Ibid.*, p. 78.

35. Walker, *The Legislative Process, op. cit.*, p. 156.

36. Zeller, *American State Legislatures, op. cit.*, p. 67.

37. See John C. Wahlke *et al., The Legislative System* (New York: John Wiley, 1962), p. 134.

38. Zeller, *American State Legislatures, op. cit.*, p. 70. See also Charles S. Hyneman, "Tenure and Turnover of Legislative Personnel," *The Annals of the American Academy of Political and Social Science*, CXCV (January 1938), 21–31.

39. See Galloway, *op. cit.*, p. 367, for comments on turnover in the House of Representatives. He states that turnover is highest for senators from the border states (p. 366).

The number of committee assignments per person in American state legislatures has ranged from an average of one in Maine and New Hampshire to an average of twelve in North Carolina. The national mean of averages has been 4.37 in the houses and 6.09 in the senates (Zeller, *American State Legislatures, op. cit.*, p. 101). C. I. Winslow found that the average number of committee assignments per member was 7.6 in the senates and 4.46 in the houses (*State Legislative Committees* [Baltimore: Johns Hopkins Press, 1931], p. 45). See Jay Doubleday, *Standing and Interim Committees of the California Legislature* (Univ. of California, Bureau of Public Administration, May 1959); Dean Mann, "The Legislative Committee System in Arizona," *Western Political Quarterly*, XIV (December 1961), 925.

40. Floyd M. Reddick, "The Eighty-sixth Congress' First Session," *Western Political Quarterly*, XIII (March 1960), table, p. 116; ————, "Eighty-seventh Congress: Second Session," *Western Political Quarterly*, XVI (March 1963), 135.

41. Zeller, *American State Legislatures, op. cit.*, pp. 70–1. See Walker, *The Legislative Process, op. cit.*, p. 148.

W. Brooke Graves, ed., *Our State Legislators*: Wm. T. R. Fox, "Legislative Personnel in Pennsylvania," pp. 32–9; Howard B. Lang, Jr., "They Legislate for Missouri," pp. 40–4; Dean E. McHenry, "Legislative Personnel in California," pp. 45–52. M. Louise Rutherford, "Lawyers as

Legislators," pp. 53–61, in *Annals of the American Academy of Political and Social Science,* CXCV (Philadelphia, January 1938). Waldo Schumacher, "Oregon's Legislators," *Commonwealth Review,* XX (January 1939), 675–82; P. Beckett and C. Sunderland, "Washington State's Lawmakers, Some Personnel Factors in the Washington Legislature," *Western Political Quarterly,* X (March 1957), 198; C. W. Hyneman, "Who Makes Our Laws?" *Political Science Quarterly,* LV (1940), 556. W. Brooke Graves, *American State Government* (Boston: D. C. Heath, 1936), pp. 178–82, found lawyers in legislatures of industrial states at 25 percent; in agricultural states, farmers 25 percent.

42. John Mason Brown, "The Trend: Lawyers in the 71st to 75th Congress," *Rocky Mountain Law Review,* X (1937), 43–52. See M. Louise Rutherford, "Lawyers as Legislators," *op. cit.,* pp. 53, 55.

43. Galloway, *op. cit.,* p. 373; see table, p. 374.

44. See Donald R. Matthews, *op. cit.* See also H. D. Anderson, "Educational and Occupational Attainments of Our National Rulers," *Scientific Monthly,* XL (1935), 516; D. R. Matthews, *United States Senators: A Study of the Recruitment of Political Leaders* (unpubl. diss., Princeton, 1953); ———, *U.S. Senators and Their World* (Chapel Hill: Univ. of North Carolina Press, 1960); Madge M. McKinney, "The Personnel of the 77th Congress," *The American Political Science Review,* XXXVI (1942), 74; G. Haynes, *The Senate of the United States* (Boston: Houghton Mifflin, 1938).

45. Galloway, *op. cit.,* p. 373, says that the typical congressman is from a town of under 50,000 population, is a lawyer who was district attorney, mayor, or a member of the state legislature. A study in 1931, by Dayton E. Heckman, of 278 congressmen from Ohio from 1868 to 1930 found that the average was probably a lawyer who had been a county prosecutor or a member of the lower house and was from a small town (cited by Walker, *The Legislative Process, op. cit.,* p. 148).

46. In 20 of the 25 chambers Hyneman studied, lawyers held more chairmanships than any other group. In Ohio and Tennessee in 1957, the proportion of lawyers in high posts in the legislature was greater than their proportion in the legislature. In his study of the Illinois and Missouri assemblies for 1957, Derge found lawyers as speakers, presidents pro tem, and in high proportions on rules committees (David R. Derge, "The Lawyer as Decision-Maker in the American State Legislature," *The Journal of Politics,* XXI [1959], pp. 408–33). See also Joseph A. Schlesinger, "Lawyers and American Politics: A Clarified View," *Midwest Journal of Political Science,* II (1957), p. 27; R. E. Agger, "The Lawyer in Politics," *Temple Law Quarterly,* XXIV (summer 1956), 434; Peyton Ford, "The Government Lawyer," pamphlet (New York, 1952); William Miller, "American Lawyer in Business and Politics," *Yale Law Review,* LX (1951), pp. 66–76; David Gold, "Lawyers in Politics," *The Pacific Sociological Review,* IV (fall 1961), 84; David R. Derge, "The Lawyer in

the Indiana General Assembly," *Midwest Journal of Political Science,*
VI (February 1962), 21; Walter I. Wardwell and Arthur L. Woods, "The
Extra-Professional Role of the Lawyer," *Americal Journal of Sociology,*
LXI (January 1956), 304; Lester Mulbrath "Lobbyists and Campaign
Politics," paper at APSA meeting, New York City, 1957, p. 19, found
that three-fourths of a sample of 100 lobbyists interviewed had been trained
in the law.

47. As quoted by the Oakland *Tribune.* The author made extensive
preliminary studies of, and interviewed, all the lawyers in the California
legislature in 1961. Most of them said they were better legislators because
they were lawyers. See Heinz Eulau and John D. Sprague, *Lawyers and
Politics* (Indianapolis: Bobbs-Merrill, 1964).

48. This section is based on the examination of numerous journals,
newspaper accounts, dissertations; numerous interviews; personal observation of the California legislature from 1959 to 1963, with attendance
three days a week during the 1961 session; Gilbert Y. Steiner and Samuel
K. Gove, *Legislative Politics in Illinois* (Urbana: Univ. of Illinois Press,
1960); Zeller, *Pressure Politics in New York, op. cit.;* Council of State
Governments, *American State Legislatures in Mid-Twentieth Century*
(April 1961); Hallie Farmer, *The Legislative Process in Alabama* (Bureau
of Public Administration, Alabama University, 1949); Frank E. Horack,
Statute Law-Making in Iowa (Iowa City: Scribner's, 1916); A. C. Han-
ford, "Our Legislative Mills: Massachusetts Different from the Others,"
National Municipal Review, XII (January, 1923), 42–3; Walter Thomp-
son, "Our Legislative Mills: Wisconsin," *National Municipal Review,*
XII (October, 1923), 602–3; Ralph S. Boots, "Our Legislative Mills:
Nebraska," *National Municipal Review,* XIII (February 1924), 113–14.
See Winslow bibliography for other references. Ernest S. Griffith, *Con-
gress, Its Contemporary Role* (New York: New York U.P., 1956);
Lawrence H. Chamberlain, *The President, Congress and Legislation*
(New York: Columbia U.P., 1946); P. S. Reinsch, *American Legisla-
tures and Legislative Methods* (New York: Century, 1907); J. Leiper
Freeman, *The Political Process: Executive Bureau-Legislative Committee
Relations* (Garden City: Doubleday, 1955); George E. Male, *The
Michigan Education Association as an Interest Group, 1852–1950* (unpubl. diss., Univ. of Michigan Press, 1951); Louis Jaffe, "Law Making
by Private Groups," *Harvard Law Review,* LI (December 1937), 201;
Frederick K. Beutel, "The Pressure of Organized Interests as a Factor
in Shaping Legislation," *Southern California Law Review,* III (1929),
10. Other books and articles on Congress previously and hereafter cited.
Report of ABA House of Delegates Midyear *Proceedings,* 1961. Various
articles and books on the professional associations. Interviews with staff
of seven congressional committees closest to the professions. Interviews,
Washington, D.C., December 1963, with staff of Washington offices of
ABA and NASW. Interview, Philadelphia, December 1963, with executive

secretary of the County Dental Society. Attendance at conventions and meetings of national, state, and local professional associations. AFT *Legislative Handbook,* 1959. Seventh Biennial Report, Board of Social Work Examiners, California, July 1, 1959. Other legislative committee and administrative board reports for 1950's and early 1960's.

49. McKean, *op. cit.,* p. 71.

50. "Politics as a Vocation," in *Essays in Sociology,* H. H. Gerth and C. Wright Mills, eds. (New York: Oxford U.P., 1946). See William A. Glaser, "Doctors and Politics," *The American Journal of Sociology,* LXVI (November 1960), 230–45.

51. *Journal of the American Judicature Society,* XIV (February 1931), 141.

52. Mann, on Arizona, *op. cit.,* p. 928.

53. Gove and Steiner, *op. cit.,* pp. 59–60.

54. *Ibid.,* p. 65.

55. William Buchanan, *Legislative Partisanship* (Berkeley: Univ. of California Press, 1963), p. 104. Gove and Steiner, *op. cit.,* pp. 62–3. The power of committees in other states varies between these extremes.

56. *Ibid.,* pp. 74, 76.

57. See Report of Assembly Interim Committee on Public Health, 1962, Vol. IX, No. 25, of Reports for 1961–63, pp. 11, 15. News accounts of one controversial incident appeared in the Berkeley Daily *Gazette,* January 18, 1961; Oakland *Tribune,* February 27, 1961 and March 6, 1961; Los Angeles *Examiner,* March 27, 1961; San Francisco *Examiner,* April 30, 1961. See also CMA *Newsletter,* Vol. V, No. 9 (September 1960).

58. Gove and Steiner, *op. cit., passim,* and pp. 72, 77, 82.

59. Interviews, Washington, D.C., September 1963; Sunderland, *op. cit., passim;* Wesley, *op. cit.*

The ABA has not always been successful in influencing the choice of judges. See U.S., Congress, Senate, Committee on Judiciary, *Nomination of Louis D. Brandeis* (whom the ABA strongly opposed), Sixty-fourth Congress, first session, 1916, I, p. 1226; and Walter Lippmann, *The New Republic,* VI (1916), 165.

60. Sunderland, *op. cit.,* p. 119.

61. Fenner, *op. cit.;* Wesley, *op. cit.*

62. Biographies (printed leaflets, mimeographed statements, typed statements) from the offices of professionals in the California legislature in 1961.

63. Interviews with staff of seven congressional committees, Washington, D.C., September 1963.

64. See Derge, *op. cit.*

65. Gove and Steiner, *op. cit.,* p. 3.

66. See Walker, *The Legislative Process, op. cit.,* p. 148, on ages of state legislators and Galloway, *op. cit.,* p. 370, on ages of congressmen.

In 1927 the median age for all California senators was 47; in 1937 it was 54 (a change had been made in the basis of apportionment, giving more representation to rural areas), with the median at 45. See John Mason Brown, "A Study of the Legal Education and Training of the Lawyers in the Seventy-third Congress," *The Bar Examiner* (September 1934), pp. 254–9; ———, "Lawyers in the 74th Congress: Their Legal Education and Experience," *The Bar Examiner* (January 1936), pp. 42–8.

67. Sacramento *Bee,* April 21, 1937, p. 5, col. 1; March 18, 1937, p. 22, col. 7.

68. See Brockman bibliography, cited in Note 1 for Chapter 1.

69. Wahlke *et al., op. cit.,* p. 160.

70. See Sunderland, *op. cit.,* pp. 165–6.

Sunderland's account of the ABA's legislative activities mentions two bills on admiralty courts proposed in 1909 but not passed until 1920, a procedural bill proposed in 1909 and passed in 1919, a bill to create a federal court of patent appeals introduced in vain in Congress for fourteen years, and efforts to pass a bill on government liens from 1916 to 1926, which did not pass until 1929 and then was pocket vetoed (pp. 104–5, 131, 152, 161).

CHAPTER 7. *The Status Society*

1. Carl Stephenson, *Borough and Town, a Study of Urban Origins in England* (Cambridge, Mass.: Medieval Academy of America, 1933).

2. See article by Austin C. Wehrwein, *New York Times,* May 10, 1959, on the professional farm managers. See also *Annals of the American Academy of Political and Social Science:* Howard R. Bowen, "How Public Spirited Is American Business?" CCLXXX (Philadelphia, 1952), and "Business Management: A Profession?", CCXCVII (1955). See Thomas P. Imse, *The Professionalization of Business Management* (New York: Vantage Press, 1962); George H. Hildebrand, "American Unionism, Social Stratification, and Power," *The American Journal of Sociology,* LVIII (January 1953), 381–390; Fox, *op. cit.*

3. See Seymour E. Harris, ed., *American Economic History* (New York: McGraw-Hill, 1961).

4. Cochran, *The American Business System,* p. 169. Martin L. Lindahl and William A. Carter, *Corporate Concentration and Public Policy,* 3rd ed. (Englewood Cliffs: Prentice-Hall, 1959), pp. 404–8.

5. Howard M. Vollmer, *Employee Rights and the Employment Relationship* (Berkeley: Univ. of California Press, 1960). There is no evidence that vocational status is as markedly linked to kinship as it was in medieval times. Americans have more social mobility. Nor do vocational status and social status necessarily exactly correspond.

6. Alzada Comstock, *Taxation in the Modern State* (New York: Longmans, Green, 1929); Harvey C. Mansfield *et al., A Short History*

of the OPA (Washington, D.C.: U.S. Office of Price Administration, 1948); Herbert Stein, *Government Price Policy in the United States During the World War* (Williamstown, Mass.: Williams College, 1939); O. W. Phelps, *Legislative Background of Fair Labor Standards Act* (Chicago: Univ. of Chicago Press, 1939).

7. See Kornhauser, *op. cit.*, and D. G. Moore and R. Renck, "The Professional Employee in Industry," *Journal of Business*, XXVII (1955), 58-66.

8. Robin M. Williams, Jr., *American Society* (New York: Knopf, 1960), p. 94, says that a large number of studies have demonstrated a correlation between economic and occupation levels and participation in formally organized associations. Mirra Komarovsky, "The Voluntary Associations of Urban Dwellers," *American Sociological Review*, XI (December 1946), 686-98, reported that in New York City well over 80 percent of professional people belonged to voluntary associations, as compared with 32 percent of the men and 9 percent of the women in the unskilled labor group.

CHAPTER 8. *Democracy and Dynamism*

1. See for examples the pronouncements of the Ecumenical Council as reported in the *New York Times* during the last quarter of 1963. See also Robert A. Nisbet, *The Quest for Community* (New York: Oxford U.P., 1953).

2. Adolph A. Berle, Jr., and Gardiner C. Means, *The Modern Corporation and Private Property* (New York: Macmillan, 1932).

3. O. Kahn-Freund, Introduction, Karl Renner, *The Institutions of Private Law and Their Social Functions* (London: Routledge & Kegan Paul, 1949), p. 20.

4. William L. Prosser, *Handbook of the Law of Torts* (St. Paul: West Publishing, 1941), pp. 20-1; ———, "The Assault upon the Citadel (Strict Liability to the Consumer)," *Yale Law Journal*, LXIX (1960), 1099. Roscoe Pound's ideas on this are summarized in M. P. Follett, *The New State*, Ch. 15, "From Contract to Community" (New York: Longmans, Green, 1923). Justice Mathew Tobriner of the California Supreme Court has written a variety of articles and opinions on phases of the new trend.

5. Clark Kerr, "The Prospect for Wages and Hours in 1975," Berkeley, Institute of Industrial Relations, Reprint No. 122 (1959). In January 1960 *Nation's Business* reported that in 1939, according to Census figures, professional workers earned 2.12 times the annual earnings of laborers; in 1957, only 1.61 times. See also Brown and Tate, *op. cit.* See Reinhard Bendix and Seymour Martin Lipset, eds., *op. cit.*; J. A. Kahl, *op. cit.*; Leonard Riessman, *Class in American Society* (Glencoe: Free Press, 1960); Robin M. Williams, Jr., *American Society* (New York: Knopf,

1960), John F. Cuber and William F. Kinkel, *Social Stratification in the United States* (New York: Appleton-Century-Crofts, 1954).

6. U.S. Department of Health, Education and Welfare, *Education in the USA, op. cit.,* p. 3.

7. Letourneau, *op. cit.,* p. 23.

8. On the early education battles, see Cubberly, *op. cit.* On medicine, see the already cited works of Fox, Carter, Hyde and Wolff, Garceau, and Kelley. These conclusions are also based on reports, professional-journal accounts, a variety of public governmental reports, and extended participant-observation in partisan political organizations.

9. Hyde and Wolff, *op. cit.,* pp. 955, 957; Fox, *op. cit.,* pp. 138-9; 142-3; Truman, *op. cit.,* p. 174; Carter, *op. cit.,* pp. 206-15; Kelley, *op. cit.,* pp. 83, 100. Not all work issues and consumer issues for the professions fit this analysis, and it should be emphasized that work issues for other vocations (*e.g.,* organized labor) may follow the consumer pattern. There are many exceptions to the general rule here hypothesized.

10. Interview with Paul Ward, California governor's legislative secretary, Sacramento, September 15, 1961. Coleman B. Ransone, Jr., *The Office of Governor in the United States* (University: Univ. of Alabama Press, 1956), personal observation, contact with office of California governor, 1958-64; Richard E. Neustadt, "Presidency and Legislation; Planning the President's Program," *The American Political Science Review,* XLIX (December 1955), 1016; ————, "Presidency and Legislation: The Growth of Central Clearance," *ibid.,* XLVII (September 1954), 662; ————, *Presidential Power* (New York: John Wiley, 1961), *op. cit.* David Truman, *The Congressional Party;* ————, *The Governmental Process, op. cit.,* pp. 215-16; Galloway, *op. cit.,* pp. 229, 280, 329, 330, 337; Griffith, *op. cit.,* pp. 59-60; Ralph K. Huitt, "Democratic Party Leadership in the Senate," *The American Political Science Review,* LV (June 1961), 333-42; Herbert McCloskey, Paul J. Hoffman, Rosemary O'Hara, "Issue Conflict and Consensus Among Party Leaders and Followers," *The American Political Science Review,* LIV (June 1960), 406; Carter, *op. cit.,* p. 208; Thomas H. Eliot, "Toward an Understanding of Public School Politics," *The American Political Science Review,* LIII (December 1959), 1043; Carol Ann C. Thompson, "The National Defense Education Act of 1958" (unpubl. thesis, Univ. of California, at Berkeley, September, 1961); Richard E. Neustadt, "Presidential Clearance of Legislation" (unpubl. diss., Harvard, June 1950); Hugh A. Bone, *American Politics and the Party System,* 2nd ed. (New York: McGraw-Hill, 1955). Of course while partisanship has been important for Medicare and federal aid to education bills, delays in passage of such bills have been to a considerable extent due to *intraparty* disagreement.

11. On state practices generally, see Zeller, *American State Legislatures, op. cit.,* pp. 199, 203-4, 204-5; Ransone, *op. cit.,* pp. 94, 140, 149, 175-7, 179; Kelley, *op. cit.,* regarding medicine; Malcolm E. Jewell, "Party

Voting in American State Legislatures," *The American Political Science Review*, XLIX (1955), 773–91. For Illinois, see Gove and Steiner, *op. cit.*, pp. 13, 32, 40, 74–5; for California, see Robert E. Burke, *Olson's New Deal for California* (Berkeley: Univ. of California Press, 1953), p. 176; R. E. Donnelly, "The Health Insurance Movement in California, 1938–48" (unpubl. thesis, Univ. of California at Berkeley, January 1949), p. 147; Buchanan, *op. cit.* The author's information about California comes from prolonged research in many sources; participant-observation in California politics, 1957–64; attendance at the 1959, 1961, 1962, 1963, and 1965 sessions of the legislature; a mimeographed sheet issued by the chairman of the Democratic legislative caucus, January 24, 1959; also interviews with Republican caucus leader, John Busterud, September 20, 1961, San Francisco; with Milton Marks, member of the Republican caucus, September 17, 1961, San Francisco; with Democratic majority leader Jerome Waldie, Antioch, Calif., summer 1961; and with the governor's legislative secretary, Paul Ward, Sacramento, September 15, 1961. William J. Keefe, "Parties, Partisanship, and Public Policy in the Pennsylvania Legislature," *The American Political Science Review*, XLVII (June 1954), 450–64.

12. Dupree, *op. cit.*

13. Quoted in Gerth and Mills, *op. cit.*, p. 71. However, see J. O. Hertzler, "Some Tendencies Toward a Closed Class System in the United States," *Social Forces*, XXX (March 1952), 314–23; G. Sjoberg, "Are Social Classes in America Becoming More Rigid?", *American Sociological Review*, XVI (December 1951), 775–83.

Index

297